Tracing Your Mississippi Ancestors

TRACING YOUR MISSISSIPPI ANCESTORS

BY

ANNE S. LIPSCOMB

AND

KATHLEEN S. HUTCHISON

UNIVERSITY PRESS OF MISSISSIPPI
Jackson

97 96 95 94   4 3 2 1

The paper in this book meets the guidelines for permanence and durability of the Committee on Production Guidelines for Book Longevity of the Council on Library Resources.

Library of Congress Cataloging-in-Publication Data

Lipscomb, Anne S.
    Tracing your Mississippi ancestors / by Anne S. Lipscomb and Kathleen S. Hutchison.
      p.   cm.
    Includes index.
    ISBN 0-87805-697-1. — ISBN 0-87805-698-X (pbk.)
    1. Mississippi—Genealogy—Handbooks, manuals, etc.
    I. Hutchison, Kathleen S. II. Title.
    F340.L56   1994
    929'.1'0720762—dc20   94-13812
                                                                         CIP

British Library Cataloging-in-Publication data available

Contents

Illustrations

Preface

The study of family histories, is a subject of particular appeal to many persons. The undertaking of research in this area, however, can sometimes be disheartening when the investigator is faced with the prospect of locating and digging through obscure and incomplete records from the past. Many experienced researchers acknowledge that the pursuit of vital data can be tedious and unprofitable, with long hours of toil and little to show for it. Those same persons, though, express a feeling of great accomplishment when they finally discover a morsel of information that supplies the missing piece to a puzzle. This book is intended to be a guide through the maze of research possibilities for anyone, veteran or novice, whose ancestors may have lived in Mississippi.

The book consists of two main sections. The first is a comprehensive review of the many resources available to one researching Mississippi ancestors, with specific information of where and how to locate them and how to use them. These resources include official records of the county, state, and federal governments and unofficial public and private documents, ranging from cemetery records to personal diaries and papers. A special feature of this section is a chapter for those gathering information on ancestors belonging to minority groups—particularly African-American and native Americans. The second half of the book, "Descriptive Profiles of Printed Sources," presents an annotated list of published books and unpublished materials that can aid the researcher of Mississippi ancestry.

The most extensive collection of genealogical resources for locating Mississippi ancestors is found at the Mississippi Department of Archives and History. At the state archives, in fact, researchers will find most of the available materials necessary for tracing one's Mississippi ancestors. Thus we have made the Missisippi Department of Archives and History the focus of this book. (It will hereafter be referred to as MDAH, the Archives, and the state archives.)

There are other valuable sources of Mississippi genealogical information elsewhere, and we have tried throughout this book to guide you to the appropriate places—local, state, and national—to find these materials. The appendix provides a complete listing of other genealogical library collections in the state, as well as important national repositories.

I

Where and How to Trace Mississippi Ancestry

ONE

Planning Your Research

The search for one's ancestors should begin sometime before you appear at an archives or genealogical library. The best starting point is your own home, where you should search for such documents as birth, marriage and baptism certificates and family Bible records, for clues to your family's heritage. If these items are not in your possession, then calls or letters to relatives are in order.

Any such calls or letters should be documented with the date of contact and the name of the person questioned or written. *Always keep a copy of your correspondence*, as well as a copy of your questions, if you are telephoning. Letters are one of the most important tools of genealogical research. Throughout your investigation, you will be writing to relatives, other researchers, courthouses, libraries, and archives. A self-addressed stamped envelope will increase your chances of getting a reply. Be sure to put your address on the letter itself and not just on the envelope in case the two are separated.

Contact older relatives first, as they are usually good sources for information and family stories, or at least for names of other relatives who might know more than they. Nancy Parkes, who wrote a weekly genealogical column for many years in the Jackson, Mississippi, *Clarion Ledger*, used to say that she would "like her descendants to know some of the more personal things about her family"; so her family history included material about people's talents, their hobbies or special interests, and their health, as well as family anecdotes, including some about relatives she remembered from her childhood. Think what a treasure chest of history that is for her children and grandchildren!

As you start to accumulate some definite names, dates, and places from your relatives, you may want to consider purchasing family chart sheets. These are work forms that can be helpful in organizing your generations and recording birth, marriage, and death dates. Family charts are certainly not mandatory, but they can be helpful in keeping the generations of a family straight. These are generally available at book stores and genealogical libraries. Should you want these charts while working in the MDAH research library, you can purchase them at the sales shop in the Old Capitol (next door).

Several very good "how to" books are available for the beginning genealogist to consult, such as Val Greenwood's *The Researcher's Guide to American Genealogy* and *Tracing Your Ancestry* by F. Wilbur Helmbold (see source list). Most public libraries have these volumes or similar ones in their genealogy sections. Advance preparation is essential if you want to have positive results in a limited time.

When you have some definite family names and periods of residence in Mississippi, then it is time to consider visiting or writing the Archives or other genealogical libraries in the state. The state archives are found at the Capers Building, 100 South State Street, Jackson, Mississippi (mailing address: P. O. Box 571, Jackson, MS 39205). The names and addresses of other genealogical libraries in Mississippi, along with other important sources of genealogical material in the nation, appear as an appendix to this book.

Using the Mississippi Department of Archives and History

Before visiting the Archives, the researcher should ascertain the hours of operation, rules, and security regulations, parking facilities, and any other necessary information. Should you need special assistance, e.g., sight and hearing impaired, please let the institution know in advance so arrangements can be made.

On your initial visit to MDAH, you will need to apply for a research card and provide some form of identification, such as a driver's license. The card will be issued immediately and is effective for five years. No pens, purses, briefcases, or personal books are allowed in the search room; lockers are available to store such items. All materials brought into the research area will undergo a security check when you leave the facility.

Since its creation in 1902, the Mississippi Department of Archives and History has made an effort to assist the genealogist. The department has the largest collection of genealogical source material in the state. With the exception of individual family histories, which are not purchased by the department, all published material concerning the state can usually be found there. However, do remember that the department was created not as a genealogical library but as an institution to house and maintain the official records of the state. If these official archives happen to contain information helpful to you as a genealogist, you are fortunate but if such is not the case do not be upset with the archivists or librarians, for they are the caretakers of these records, not the creators! Also keep in mind that while your family's history is interesting to you and you may feel an impulse to share it, the staff members are not genealogists and unfortunately do not have the luxury of spending an extended period of time with any one patron.

Neither is the MDAH library a lending library; it is a research facility with rigorous and strictly enforced regulations for the protection of the documents.

Written requests are accepted at MDAH as at many other genealogical libraries, but remember that most such departments have small staffs and can only spend a limited amount of time per letter, so be specific about who and what you want searched. At the Mississippi Archives, out-of-state researchers are charged a nominal fee and research time is one hour per letter. In-state residents do not pay the research fee, but the time per letter is still one hour. All photocopying fees must be paid before copies are obtained. Historically, public records have been maintained according to race. So that records can be examined in an efficient manner, always include the race of your ancestor in your written query to an archival repository.

Every archives research facility has unique "finding aids" peculiar to their institution, and the Mississippi Archives is no exception. There are seven distinct finding aids that will need to be examined at some time during the search for your family heritage:

1) Biographical index. This source provides an index to the names of individuals mentioned in various sources on early Mississippi history. Some of the sources indexed include Goodspeed's *Biographical and Historical Memoirs of Mississippi; Bench and Bar of Mississippi; Courts, Judges, and Lawyers of Mississippi 1798–1935*; Mississippians who fought in the War of 1812 and the Mexican War; newspaper notices of marriages and deaths in early Natchez, Holly Springs, and Jackson; and many others. This index has for many years been located in a card catalog, with cards in alphabetical order by surname with the source of information on that family or individual and page indicated on the card. The source is presently being computerized and the information placed on microfiche cards. The entire biographical index will eventually be on microfiche.

2) Subject file.   This is a clipping or pamphlet file of ephemeral material on persons, places, and events in Mississippi history. The contents may consist of a single item or many files on a particular person or event. Subjects range from Elvis Presley to Greenwood Leflore and cemeteries in Leflore County to the Tombigbee Waterway!

3) Book card catalog.   All published (and some unpublished) monographs are listed by author, title and subject. The majority of the book collection is in a closed stack area of the library; however, the Mississippi genealogical books that should be most helpful are usually found in the Search Room. These books which are designated in the card catalog with a plastic slip-cover that says "Search Room," are located on open shelves so that you can help yourself. Books that are not in the Search Room must be requested by filling out a call slip.

4) Private manuscripts.   Nongovernmental records created by individuals, churches, schools, etc., are described in a series of notebooks and listed by the title of the collection. The description usually explains the size, general contents, and restrictions, if any. The call number for manuscripts is preceded by a "Z" and is on the cover sheet of all of the descriptions. Since all of the manuscript collections are stored in a closed stack area, a call slip is necessary for retrieval of this material.

5) Guide to official records.   Each state agency is assigned a record group (RG) number; as papers/records are received from an agency, they are described under the appropriate RG number in the guide. A series of notebooks arranged by record group number serves as an index to these materials. An alphabetical list of each state agency and its appropriate record group number is located in the front of each official record notebook. As this book goes to press, the descriptions for individual record groups are being revised. In the future they will be accessed by series and location number. A conversion chart from the old arrangement to the new one will be in each official record notebook. The most difficult task in working with official records is trying to determine which record groups would be helpful to the genealogist and which agency would have created them. Several will be singled out in this volume.

6) Non-book catalog. You will become very familiar with this catalog as you use the Archives library, since it is here that you will find the county records, maps, photographs, and newspapers, as well as an index to the Mississippi Genealogical Society's *Mississippi Cemetery and Bible Records* (see source list).

7) Computer catalog. To gain access to material processed after May 1992, you will need to examine this finding aid. At present this catalog includes books, maps, photographs, and manuscripts and will in time include descriptions of official records. The easiest way to conduct a search is by entering a key word or surname of your family. A full description of the material and the call number needed for retrieval will appear on the terminal screen. Other "how to" information appears on the terminal screen as it is needed.

The time will come when you have uncovered all of the information that is available in Mississippi about the family you are researching. If you have been successful, you will have picked up some clues about their former place of residence. When you have determined the state but not the county from which your ancestors migrated, you will need to consult some general statewide index source material for that state in order to pinpoint a county. The amount of such material available at MDAH varies according to the state. Over the years, when monies have been available, books and other resources pertaining to the southeastern states have been purchased. These are helpful in documenting migration routes to Mississippi.

Besides having all of the Mississippi census records from the provincial period to 1920, the Archives also has those federal census records through 1850 for Alabama, Georgia, Louisiana, North Carolina, South Carolina, and Tennessee, and through 1840 for Maryland, Virginia, and Kentucky. Other examples of such source material are statewide indexes to wills and marriages. These references may not give you the specific material you need but point you to the county in which your ancestor lived. Once you have found that, the cycle begins again and you search all available county records in hopes of tracing the family line back another generation or two.

TWO

Basic Sources

FEDERAL CENSUS

The United States federal population census schedule is the backbone of genealogical research and thus probably the best single source for the beginning genealogist to consult. (Even so, remember that a census record, though official, may not be entirely accurate and must be used with caution: the person giving the information to the census taker may not have been a family member but a neighbor or other acquaintance.) The most recent census available for research by the public is the one taken in 1920. If you had relatives in Mississippi at that time, this should be your point of departure. To protect the privacy of individuals listed on the census, the U. S. Bureau of the Census does not release census schedules until seventy-two (72) years after they are taken, so the 1930 census will not be available to the general public until 2002! Federal census schedules pertaining to Mississippi available for research at the state archives cover the period from 1820 to 1920. All of the federal population schedules are microfilm copies from the National Archives. If you do not know the names of relatives who would be on the 1920 census but need a more recent one, you can write to the Bureau of Census in Pittsburg, Kansas (see appendix for the address). For a fee they will send you information on one person, though not the entire family.

Most professional genealogists recommend that the search for family roots proceed from the known to the unknown, starting with oneself, one's parents and grandparents, and so on back to earlier relatives. Since each successive census provides more information, you will find that as you proceed in reverse chronological order, less and less material will be available. So take advantage of the more recent schedules and study them carefully for all of the information provided!

Starting with the 1920 census, you will find that the census is indexed, but the index is on microfilm and is not in alphabetical order. For the years, 1880, 1900, 1910, and 1920, the Soundex index may be used to identify which census schedules include family members. This index is a coding system whereby names are grouped phonetically so that similar sounding names, such as Smith and Smythe, will be found together in the same code. This code system has proven most helpful, as many census takers (and their clients as well) could not spell and so recorded the names as they heard them. The Soundex is composed of the first letter of the surname followed by three digits. The first letter of any surname determines the main alphabetic section where the index card belongs. To determine the code numerals, use the following table in conjunction with the subsequent explanations:

1 — B F P V
2 — C G J K Q S X Z
3 — D T
4 — L
5 — M N
6 — R

The letters a, e, i, o, u, y, w, and h are *not* coded. The first letter of a surname is *not* given a code number. Every Soundex must have a letter and three digits; thus, the code for both Smith and Smythe would be: S530, as we cannot code the i or the h in Smith, or the y, h, or e in Smythe. Also, when two letters in the same numeric range fall together, the two are coded as one, so that, for example, Kelly=K400, since we would not code the e and y and would code only one l. Other examples of this same rule would be: Ezelle=E240 and Black=B420. Some names have only vowels after the first letter of their name; for those particular names zeros would be added after the initial letter: Lee=L000 or Shaw=S000. Within the microfilm, you will find many different names with the same code. The index cards will be arranged alphabetically by the *given* name, not the surname.

After you have located your relative on the Soundex card, record the county, enumeration district number (ED) and sheet as given on the card

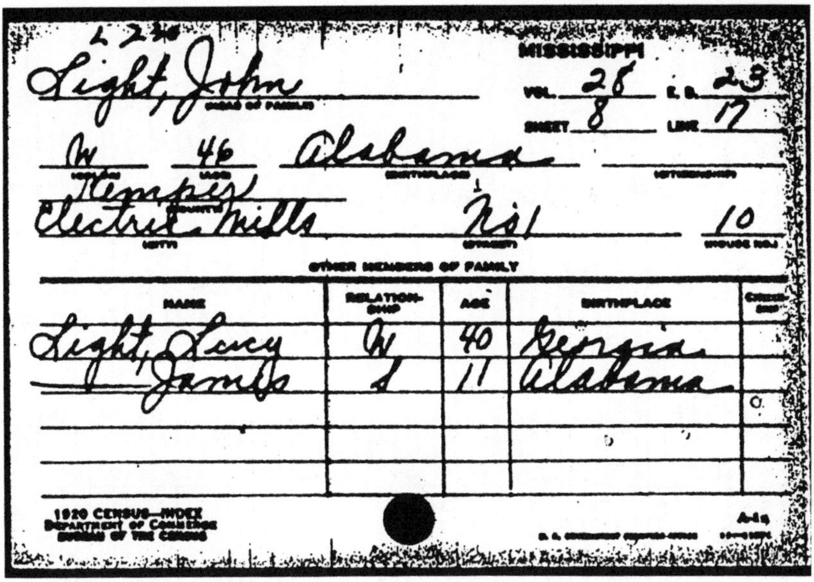
L230

MISSISSIPPI

Light, John
(HEAD OF FAMILY)

VOL. 28 E.D. 23

SHEET 8 LINE 17

W 46 Alabama

Kemper

Electric Mills N 31 10

(CITY) (STREET) (HOUSE NO.)

OTHER MEMBERS OF FAMILY

NAME	RELATIONSHIP	AGE	BIRTHPLACE	CITIZENSHIP
Light, Lucy	W	40	Georgia	
James	S	11	Alabama	

1920 CENSUS—INDEX
DEPARTMENT OF COMMERCE
BUREAU OF THE CENSUS

A-1a

Figure 1: 1920 Soundex card for John *Light* (L230) living in Kemper County, ED 23, and sheet 8

(fig. 1). The family members who are living in that household and their places of birth will also be given on the card. Note, for instance, in figure 1 the Soundex card for John Light (L230). He is living in Kemper County in enumeration district number 23, and he will be found on page 8 of the census schedule. His household consists of his wife Lucy, age forty, born in Georgia, and his son James, age eleven, born in Alabama. Frequently patrons stop after locating their relatives' Soundex card, forgetting that it is just an index that leads to another source, the census schedule itself, which usually gives much more information.

The census schedules are on microfilm and can be found in the microfilm room. They are arranged first by census year and then usually alphabetically by county. Researchers may help themselves to the census microfilm after they have ascertained which county they will need. The counties are filmed in the order indicated on the microfilm box labels. After you are in the correct county, look for the ED number at the top of the page. These numbers are usually in chronological order unless a note on the box indicates otherwise. Once you are in the correct district, proceed to the sheet (or page) number as it was given on the Soundex card. Be aware that each page has an A and B; if your family is not on the page cited, advance

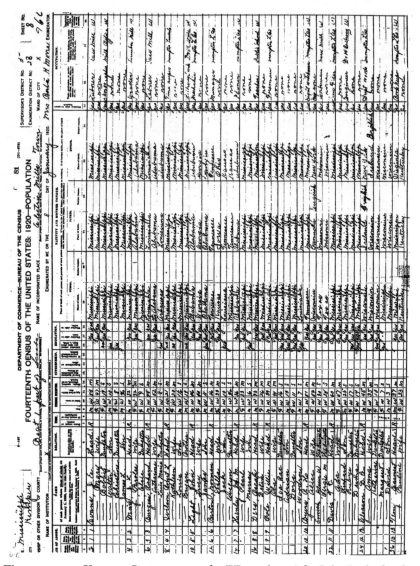

Figure 2: 1920 Kemper County census for ED 23 sheet 8 for John Light family

one page and it should be there. (fig. 2; note previously mentioned John Light family).

Copy all of the information given. Even if you do not think it is important, it may prove helpful later, and you certainly do not want to have to search for the record again! Be sure to copy the source information, that is, census year, county, ED, and page, in case you need to refer to it again. Census information cannot necessarily be trusted for names and ages do not always correspond to other records or family tradition, but it is a beginning and should be saved until other sources can definitely refute it.

Do not be discouraged if your relative is not on the census index. If you have the time and know the county, read the census through line by line. If your relative was not at home when the census taker called, or if the census enumerator did not locate his home, the person may have been missed on this particular census altogether. With luck, however, you will locate another relative living in a household with his family. In such a case, the ages of each family member will be given (this could play an important part in determining the right family if it is a common surname), as well as place of birth of each individual listed, place of birth of each individual's parents, and other helpful information. Frequently, researchers take down only this sort of information, but it is a good idea to copy everything given. Even better, photocopy the entire page and a page or two on either side of your family. Neighbors often turn out to be relatives and many times settled an area together, traveling from one state to another in community groups.

1920

When you are taking notes, be sure to note the comment at the top of the name column on the 1920 schedule. The census lists only those persons whose place of residence on January 1, 1920, was with this family. Children born after January 1, 1920, were omitted, meaning that this is actually a census of 1919.

The census is taken every ten years and if your ancestors were still in Mississippi (determined by noting their place of birth statement), you will want to examine each and every census until you have proof that they were not living in Mississippi.

1910

The next federal census for Mississippi that should be checked is the one taken in 1910. The census day was April 15, 1910, and all information given relates to that day. This census is also indexed by the Soundex system. Once you have the code for your surname, it remains the same through each census requiring it. The 1910 census itself is different from the 1920 census in several ways that could prove beneficial to the family historian. Questions asked included number of years married, number of children born to the mother, number of living children, and whether there was a Union or Confederate veteran in the household.

1900

The 1900 census is much the same as the 1910 with a couple of notable exceptions. In the 1900 census the birth month and year are given. However, the census day is June 1, 1900. If a member of the family died on June 30 and the census taker visited in July, the person who was then deceased should appear on the census! No question concerning veterans appears on the 1900 census. This census is also indexed by the Soundex system.

1890

In 1921 a fire in the department of commerce building in Washington, D.C., destroyed most of the 1890 federal census. Of the few schedules that survived, none is for a Mississippi county. In addition to the federal population census, however, in 1890 another census was taken of Union veterans of the Civil War and their widows. There is a published index to this source, and close examination of the key reveals that this census contains much more information than its title suggests (fig. 3).

1880

When you prepare to use the 1880 federal census, be aware that while the census is complete, the index to it is only a partial one. Only families with children ten years old or younger are on the index. Singles, childless couples and families with older children are omitted from the Soundex index altogether. Again, if you know the county of residence and have the time and patience, you should assume that your ancestors were left off the Soundex and "read" the census schedule.

KEY TO USING THE 1890 CENSUS OF UNION VETERANS

-W- OR -WID- = WIDOW OF UNION OR CONFEDERATE VETERAN
-DEC- = UNION VETERAN IS DECEASED
-C- OR -CONF- = CONFEDERATE VETERAN
-AKA- = ALIAS OF UNION OR CONFEDERATE VETERAN WHILE IN SERVICE.
-F- OR -FOR- = FORMER WIFE OF UNION OR CONFEDERATE VETERAN, USUALLY
        REMARRIED WITH DIFFERENT SURNAME.
-X-   = NAME IS CROSSED OUT WITH NO EXPLANATION

-1812- = VETERAN OF WAR OF 1812
-MEX-   = VETERAN OF MEXICAN WAR (1847)

Figure 3: Key to published 1890 Union veterans index that indicates census includes much more than the title suggests

The 1880 census was the first one to show the relationship between the head of the household and the other people listed in that household. In the 1870 census records and those preceding it, no relationships are given, so you must guess or find proof elsewhere about the relationships (if any) of the people listed as a household.

In 1880 the federal government also took a special census of handicapped or dependent persons. This material, on two rolls of microfilm is entitled "Defective, Dependent, and Delinquent Classes." Arranged by county, the census lists persons who might have been dependent on the county and/or other individuals to support them. These "classes" included those who were blind, deaf, mute, homeless children, paupers, and imprisoned.

1870

The 1870 population census was the first federal census taken after the Civil War. For the first time, all persons, regardless of race, were included, with the exception of Indians living on reservations and the wandering tribes out west. The census day was June 1, 1870; all information recorded was as of that day even if the census taker visited in July.

The index for the 1870 census is in a published volume. (The publisher, Accelerated Indexing Systems, is a frequent producer of computer generated census indexes, future references in text and in the source list will simply cite AIS.) Names are in alphabetical order; however, only the head of the household is listed in the index. The information provided includes the county of residence and the page on the National Archives microfilm where that person will be found. Remember always to check for a variety of spellings of your surname if you are unable to locate it using today's spelling. If you are searching for a Native American ancestor, you will find that many are listed in this volume simply under the term "Indian," followed by a given name. The Soundex system is not available for 1870 and earlier years.

You will note in the example of the 1870 census (fig. 4) that the amount of information is considerably less than that given in the 1920 census. (Also notice the spelling of the name Right. If you had wanted to Soundex it to search another year, would you have looked under W623 [Wright] or R230 [Right]? Both codes should be examined.)

1860

After examining the 1870 census information for your family and making a copy of the entire page, proceed to the 1860 census indexes. Three counties

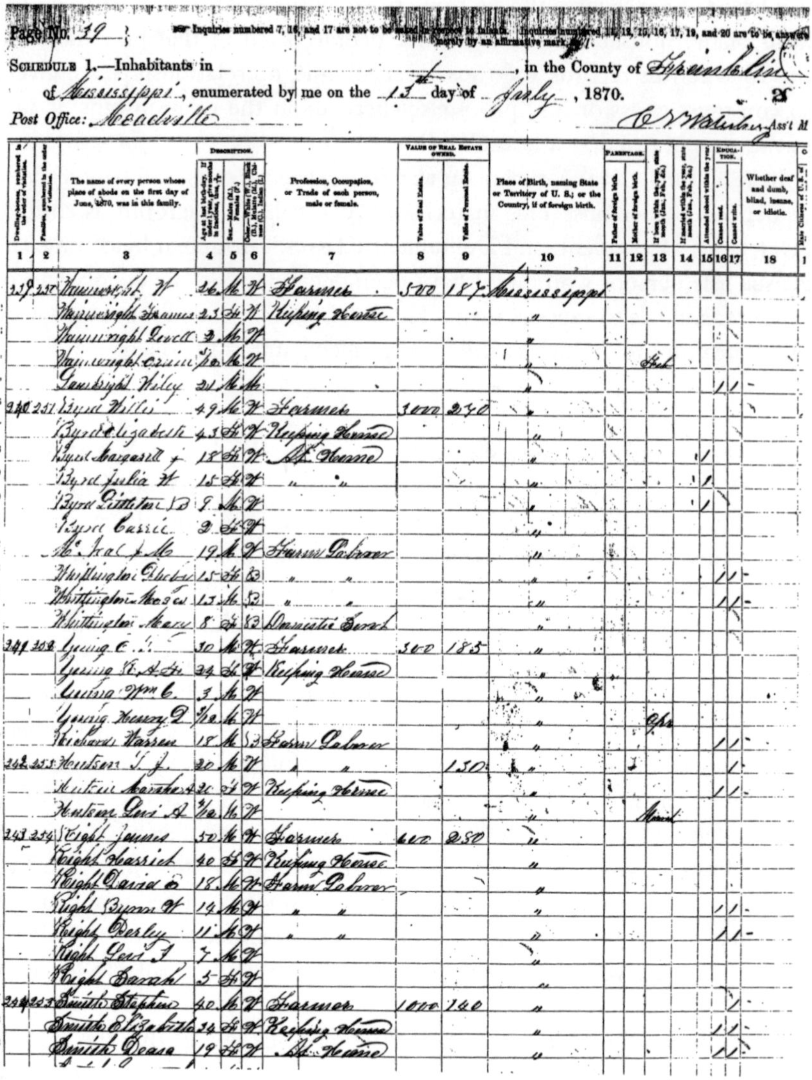

Page No. 39 } Inquiries numbered 7, 16, and 17 are not to be asked in respect to infants. Inquiries numbered 11, 12, 15, 16, 17, 18, and 20 are to be answered (if at all) merely by an affirmative mark, as /.

SCHEDULE 1.—Inhabitants in ______, in the County of Franklin, State of Mississippi, enumerated by me on the 13th day of July, 1870.

Post Office: Meadville — C. W. Waterbury, Ass't M[arshal]

Dwelling-houses (1)	Families (2)	Name (3)	Age (4)	Sex (5)	Color (6)	Profession, Occupation, or Trade (7)	Value of Real Estate (8)	Value of Personal Estate (9)	Place of Birth (10)	11	12	13	14	15	16	17	18
239	250	Wainwright J. W.	26	M	W	Farmer	500	187	Mississippi								
		Wainwright Frances	23	F	W	Keeping House			"								
		Wainwright Lovell	2	M	W				"								
		Wainwright Erwin	?/12	M	W				"			Feb					
		Lambright Wiley	21	M	M				"						/	/	
240	251	Byrd Willis	49	M	W	Farmer	3000	270	"								
		Byrd Elizabeth	43	F	W	Keeping House			"								
		Byrd Margaret J	18	F	W	At Home			"					/			
		Byrd Julia W	15	F	W	" "			"					/			
		Byrd Littleton B	9	M	W				"					/			
		Byrd Carrie	2	F	W				"								
		McNeal J M	19	M	W	Farm Laborer			"								
		Whittington Phebe	15	F	B	" "			"						/	/	
		Whittington Moses	13	M	B	" "			"						/	/	
		Whittington Mary	8	F	B	Domestic Servant			"								
241	252	Young C. J.	30	M	W	Farmer	300	185	"								
		Young R. A. F.	24	F	W	Keeping House			"								
		Young Wm C.	3	M	W				"								
		Young Henry D	?/12	M	W				"			Apr					
		Richards Warren	18	M	B	Farm Laborer			"						/	/	
242	253	Hutson T. J.	20	M	W	" "		130	"							/	
		Hutson Martha A	20	F	W	Keeping House			"						/	/	
		Hutson Levi A	?/12	M	W				"			March					
243	254	Right James	50	M	W	Farmer	600	250	"								
		Right Harriet	40	F	W	Keeping House			"								
		Right David C	18	M	W	Farm Laborer			"								
		Right Byron W	14	M	W	" "			"						/	/	
		Right Dorley	11	M	W	" "			"						/	/	
		Right Levi F	7	M	W				"								
		Right Sarah	5	F	W				"								
244	255	Smith Stephen	40	M	W	Farmer	1000	140	"							/	
		Smith Elizabeth	34	F	W	Keeping House			"						/	/	
		Smith Deasa	19	F	W	At Home			"						/	/	

Figure 4: 1870 census of Franklin County (notice the spelling of Right [Wright])

are missing from the Mississippi 1860 census, Hancock, Sunflower, and Washington. There are two published 1860 indexes; MDAH has both (see source list). If you are unable to locate your relatives in one index, be sure to check the second book; that compiler might have found the family. Remember that indexers make errors too, and with the variances in handwriting styles, mistakes can be made in the transcribing and reading of names. Again, if you locate your ancestor in the printed index, you will also find the county of residence as well as the census microfilm page number. One confusing aspect of using the 1860 indexes is that the index by Kathryn Rose Bonner refers to the page number as indicated by the words "page number" at the top of the census schedule, and the index by AIS (see source list), leads you to the page number that runs consecutively through the roll. When in doubt (or if you cannot locate the citation on the first attempt), check each page number, left and right at the top of the page.

1850

Working on the assumption that your ancestors are still being found in the census records and that Mississippi is still listed as the place of birth, you will now want to examine the 1850 printed census index. MDAH has two published indexes to the 1850 Mississippi census, and they are quite different. The AIS volume, lists the head of household by surname and given name, the county of residence, and the microfilm page number. The second source, by Norman Gillis, lists only the surname, the county, and a number. The number cited is *not* the page number, but rather the family number. The family number is the number to the left of each household on the microfilm. Family number 125 in Hinds County would indicate that this family was the one hundred twenty-fifth family visited by the enumerator in that particular county. Again, if your ancestors are not found in the first index, always check the second on the chance that that transcriber found your family and read the name correctly.

The 1850 census schedule was the first to include the names (or initials) of all of the members of the household. It is particularly important to notice the ages on the 1850 schedules because the next census (1840) gives only sex and age ranges of individuals living in the household.

Minority individuals who were free men would normally be included in the census schedules prior to the Civil War. Slave schedules were taken in 1850 and 1860; see the chapter on minority source material for information on this census.

In addition to the federal population census for the years 1850–1880, there were also agriculture, industrial and mortality schedules. The agriculture and industrial records are probably not used as often as they should be because they are not indexed and because at first glance the information does not look particularly helpful. However, if your ancestor is not on the population schedule when you think he should be, a perusal of the agriculture/industrial census schedule may at least document that he was in Mississippi during a particular time period. These schedules are arranged by county and only the head of the household is listed. (For information on mortality schedules, see chapter 3.)

1840

The census index of 1840 is also published and there are two indexes that can be examined. See the source list in the second part of this book for these volumes. The information provided on the 1840 census is much less detailed than that found on the schedules discussed thus far (fig. 5a). One unique entry on the 1840 schedule is the inclusion of the question "name of pensioner" in the household. This item alone could provide another name in a previous generation as this pensioner would more than likely have been a Revolutionary War or War of 1812 veteran! Note the family of Jacob Holland on the census schedule depicted as example of this item (fig. 5b).

The number of free Negroes and the number of slaves per age group is also included in the 1840 schedule. If a free Negro was living as head of a household, he would be listed individually and not just in the number category mentioned above.

1830

The 1830 census is like the 1840 except that no pensioner information is included. The printed index by Irene and Norman Gillis is a reproduction of a portion of the schedule that lists the white population. This example of the Gillis 1830 index page clearly shows the drastic change in the amount of census information given (fig. 6).

The 1830 Pike County census was evidently lost; the Gillis volume includes a tax list for 1831 to help restore some of that information. The 1830 index produced by the AIS does include the free black population in addition to the white inhabitants.

1820

Since Mississippi became a state in 1817, the 1820 census is the first federal population census available for research. This census also has several published indexes; these are listed in the second part of this book.

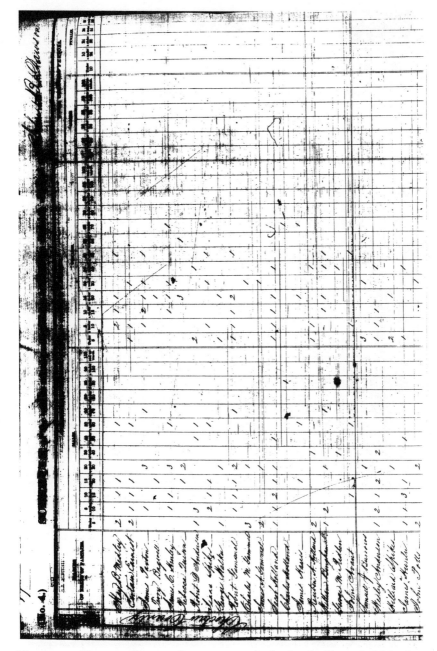

Figure 5a: Choctaw County 1840 census; only the head of household is given

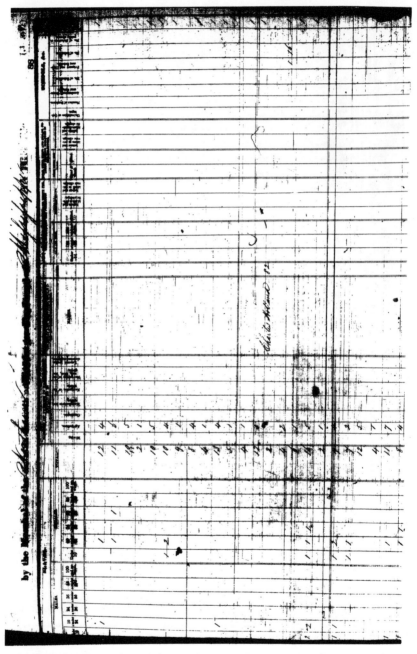

Figure 5b: 1840 Choctaw County census which includes pensioner Charles Holland, age 82

MISSISSIPPI CENSUS - 1830		WHITE MALES					WHITE FEMALES				
FAMILY HEAD	COUNTY	UN 10	10 to 20	20 to 40	40 to 60	60 & OV	UN 10	10 to 20	20 to 40	40 to 60	60 & OV
Kendrick, Alan	Monroe	1	2	0	0	0	0	0	0	1	0
Kendrick, Joseph	Monroe	5	0	1	0	0	0	0	1	0	0
Keneday, Jesse	Franklin	0	2	1	1	0	1	0	1	0	0
Kenedy, Andrew	Hancock	0	1	0	1	0	0	0	0	0	0
Kenedy, Nathan	Lawrence	3	2	1	0	0	2	1	1	0	0
Kenida, William	Jefferson	0	0	1	0	0	0	0	1	0	0
Kenison, Isaac	Franklin	0	0	1	0	0	0	0	0	0	0
Kenison, Jno.	Franklin	1	2	1	1	0	2	3	1	1	0
Kenison, William	Franklin	2	0	0	0	1	4	0	1	0	1
Kennady, John	Amite	0	0	1	0	0	0	0	0	0	0
Kennason, William	Claiborne	3	2	1	1	0	0	1	1	0	0
Kennedy, Alfred	Monroe	0	0	1	0	0	0	0	0	0	0
Kennedy, Benjamin	Copiah	1	0	1	0	0	0	1	0	0	0
Kennedy, Wm. P.	Monroe	0	0	1	0	0	0	0	1	0	0
Kent, Jonathan	Hinds	2	2	0	1	0	2	0	0	1	0
Kent, Laban	Hinds	0	3	2	1	0	1	1	1	1	0
Kent, Uriah	Hinds	2	0	1	0	0	2	0	1	0	0
Ker, Jno.	Adams	3	0	2	0	0	2	1	1	0	1
Ker, Jno. C.	Adams	0	0	1	0	0	0	0	0	1	0
Kerby, William	Yazoo	0	0	0	1	0	0	1	0	1	0
Kernan, Jno.	Amite	2	0	2	0	0	2	0	1	0	0
Kerr, Jacob	Adams	0	0	1	0	0	0	1	1	0	0
Kerr, James	Yazoo	0	1	3	1	0	1	2	0	1	0
Kesler, Daniel	Yazoo	1	0	3	0	0	1	1	3	0	0
Keston, James	Lowndes	0	1	1	0	0	3	2	1	0	0
Keys, William	Covington	3	1	1	0	0	1	0	1	0	0
Kilburne, James	Copiah	1	0	1	0	0	2	1	0	0	0
Kilburne, Zadoc P.	Claiborne	1	0	1	0	0	0	0	1	1	0

Figure 6: 1830 census as published in Gillis book

State Census

Mississippi researchers are fortunate in that many of the census schedules taken by the state also survive. These were frequently taken in years
between the federal census counts. Even though the head of the household
is usually the only family member listed, these documents can definitely
help to pinpoint the time period of a family's residence in a particular
county. (Surprisingly, the 1866 state census for Tallahatchie County lists
everyone in the household.) Several of the state census schedules have
recently been indexed and, although not complete, they are helpful. (These
indexes are included in this book's source list.) To determine what state
census records exist for the county you are interested in, examine Record
Group 28, Office of the Secretary of State, for a list of holdings.

PRE-STATEHOOD CENSUS

To document a family's residence in Mississippi in the years before 1817, researchers may check several territorial census schedules as well as a few census records from the Spanish Provincial period. These early census records list only the names of the head of the household. The territorial census records have been microfilmed and are available to researchers in the microfilm room. An important point to remember when working with the territorial records is that the state of Alabama was once part of the Mississippi Territory and that there are Alabama counties with the same names as some present-day Mississippi counties, e.g., Washington, Clarke, Madison, Monroe, and Montgomery. Any time you find records indicating such a county in Mississippi as the place of residence before 1817, remember that research may be needed in one of the Alabama counties. A helpful source to check for information about these early residents is Norman Gillis's *Early Inhabitants of the Natchez District* (see source list). Despite the title, it actually covers more than the Natchez District. The majority of Gillis's information is taken from secondary source material, but this is still a time saver and might possibly verify a name and county that will be helpful to you. When a territorial census was missing, frequently a territorial tax roll was used to document a person's residence (see section in this chapter on tax records). There are several Spanish census lists available in the Spanish Provincial Archives, in addition to the 1792 list that Gillis included. These records may be found in Record Group 26; however, many of the Spanish records have not been translated.

COUNTY RECORDS

After a thorough examination of the population census schedules, you will have a pretty good idea of when your ancestor resided in a particular county. The next step is to consider the non-book catalog of county records, but before you begin a search of the county records, you will want to consult *The Handy Book for Genealogists* by George B. Everton, Sr. (see source list). This volume is particularly valuable in documenting the date of the formation of each county and the names of the parent counties (county or counties from which it was created). Most genealogical source materials are arranged by county, so it is important to know when a county was created and from which existing counties, if any. A family that stayed in the same place may appear in the records of several counties, just because of a change in the county boundary lines. Published by the Historical Records Survey, *State and County Boundaries of Mississippi* (see source list) cites the laws creating the changes as well as the changes themselves. This volume also includes some helpful maps showing the stages of county development within the state.

With the assistance over the years of the Church of Jesus Christ of Latter-day Saints, the collection of county record microfilm at MDAH has expanded. These volunteers work tirelessly to preserve the county records for use by future generations. Microfilm copies of the Mississippi county records are also available through the services of that church's Family Research Library in Salt Lake City (see appendix for address).

The holdings and dates vary from county to county but, for the most part, the collection of county records consists of marriage records, wills, deeds, and tax records. With the exception of the tax rolls, the records are *usually* indexed by name with a citation of the volume and page where the record can be found. The holdings list of county records at the Archives is located in the non-book catalog. Figure 7 is a sample of the county record cards for Holmes County.

Nineteenth-century Mississippi marriage records rarely have material of genealogical value other than the names of the bride and groom and the date of the marriage. If either of the parties involved was underage at the time of the marriage, however, a letter or notice of permission from a parent or guardian would be tipped into the marriage book. Another clue on a marriage record is the cosigner of the marriage bond. In Mississippi someone had to guarantee bond of two hundred dollars before the marriage in case it failed to take place. Frequently, the father of the bride or groom, or perhaps a brother, cosigned on the bond.

Although wills, of course, document the disposition of the belongings of the deceased, it is important to remember that they also usually document relationships, and some may even provide a clue to a former place of residence. The family researcher often searches in vain for wills, as they were not as common in the nineteenth century as they are today. If you cannot locate a will for your ancestor, you will need to search the files at the county courthouse for the estate papers. Estate papers are loose papers relating to the disposition of the estate of the deceased, and there are many more of these records than there are wills. Since these are loose papers of varying size and color, it is not practical to microfilm them. However, MDAH does have the estate papers of one county, Copiah, on microfilm so you can see what type of information is provided. By examining this

```
Film
     Holmes Co., Mississippi.  Chancery Clerk.
          Deed records, 1833-1887; deed index, 1833-
     1893.  Lexington, Miss., filmed by Reproduction
     Systems for G. S., 1971.
          24 rolls, 35mm.  Index.  Handwritten.
1         Deed index      v. 1-2    1833-1893
2         Reverse index      1-2    1833-1893
3         Deed records       A      1833-1837
4          "      "         B-D     1837-1839
5          "      "         E-F     1839-1843
6          "      "          G      1839-1845
7          "      "          H      1845-1846
```

```
Film
     Holmes Co., Mississippi.  Chancery Clerk.
          Index to wills, 1833-1977.
     Lexington, Miss., filmed by MDAH, 1977.
          1 roll, 35mm.
138       Index to wills              v. 1      1833-1977
```

```
Film
     Holmes Co., Mississippi.  Circuit Clerk.
          Marriage records, 1884-1918; index to mar-
     riages, 1884-1967.  Lexington, Miss., filmed
     by Reproduction Systems for G. S., 1971.
          12 rolls, 35mm.  Index.  Hand and typewritten.
26   Whites index      v. 1        1884-1967
29   Blacks index         1-2      1899-1943
27   White marriages      G-H      1884-1901
28    "        "          1-2      1901-1918
30   Black marriages       K       1889-1890
      "        "           H       1893-1895
31    "        "          1-2      1895-1898
```

Figure 7: County records for Holmes County as given in the non-book catalog

county's holdings, you can see what might be available for your research in the county courthouse of your ancestor's home county.

Deed records are also found in the county records file, and will be discussed with the land records in chapter 5.

Since the publication and television production of *Roots* by the late Alex Haley, a new interest in the pursuit of family history has arisen, and to accommodate that interest, many indexes to county records have been published. Those published relating to Mississippi county records may be found in the MDAH library book card/computer catalog. To determine if a book on a particular county's marriage records has been published, search the catalog, looking for the subject "MARRIAGE RECORDS." Once you have found this general heading, continue looking until you locate the geographical subdivision—Copiah County, for example: "MISSISSIPPI—COPIAH COUNTY." If the library has a book on Copiah County marriages, it should be found under the heading that reads "MARRIAGE RECORDS—MISSISSIPPI—COPIAH COUNTY." Some counties may have more than one book listed; remember to search all of them, as one transcriber may have been able to decipher a name while another may have had difficulty. Figure 8 shows examples of subject entries from the book card catalog. Other subject approaches to information include wills, deeds, genealogy, etc.

The book catalog cards that refer to the most heavily used Mississippi genealogical books will have a plastic slip on the cards with the words "Search Room" in red across the top. These books are shelved in Dewey Decimal (numerical) order along the walls of the library research room. All of the other books (those lacking the plastic sleeve) are shelved in a closed stack area and must be requested with a call slip (fig. 9).

Tax Records

The majority of the department's tax records since statehood have been microfilmed and are listed with the county records in the non-book catalog. The tax rolls are filed in alphabetical order by county in the microfilm room. The territorial tax rolls have also been filmed and are in the microfilm room, but they are filed with the territorial auditor material in Record Group 3. The tax records are frequently used to verify a person's residence in the territory/state when a census record may not have survived; these records should be viewed cautiously for the individual may indeed have owned property in a Mississippi county but have lived in another county

Room

929.3
M69b
B478

MARRIAGE RECORDS - MISSISSIPPI -
BENTON COUNTY.
Benton County, Mississippi, 1871-1900.

Search
Room

929.3
M69bo
B6895
v.2

MARRIAGE RECORDS - MISS. - BOLIVAR COUNTY.

Bolivar County, vol. 2, 1866-1904 / Katherine Clements Branton, Alice Clements Wade, co-editors. -- [S.l. : s.n.], 1990.
ii, 243 p. ; 29 cm. -- (Early Mississippi records)

1. Marriage records - Miss. - Bolivar County. 2. Registers of births, etc. - Miss. - Bolivar County. 3. Court records - Miss. - Bolivar County. 4. Bolivar County, Miss. - Genealogy.
I. Branton, Katherine Clements. II. Wade, Alice Clements.
III. Series.

Search
Room

929.3
M69c
I38

MARRIAGE RECORDS - MISSISSIPPI -
CALHOUN COUNTY.
Index to marriage records, Calhoun County, Mississippi, Dec. 30, 1922, thru Dec. 10, 1946, also rerecorded 1800-. -- [S.l. : s.n., 19--]
[77] leaves ; 30 cm.

Reproduction of typescript.

1. Marriage records - Mississippi - Calhoun County. 2. Calhoun County, Mississippi - Genealogy.

Search
Room

929.3
M69ch
C533

MARRIAGE RECORDS - MISSISSIPPI -
CHICKASAW COUNTY.
Chickasaw County, Mississippi, 1863-1900, computer indexed marriage records.

Search
Room

929.3
M69cop
G481c

MARRIAGE RECORDS - MISSISSIPPI -
COPIAH COUNTY.
Gillis, Irene S.
Copiah County, Mississippi, marriages, 1823-1865.

Figure 8: Subject approach to search for marriage records in the book card catalog

NAME	RESEARCHER NO.	DATE

BOOKS:

Call No. _____ Volume No. _____

Call No. _____ Volume No. _____

Call No. _____ Volume No. _____

Call No. _____ Volume No. _____

Call No. _____ Volume No. _____

SUBJECT FILES:

Subject _____

Subject _____

Subject _____

Subject _____

Subject _____

NEWSPAPERS:

Town _____ Title _____ Date _____

Town _____ Title _____ Date _____

Town _____ Title _____ Date _____

Town _____ Title _____ Date _____

Town _____ Title _____ Date _____

COUNTY RECORDS:

County _____ Roll No. _____

County _____ Roll No. _____

County _____ Roll No. _____

County _____ Roll No. _____

County _____ Roll No. _____

MISCELLANEOUS: (Recordings; video, audio, etc.)

Figure 9: Call slip used to request items in closed stacks

or even out of state. Therefore, a person might appear on the tax list but not be on the census because he did not actually reside in that county. Or, an individual might be shown on more than one county tax list, in which case it becomes your task to determine where he resided.

In addition to helping locate an individual in a particular area and time, tax records can also be used to ascertain a person's death, since when someone died, his estate would be taxed. These records can also help determine the name of an individual, who would be more likely to give his complete name than a nickname or initial to the tax assessor. The years available for any one county vary greatly, since after the tax was collected, the volumes were often discarded.

While the state archives has a basic collection of the county records helpful to genealogist's, at some point you will need to go to the county courthouse to search records that have not been filmed. Remember that most courthouses will not have the staff to assist you personally; however, if you are unable to get assistance there, do not be discouraged! Contact MDAH or the local public library to see if the county has an active genealogical/historical society. If it does, perhaps some of the members will be willing to plunge into the old courthouse records for you. At the state archives, a list of private researchers is available upon request.

EDUCABLE CHILDREN

After the Civil War, in order to determine how much revenue would be needed to educate all of the children of the state, a census was taken of schoolage children. The state superintendent of education was to provide the number of children annually to the auditor; the auditor would then apportion the school revenues based on the number of students (*Laws of Mississippi* 1873). In 1878, the law was changed and the county assessor was directed to make a list of the schoolage children giving "the name, age, sex, and color of each child, also the election district, and if in a city or town, the ward in which such child resides."

The educable children list's from 1885 on are even more helpful to the family historian, for the name of the parent or guardian of each child was added that year. If you notice the years for which the Archives has the list of schoolage children, you will realize that by using the 1885 and the 1892 educable children list (for those counties where the lists are available), you will have a good replacement for the record of families with children who should have appeared on the 1890 federal census that burned up.

After these records were used by the auditor and the state superintendent of education, they were turned in to the Office of the Secretary of State (Record Group 28); this is the location of many of the early educable children lists. Naturally, after the creation of the department of education, the educable children records were filed with that department (Record Group 50). In recent years, educable children lists have also been appearing in the county microfilm files and in published works, so there are really four places to check for holdings of these records (RG 28, RG 50, the card/computer catalog and the non-book catalog of county records).

The Archives does not have all of the records of educable children. Many of these records are still in the care of the county superintendent of education in the various counties. If you do not see your county listed in the MDAH holdings, contact the county education office to determine the location of this invaluable resource. (MDAH has telephone numbers and addresses for each county education office.)

THREE

Vital Records

Birth and death records were not officially kept by the state of Mississippi until November 1912. Before that time, some municipalities and counties did have registers, though the majority did not keep records until they were required to do so. To find out if these local vital records exist in your county of interest, contact the county chancery clerk, or in a local community, the city clerk.

BIRTH RECORDS

The Archives Department does not have any official birth certificates. The State of Mississippi did not officially keep birth records until November 1912, records from that date to the present are in the custody of the Mississippi Department of Health, Vital Records Section (see appendix for address). However, some certificates of birth that were kept by Pass Christian midwives can be found in the Department of Health files (RG 51). These certificates which were to be filled out and forwarded to the beat health officer or county health officer, are the only midwives' reports presently located at the Archives. The certificates contain the date of birth, sex and color of child, names and places of birth of the parents as well as their color and occupations, remarks, informant's name, and the date when the form was completed, and the certificate number. Strangely, the certificate does not give the name of the child. These certificates have been transcribed by MDAH staff and are available in the library research room with the Hancock County books. They cover the period 1895–1902.

Birth information relating to the Choctaws Indians living on the reservation during the period from July 1924 through 1938 may be found on the Indian census microfilm labelled 1924–1932 and 1933–1937. Since these are federal records it is not known if these births appear in the files at the Mississippi Department of Health.

Baptism records are sometimes helpful in determining birth information. Numerous church records can be found in the Archives. They often contain valuable data relating to baptisms, marriages, and deaths. (Church records will be discussed more fully in chapter 6.)

DEATH RECORDS

While there are no copies of official birth records at MDAH, there are microform copies of the state's official death records from November 1912 to 1937. These are indexed by years; some are in alphabetical order and others are arranged by the Soundex Code (see chapter 2 for a discussion of this code). The index usually gives the name of the deceased, race, county, death certificate number and year of death. A library staff member would need the death certificate number and the year of death to pull the record for you. Death certificates provide the date and place of birth of the deceased, as well as the names of the parents and their places of birth (assuming all this information was given to the attending physician or health officer). The death records at MDAH are located in RG 51, the Department of Health. Additionally, death records for Choctaw Indians living on the reservation have been found among the microfilmed census schedules of 1926–1937. The death rolls as they are called, skip some years but include deaths from July 1, 1924 through December 31, 1938.

Some counties and cities have death records for years before 1912; this was found to be true in Jackson. Death certificates for the years 1909–1912 were found in the Jackson Municipal Archives. These have been transcribed and are cataloged in the library book collection. In addition to Jackson's death records, the Archives also has the early Sexton Reports (1836–1859 and 1870–1873) from the city of Natchez. Access to these microfilm records is through the non-book catalog under Natchez Municipal Records.

Another source that can be used to verify a death date is a funeral home register. In addition to the expected information about the date of death and place of burial, some registers contain the following about the deceased: occupation, date of birth, and names and places of birth of the parents. At present MDAH has funeral home records from the Fisher Funeral Home in Vicksburg (1854–1921); the Hartman-Henderson Funeral Home in Brookhaven (1927–1970), the C. O. Pate Funeral Home in Tate County (1928–1967), and in Jackson, Baldwin Funeral Home (1929–1969), Hardy Funeral Home, (1906–1929), Memorial Funeral Home (1952–1960), and Taylor Funeral Home (1924–1952). The funeral homes in Jackson, especially Hardy and Taylor, handled funerals for both blacks and whites for many years. This was a common practice in the early years and still is in many communities.

Finally, the federal mortality schedules may be used to help establish a death date. However, remember that these records only give information about persons who died during the twelve months preceding the census year, so they actually just cover one year out of ten. Thus, for example, the 1850 Mortality Schedule covers the period from July 1, 1849, through June 30, 1850. Many people were undoubtably omitted; in fact, census authorities estimate that 40 percent of the persons who died during that period were left off the schedules! The Archives has mortality schedules on microfilm for 1850, 1860, 1870, and 1880, and each now has a printed index. While the printed index is easier on the eyes (many of the microfilm copies are light and difficult to read), researchers should beware of depending too heavily on an index since some of them do not give all of the information available on the actual schedule. The 1880 index *does not* include the birth place of the deceased or of his parents, yet this information is on the schedule. The 1870 index provides the family number where the deceased individual's family may be found on the corresponding 1870 population schedule. Both of these omissions in the indexes could be critical to the family genealogist, so remember never to depend solely on an index; always examine an actual copy of a document if it is available for research.

Any discussion of mortality in Mississippi (or elsewhere in the South) must include a mention of the numerous epidemics, yellow fever and others, that ravaged the state. Yellow fever was a constant threat to the early settlers, with the highest number of deaths occurring in 1823, 1853 and 1878. Dunbar Rowland gives a good summary of the disease and its effects in volume 2 of his history of Mississippi. Several books have been published listing these deaths; they can also be found in some of the subject file clippings and other newspaper accounts.

For death records since 1937, and for all birth records, contact: the Mississippi Department of Health, Vital Records Section, P. O. Box 1700, Jackson, Mississippi 39215.

MARRIAGE AND DIVORCE RECORDS

Marriage records in Mississippi are readily available for researchers to explore. While most of the original marriage books are in the various county courthouses, microfilm copies are accessible in the Archives as well as in many Mississippi libraries. The extent of the collection varies from county to county, since over the years some records may have been destroyed in courthouse fires. In the Archives collection, the marriage records are filed by county, and all are indexed to some degree. Those who do not know the county where the marriage took place can try Mississippi's statewide marriage index, which was compiled by the Works Progress Administration workers. It is indexed by the groom's name; access is through the Soundex (see explanation in chapter 2). This index provides the researcher with the names of both parties, the date of the marriage or when the license was secured, the county, book, and page where the record can be found, and the name of the minister or court official. With this citation, you could then proceed to the county record files to see if MDAH has the marriage data for that particular period. If you are unable to use this source at the Archives library, you may get it on loan from the Mississippi Library Commission (see appendix for address). The Library Commission will send their microfilm on interlibrary loan to other libraries, so determine which Soundex roll you need and ask your librarian to request that roll for you. Be aware when you are using the Soundex marriage rolls that there are two sets of these records, one with primarily white marriages and the other with a mixture of blacks and whites. If you do not locate your ancestor on one set, always examine the second copy.

Additionally, there are now many published indexes to the county marriage records (these will be listed in the bibliography of source materials). To locate the published volumes at the Archives library, look in the book card/computer catalog under "MARRIAGE RECORDS—MISSISSIPPI."

Many researchers come to the Archives searching for divorce records. Before 1859, divorce proceedings were introduced as private bills in the legislature. References to these are found in the books *Index of Mississippi Session Acts 1817–1865* and *Index to the Laws of the Mississippi Territory* (see source list). After 1859, divorce proceedings were filed in the chancery clerk's office of the county in which the divorce took place. As a rule, these later records are not available for research at the Archives, but always examine the county record holdings since new records are being microfilmed and added all the time. Also, numerous references to divorces can be found in the various newspaper abstract books, and many of these divorces are not mentioned in the *Index of Mississippi Session Acts 1817–1865*.

OTHER SOURCES

Newspapers should not be overlooked as sources for vital record information. In addition to the biographical index, there are numerous books that index marriage, death and even divorce notices which have appeared in newspapers. (Some of these will be given in this book's annotated source list.) To locate these volumes in the Archives library card/computer catalog, search under the key words, e.g., marriage and/or divorce.

The Historical Records Survey program of the Works Progress Administration provided numerous guides and indexes to Mississippi sources. One source, the *Guide to Vital Statistics Records in Mississippi*, was originally compiled in an effort to locate sources of vital records as part of the war effort. It is discussed in chapter 6 on researching cemeteries and churches.

FOUR

Military Information

Many researchers come to the Archives seeking military service information. For the most part, the MDAH collection of military records pertains to the nineteenth century but there are some bits and pieces that might be useful for those doing research on the military in the twentieth century.

Twentieth Century Wars:
World Wars I and II, Korea, Vietnam

There are no service or personnel records for veterans of Vietnam, Korea, World War II and World War I at the Mississippi Archives but you can find these by writing Military Personnel Records, 9700 Page Blvd., St. Louis, Missouri 63132. A fire in that facility a few years ago, unfortunately destroyed some records. Also, if you are seeking discharge papers of a serviceman for the period of the Korean conflict and Vietnam, you may contact the Mississippi Veterans Home in Jackson (see appendix for address).

The Archives has a list compiled by military service of the men and women who were killed in twentieth-century military conflicts (World War I through Vietnam). The information varies from person to person because it was gathered from many different sources. Usually, it provides name of soldier, serial number, organization at the time of death, and the date of death; however, sometimes family members, or next of kin, are given.

Since the World War I and World War II lists are not indexed, it is time-consuming to search them. However, if you locate the name and serial number of your relative, the Military Personnel Records in St. Louis should be able to assist you in acquiring more information.

The first draft registration was held in 1917. World War I draft cards are not in the state archives, but can be found at the National Archives, Southeast Region (see appendix for address). To request a search, you must provide the full name of the individual and his city or county of residence at the time of the registration. A nominal fee is charged for this service. Additionally, the Mississippi Veterans Home does have some draft records for individuals who served in World Wars I and II.

If your relative did not die in World War I and you just need some basic information about him, the Archives does have a "Master Index of World War I Veterans" (for Mississippi) on microfilm; again, the information provides the name of the soldier, hometown, race, and serial number. This source is described in the manuscript collection guide. With this information you can also write to the St. Louis office for a copy of a service record.

Lists of soldiers who participated in World War I are often found in the county histories compiled by the Works Progress Administration in the 1930s. These files are found in MDAH in Record Group 60. Every WPA county history has a chapter on wars, but the information varies; some have only a list (or partial list) of county veterans, while others have veterans' remembrances and even copies of letters written home during the conflict. Additional information on the various wars follows the county historical material in the WPA finding aid description (RG 60).

Spanish-American War

The Spanish-American War records are housed at the National Archives (see appendix for address); however, the Mississippi adjutant general's annual report for 1898–1899 does list all of the Mississippi participants. Also, the Veterans Affairs Board (Record Group 44) has records on *some* of the Mississippi veterans who served in the Spanish-American War and World Wars I and II. Information on the Spanish-American veterans includes name, rank, residence, regiment, date of enlistment and date mustered out. For veterans who served in World Wars I and II, name, county of residence, branch of service, date of death, name of cemetery and location of cemetery are given. Remember that this does not include all who served.

Veterans of the Spanish-American War are arranged alphabetically by name, and veterans of World Wars I and II are alphabetical by county and then by name.

CIVIL WAR: CONFEDERATE RECORDS

The Confederate records are some of the most popular items at the Archives. Since over eighty thousand Mississippians participated in the Confederate army, it is no wonder that there are many descendants who are curious about their relatives' part in the war. The service records of Mississippians who fought for the Confederacy are found on microfilm in the microfilm room. An accompanying index is also on film. The index consists of individual cards microfilmed in alphabetical order. The only information on the index cards is the soldier's name and his military unit (fig. 10).

The service records are then found under the name of the unit. A guide citing each unit and the appropriate microfilm roll number is available in the microfilm reading room. The service records are in alphabetical order within each unit. While these records may prove interesting reading, they rarely provide family information. For the most part, the service record gives the location and date of enlistment; more information is provided if the soldier was wounded, captured, or killed (fig. 11). There are rare instances in which probate records can be found filed with a service record; in such a case, family members may be found listed as next of kin.

A very few Mississippians served in the Confederate navy and marine corps. The records for these units are on seven rolls of microfilm in the reading room; the cards are filmed alphabetically. These service records include men from all Confederate states, not just Mississippi.

Those looking for a soldier who was a prisoner of war will find the records of the northern prisoner-of-war camps on microfilm in the reading room. An accompanying guide to this source is also available.

A more extensive description of the MDAH Confederate archives, including muster rolls, other original records, and some discharge papers, may be found in Record Group 9, Confederate Records.

PENSION

The survivors of the Confederate army who were in financial distress in the early 1900s were eligible to apply for a pension. Pensions were issued in the state where the veteran or his widow was residing at that time (not necessarily the state where he entered service). The pension applications are in RG 29, Office of the State Auditor, and have been microfilmed in alphabetical order for easy access. Additionally, pension application files found in the various county courthouses are now being filmed by the Church of Jesus Christ of Latter-day Saints; doublecheck the non-book catalog under the county name to determine if any applications have been filmed from your county of interest. The pension applications ask numerous questions, such as name, age, county of residence, marital status, service-related information, and with whom the person was living.

Researchers who come to MDAH seeking service records are frequently unable to locate their relatives in the Mississippi index to service records. If this happens to you, examine the pension applications, for you may find that your relative lived in Mississippi after the war but served with a unit from another state. The unit's name and commander should be included on the pension application and with that information you could write to the appropriate archives asking for assistance. Mississippi's archives does have published abstracts of the service records of Confederate soldiers from Georgia, Louisiana, and North Carolina.

The records of the pension payments to the veteran are another source found in Record Group 29. An examination of these records, frequently makes it possible to determine an approximate date of death for the veteran or his widow. However, these records are not indexed, so this can be an extremely tedious search.

OTHER CONFEDERATE SOURCES

Numerous diaries and journals were kept by Mississippi soldiers during the Civil War. These are usually arranged by the veteran's (author's) name in the manuscript finding aid. The Archives also has a list by unit of the manuscript collections that contain diaries kept during the war. This unit list is kept at the reference desk and may be requested there. The manuscript collection also contains the papers of the United Daughters of the Confederacy, ten volumes of membership records covering the period 1897 to 1937. Many of the persons applying for membership in the UDC are the actual wives and daughters of the veterans. Each volume is indexed, but by the member's name, not the soldier's.

Researchers frequently know a local name, that is, a nickname or local designation of a company unit in which an ancestor may have served. In order to translate that nickname into a unit's official name, refer to William F. Amann's *Personnel of the Civil War* (see source list). For instance, the

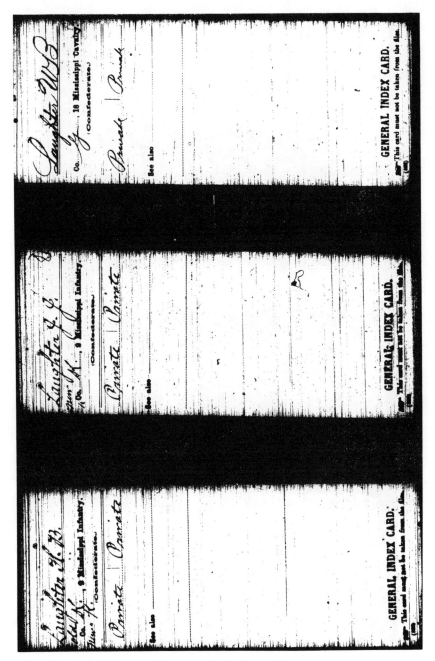

Figure 10: Confederate military service index cards

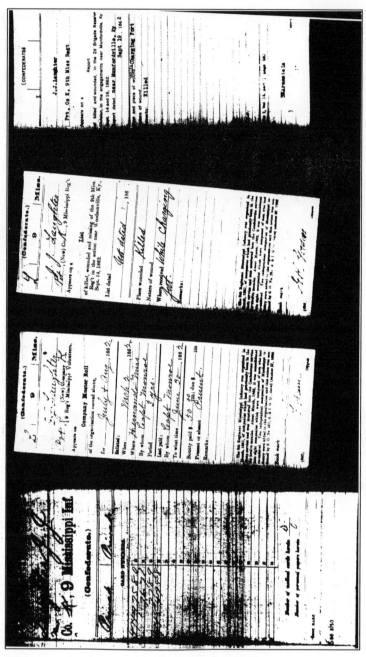

Figure 11: J. J. Laughter Confederate service record

"Jasper Avengers" would not be found on the National Archives microfilm, but using Amann's book you find that this unit really referred to Company H of the 37th Mississippi Infantry. Of course, the more expedient way to determine an ancestor's unit of service would be to examine the aforementioned index on microfilm.

Case Files of Applications from Former Confederates for Presidential Pardons, 1865–1867 are files of letters arranged in alphabetical order by the name of the applicant. The information given usually includes name, county of residence, age, whether he was a secessionist or not, and whether he was active in the war. Sometimes family members are mentioned, and in many cases accompanying letters will tell of the applicant's good character. These letter files are on microfilm in the microfilm reading room (fig. 12).

Another useful WPA project that may help the family historian is the survey of military grave registrations. Though the majority of the findings are Confederate graves, Union veterans were also recorded. These grave registrations are on microfilm. The entries are arranged by war, and within the war the entries are alphabetized by the name of the soldier. The Confederate grave registrations have been indexed by Betty Wiltshire. This index is cataloged and accessible through the library computer catalog.

CIVIL WAR: UNION RECORDS

Although few white Mississippians (around five hundred) fought on the Union side in the Civil War, there are four rolls of microfilm of service records. The index to the service records of white Union soldiers from Mississippi is similiar in format to the Confederate index. The name, rank, and unit is given on an index card. The index, however, is not really needed for Mississippi's soldiers because it only refers to one unit, the First Battalion of Mississippi, Mounted Rifles. The information given in the Union service record is similiar to that in the Confederate, with the notable exception of two forms: 1) a declaration of recruitment that gives the age, occupation and a physical description of the recruit, and 2) a volunteer enlistment form that asks place and state of birth in addition to the previously mentioned information. The records of the U. S. Colored Troops that may have served from Mississippi are still in the National Archives and have not been microfilmed. *The War of the Rebellion*, series 3, volume 5, states that approximately eighteen thousand blacks from Mississippi served with the Union forces. According to Ronald F. Davis's *The*

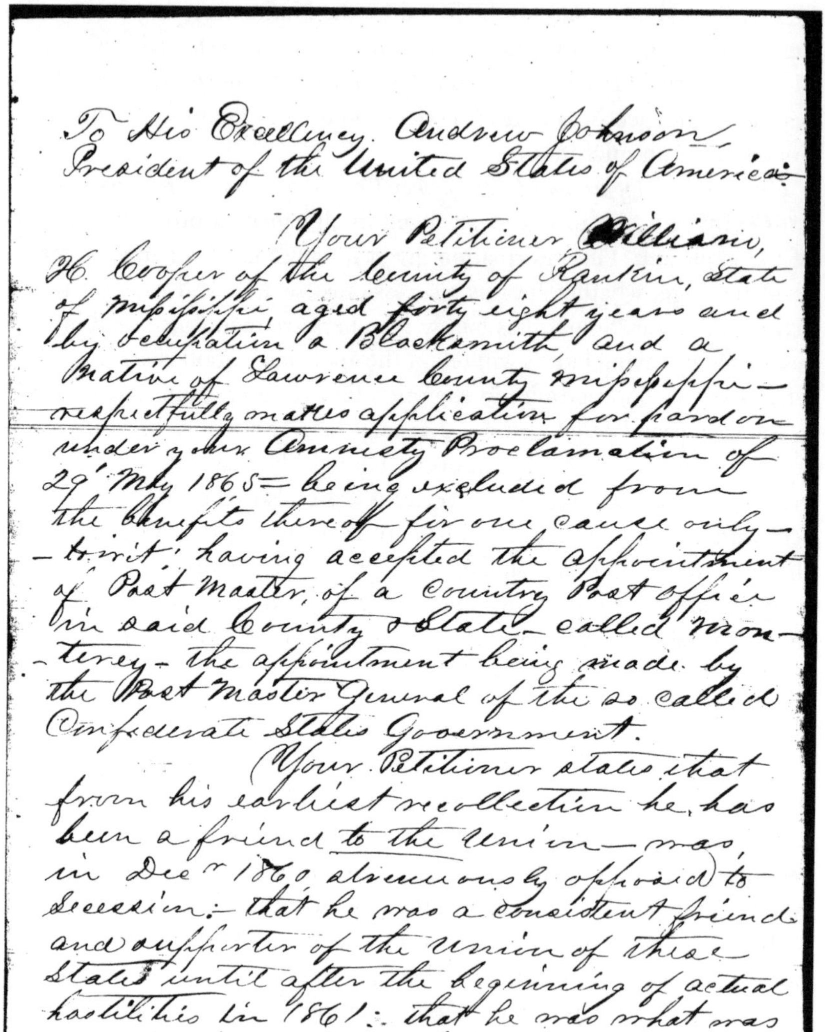

To His Excellency Andrew Johnson,
President of the United States of America:

Your Petitioner William H. Cooper of the County of Rankin, State of Mississippi, aged forty eight years and by occupation a Blacksmith, and a Native of Lawrence County Mississippi— respectfully makes application for pardon under your Amnesty Proclamation of 29th May 1865— being excluded from the benefits thereof for one cause only— to wit: having accepted the appointment of Post Master, of a Country Post office in said County & State called Monterey— the appointment being made by the Post Master General of the so called Confederate States Government.

Your Petitioner states that from his earliest recollection he has been a friend to the Union— was, in Decr 1860 strenuously opposed to Secession:— that he was a consistent friend and supporter of the Union of these States until after the beginning of actual hostilities in 1861:— that he was what was called an "old line whig"— a Union man: that in 1860 in the Presidential Contest he voted for Bell & Everett, and in December of that year, gave his vote & influence against the secession Candidates for the Convention. Your Petitioner states that

Figure 12: Application of William Cooper for a Presidential pardon (facing pages)

the never volunteered, or took up arms
in the Confederate Army, until Com-
-pelled to do so in November 1864 and
served about two months — that he
accepted the appointment above named
to escape Conscription, and for no other
reason, and thereby kept out of the
military service until the Congress passed
an Act declaring all Post Masters liable
to military Service, under the age of 50
years, who were not appointed by the
President; — that he received no such
appointment, and was consequently forced
into the service in Nov 1864, as above
named.

Your Petitioner States further that
his property, real & personal is not worth
more that Five hundred dollars, and that
he has a wife & Seven Children entirely
dependent upon him for support.
That he desires to remain within the limits
of the United States, and demean himself
as a quiet, peaceable & orderly citizen,
and aid as far as he can to restore order
and Civil Government, and abide
by and accept the situation as good citizens
should.

Your Petitioner has taken the amnesty
oath, which is herewith transmitted
Your Petitioner prays that your
Excellency will grant him a pardon
&c. and in duty bound &c.
Brandon Rankin Co Miss   William H. Cosker
July 22nd 1865

			Sample of Individuals Born in Adams County 58th. Colored U. S. Infantry: Co. E			

NAME	AGE	OCCUPATION	OWNER	MARRIED	REMARKS
Richard Austin	24	Gardener	General Quitman	S	Appt Sergeant
Prince Albert	40	Coachman	Philip Nicholes	M	
Frank Burris	20	Field Hand	Thomas McGowin	M	Died, July 1864
Walter Bradley	25	Gardener	Major Chotah	M	
Elias Docker	22	Gardener	Benjamin Chase	S	
William Dorsey	18	Field Hand	Thomas McGowin	M	
Jacob Ellis	20	Field Hand	Sam Courin	?	
David Fletcher	20	Field Hand	Major Chotah	S	Died, March 1864
Anthony Farass	22	Field Hand	Samuel Haubert	S	
William Gray	23	?	Henry Chotale	S	
Jeff. Harding	40	?	Frank Reynolds	M	
Scott Simon	40	Field Hand	Johnson Rucker	?	Deserted, Sept. 63
Screws Simon	27	Field Hand	Johnson Rucker	M	Deserted, Sept. 63
Wallis Stevens	21	Butler	Richard Chotah	M	Died, May 1864
Charles Vessles	19	Butler	General Quitman	S	Corporal
George Walters	28	Field Hand	?	S	Died, Sept. 1863
Edward Whites	44	Field Hand	Judge Turner	M	
Joe Witherspool	45	Field Hand	Girard Stanton	M	
William Wood	22	Field Hand	Samuel Graham	S	Died, Sept. 1863
Geo Washington	38	Groom	A. L. Bingaman	M	Murd by Guerillas
Nathan Wright	21	Field Hand	John Rucker	S	
George Wright	28	Field Hand	John Rucker	M	Deserted, Oct. 63 Returned, June 65
James Wright	24	Field Hand	John Rucker	M	Deserted, Oct. 63 Returned, June. 65
Albert Nichols	18	Field Hand	Free	?	Corporal
Joseph Hinton	26	Field Hand	Jonathan Day	?	Died, Dec. 1865
John Jefferson	24	Butler	Mr. Martin	?	
David Stephens	44	Gardener	Major Chotah	?	

Figure 13: Muster roll information on U. S. Colored Troops as found in the National Archives

Black Experience in Natchez 1720–1880 (see source list) there is a wealth of important information to be found on African-American veterans in the Muster Books and Regimental Description Records in Record Group 94 at the National Archives (fig. 13).

When Congress finally created legislation in 1871 that would eventually offer assistance to the pro-Union southerner, over twenty-two thousand cases were filed with the Southern Claims Commission for reimbursement of losses. Mississippi's Archives has only the index to these files, but if you find your relative listed, you can write to the National Archives for the case file. Southerners who fought for the Confederacy also tried to make claims, and even the claims that were not accepted will be on file.

MEXICAN WAR

From 1846 to 1848, many Mississippi men were engaged in the activities surrounding the Mexican War. Each man who served in a Mississippi unit is listed in the biographical name index of the Archives library. The information given on the index card/fiche is simply the soldier's name, rank, and military unit; the service records are arranged on microfilm by unit, and within the unit, they are alphabetical by the soldier's name.

Both the pension applications and the land warrants relating to the Mexican War are in the National Archives. However, beginning in volume 5, number 2, of the *Mississippi Genealogical Exchange* (see source list), the pensioners of the War of 1812 and of the Indian and Mexican wars are listed with name, post office address, date of original allowance and the certificate number. With this information, you can write the National Archives for a copy of the file. This listing includes only those pensioners who were still on file January 1, 1883. MDAH also has a set of published volumes with this information entitled, *List of Pensioners on the Roll January 1, 1883* (see source list).

WAR OF 1812

From 1812 to 1814, residents of the Mississippi Territory found themselves caught in a conflict between the French and the English. Names of Mississippians who fought in the War of 1812 can be found in the biographical name index, as well as in *The Mississippi Territory in the War of 1812* by Mrs. Dunbar Rowland (see source list). As with the previously mentioned war records, once you know the unit of service, you can search the service records on microfilm in the microfilm room; they are in alphabetical order by the name of the soldier. The information provided is usually just the place and date of enlistment, unless the soldier was wounded, taken prisoner, or died, in which case that information is also given. The war record itself does not give much family information, but because of the war service, many veterans were eligible for bounty land warrants. No bounty land warrants are in the Mississippi Department of Archives and History, but they are at the National Archives in Washington. The War of 1812 pension files are also at the National Archives. The pension application can give valuable genealogical information, such as, veteran's age and place of residence and even the wife's name, if he was married. The *Mississippi Genealogical Exchange*, volume 8, number 1, contains part one of an alphabetical list of every War of 1812 pensioner who had a Mississippi connection either through serving from the state or through residence there. The abstract gives an abundance of genealogical information, such as residence, wife (including maiden name), date of marriage (and previous marriages), death and place of death of soldier/wife. The series continues in subsequent issues. Another pension-related published book at the Archives is *The Pension Roll of 1835* (see source list) in which each individual receiving a pension at that time is listed with his rank, unit, age, and in some instances, death date.

MISSISSIPPI TERRITORIAL MILITIA

Miscellaneous muster rolls of the militia of the Mississippi Territory can be found in the papers of the Territorial Governor (Record Group 2) and in the papers of J. F. H. Claiborne (z239m). The manuscript and official records guides will indicate the appropriate boxes to search but, within the boxes there is no discernible order to these documents. However, they can be of great help in determining whether a male individual was in the territory in the late 1790s or early 1800s.

AMERICAN REVOLUTION

Revolutionary War service records are not available at the Mississippi Archives, but many records relating to the war are. The *Index to Revolutionary War Soldiers* is available for research on microfilm. The soldiers are listed in alphabetical order on individual cards with their military unit indicated on each card. With the ancestor's name and unit of service, you can write to the National Archives for a copy of his service record. While MDAH has books relating to the pension files of the Revolutionary War, the actual pension and bounty land records are available through the National Archives. Both the *Mississippi Genealogical Exchange* (volume 1 and subsequent) and the *National Genealogical Society Quarterly* (MDAH collection begins with volume 31, 1943) have printed abstracts of pensions drawn by Revolutionary War soldiers or their widows who have lived in Mississippi.

Numerous veterans of the American Revolution were among Mississippi's pioneers. The Mississippi Society of the Daughters of the American Revolution published *Family Records: Mississippi Revolutionary Soldiers* (see source list) which collects family records of some of the Revolutionary War soldiers or their families who were known to have moved to Mississippi after the war. The information given comes totally from the families and no attempt was made to verify it; therefore, some of the reference citations are unfamiliar, even to the MDAH staff.

The membership application forms of the Mississippi Society of the Sons of the American Revolution have been deposited at the Archives since the 1980s. These forms have been bound and are accessible through the library catalog. The entries within the volumes are alphabetical by the name of the soldier. The information given usually includes the applicant's line of descent from the Revolutionary War soldier, a summation of the ancestor's service in the war, the names of the spouse, children and grandchildren of the applicant, military service of applicant, if any, and finally, the references used to document the person's service record. These applications have been given over a period of years, so there are several bound volumes with the names from A to Z. Always check to see all of the volumes for whatever letter pertains to your ancestor.

FIVE

Land Records

To document land ownership in Mississippi, you must once again proceed from the known to the unknown.

DEEDS

First, determine a county of residence for an individual from the available census schedules; then search the deeds in the county records. The actual deeds and indexes to them are kept in the office of the chancery clerk in the county where the land is located, and may be consulted there. The Mississippi Department of Archives and History has microfilm copies of most existing deeds up until the early 1900s. Fires have occurred in many of Mississippi's courthouses over the years. If there was a courthouse fire, it is likely that some portion of the county records were destroyed and those records will not be at the Archives or in the county. *Survey of Records in Mississippi Court Houses* (see source list) is an excellent source for determining what records are available and also what records may have been lost in a courthouse fire. (Naturally, fires occurring since the date of publication are not included.)

The deed holdings for the various counties are filed at MDAH in the non-book catalog under the name of each county. Deeds are indexed, usually by both the grantor (person selling the land) and grantee (person buying the land). When you locate the deed index within your desired

```
Film
       Neshoba Co., Mississippi.  Chancery Clerk.
              Deed records, 1835-1888; general index to
       deeds, 1835-1892.  Philadelphia, Miss., filmed
       by G.S., 1972.
              10 rolls, 35mm.  Index.  Handwritten.
   1          General index to deeds  v. 1-2   1835-1892
   2          Deed records                A-D   1835-1839
   3            "     "                    E-G   1839-1852
   4            "     "                    H-J   1847-1857
   5            "     "                    K     1857-1859
   6            "     "                    L-M   1859-1870
   7            "     "                    N-O   1870-1874

                                          Card 1 of 2
```

MISSISSIPPI DEPARTMENT OF ARCHIVES AND HISTORY
Non-Manuscript Materials — Call Slip

Limit — 5 Items

NAME	RESEARCHER NO.	DATE

BOOKS:

Call No. _____ Volume No. _____

Call No. _____ Volume No. _____

Call No. _____ Volume No. _____

Call No. _____ Volume No. _____

Call No. _____ Volume No. _____

SUBJECT FILES:

Subject _____

Subject _____

Subject _____

Subject _____

Subject _____

NEWSPAPERS:

Town _____ Title _____ Date _____

Town _____ Title _____ Date _____

Town _____ Title _____ Date _____

Town _____ Title _____ Date _____

Town _____ Title _____ Date _____

COUNTY RECORDS:

County _Neshoba_____ Roll No. _____

County _____ Roll No. _____

County _____ Roll No. _____

County _____ Roll No. _____

County _____ Roll No. _____

MISCELLANEOUS: (Recordings; video, audio, etc.)

Figure 14: County microfilm card in the non-book catalog indicates the deed index is on roll 1; this figure illustrates the use of the call slip to acquire this record

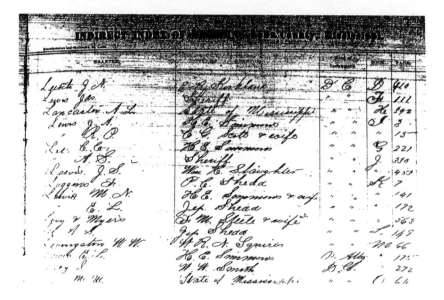

Figure 15: Deed index indicates the Kirkland deed is found in Book D page 410

county, you will need to request the corresponding roll of microfilm (fig. 14). Those doing research at the chancery clerk's office should consult with the clerk's staff for specific information about the location of deed books and indexes. In general, however, the procedure that follows, of first finding the names in the index and then locating the actual record in a deed book, will be applicable there.

As you begin to examine the index you will realize that when the term "indexed" is used with county records, it means that all of the surnames beginning with a particular letter are arranged together, but the individual surnames are rarely in alphabetical order! The index will give the grantor, grantee, volume, and page where the deed can be found. Sometimes the date of the transaction is also in the deed index. You will want to examine all of the deeds (of the right time period) for persons of your surname in the grantor/grantee index. If you find numerous references to your surname, begin your search with the latest known ancestor's date of death or departure from the state and work backwards to the earliest land granted to someone of that surname.

After locating the book and page reference in the index microfilm, return to the non-book catalog and reexamine the Archives holdings of deed records for your county to determine if the department has the microfilm for the particular volume cited in the index. In figure 15, you can see that the Kirkland deed is located in book D, page 410. On the county reference cards note that book D will be on microfilm roll number 2. To view this record at MDAH, fill out another call slip, listing in the county records portion whichever film number corresponds to the volume cited (fig. 16). At the chancery clerk's office you will read the actual deed book and not a microfilm copy.

Normally the deed record will provide the names of the grantor and grantee, the location of the property, and the amount of money given for the land. Some deeds, however, list the purchaser's former place of residence, and some even mention other members of the family by name, especially a deed of gift to an individual's heirs. Be aware that land could be passed by inheritance and not be mentioned in the deed books.

Many deeds that predate the Civil War can be a very useful primary source for family historians tracing their African-American roots. Slaves were considered property, and, as such, were frequently mentioned in deeds, and wills, and inventories of estates. (Unfortunately, the slave names are not in the index; remember the index includes only the grantor and grantee.) African-American genealogists will also want to pay close attention to the deed records for another reason. Mortgage records, in the period soon after the end of the Civil War, contain records for many freedmen obtaining property. The information given in the mortgage record can be very similiar to a freedmen's contract, with family members and even ages frequently being given. These records are usually still in the county courthouse, but a few have been filmed and are found with the county records in the Archives.

Sectional indexes are another tool used in deed research. This record shows a detailed list of who has owned a particular section of land over the years. This list of land ownership is the easiest way to do a title search. But remember, when using the sectional index, you must know the land description: that is, the exact township, range, and section of a particular piece of land. These indexes are also housed in the county chancery clerk's office but MDAH does have copies for some counties. If you see in the non-book catalog that a sectional index has been filmed for your county, you can request the microfilm as you did for the index and the deeds.

TRACT BOOKS

After you have gone back to the earliest deed records or to the sectional index (assuming there is one), with the land description in hand you will want

```
Film
      Neshoba Co., Mississippi.  Chancery Clerk.
          Deed records, 1835-1888; general index to
      deeds, 1835-1892.  Philadelphia, Miss., filmed
      by G.S., 1972.
          10 rolls, 35mm.  Index.  Handwritten.
  1       General index to deeds  v. 1-2   1835-1892
  2       Deed records                A-D   1835-1839
  3          "        "               E-G   1839-1852
  4          "        "               H-J   1847-1857
  5          "        "                K    1857-1859
  6          "        "               L-M   1859-1870
  7          "        "               N-O   1870-1874
```

MISSISSIPPI DEPARTMENT OF ARCHIVES AND HISTORY
Non-Manuscript Materials — Call Slip

Limit — 5 Items

NAME	RESEARCHER NO.	DATE

BOOKS:

Call No. _____ Volume No. _____

Call No. _____ Volume No. _____

Call No. _____ Volume No. _____

Call No. _____ Volume No. _____

Call No. _____ Volume No. _____

SUBJECT FILES:

Subject _____

Subject _____

Subject _____

Subject _____

Subject _____

NEWSPAPERS:

Town _____ Title _____ Date _____

Town _____ Title _____ Date _____

Town _____ Title _____ Date _____

Town _____ Title _____ Date _____

Town _____ Title _____ Date _____

COUNTY RECORDS:

County _Neshoba_ _____ Roll No. _2_ _____

County _____ Roll No. _____

County _____ Roll No. _____

County _____ Roll No. _____

County _____ Roll No. _____

MISCELLANEOUS: (Recordings; video, audio, etc.)

Figure 16: County microfilm card shows that vols. A–D will be found on film 2; request roll 2 on the call slip

to use the federal tract books. The tract books record the first purchase of land from the United States. They are really federal sectional index books and are very similiar to the county sectional index in appearance. After the federal government sold the land and issued a patent, the land was no longer its concern; subsequent transactions for that land were located in the individual county deed records. Although these tract books record only the first purchase of land, in counties where the deed records are lost, these federal records may be all you have to go on. *The most important thing about these records is that they frequently lead to other information.*

The tract books are found at MDAH in the records of the Secretary of State, the Land Office Section, or RG 28, SG 1. To determine which roll of microfilm you need in this Record Group, using the tract map, you should plot the land description, that is section, township and range, as you recorded it from the deed record search. (If you have trouble remembering which way the townships and ranges run, remember: uptown and downtown—township runs north and south; and "out on the range"— range runs east and west.) You need to know the approximate area or the meridian and base line to be sure you are in the correct portion of the state (land descriptions in the county records frequently neglect the meridian and base information, but if you know the county you already know the area). Remember also that while county boundary lines may change, the township and range citations do not! After plotting the description, write down the volume number and locate the microfilm number on the conversion chart on the back of the tract map. By using the tract map to plot the land description, Section 30, Township 10 North, Range 13 East, on the Choctaw meridian or in Neshoba County, you would find yourself in the area marked "C 2" (fig. 17). Then, using the tract book conversion chart, you will see that volume C 2 converts to microfilm roll number 92 (fig. 18).

Since this record is from the Office of the Secretary of State, you would find this microfilm shelved in the microfilm room with Record Group 28, Sub-Group 1. If you are lucky enough to find your ancestor listed in the tract books, you will want to copy all of the information given about him and send that to the U. S. Department of Interior, Bureau of Land Management, to see if there is a patent for this individual (fig. 19). In 1993 the Bureau of Land Management completed an automated indexing project which included the tract books of Mississippi. This name index is not yet available at MDAH, but it is available on computer disc through the BLM. You may now query the Bureau of Land Management directly to determine what individuals first received the land from the federal

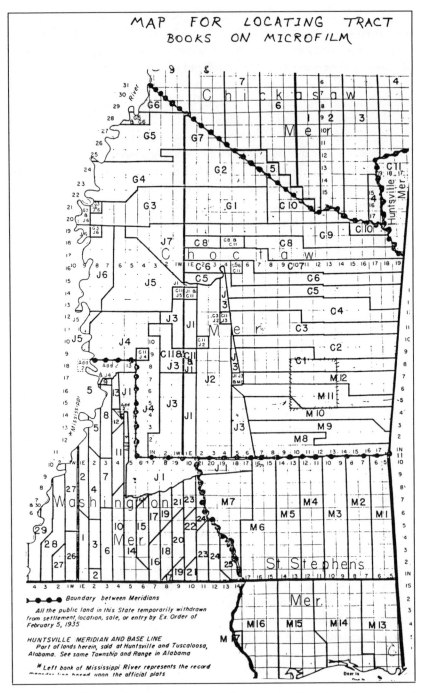

Figure 17: Plotting the land description Section 30, Township 10 north and Range 13 east, you will find that you are in the section marked "C 2"

MF ROLL #	FROM VOLUME	PAGE	TO VOLUME	PAGE	
					TRACT BOOKS FOR THE STATE OF MISSISSIPPI
90	1	1	5	682	CHICKASAW
91	6	683*	9	end	
92	C1	1	C4	159	CHOCTAW
93	C4	160	C8	99	
94	C8	100	C11	end	
95	G1	1	G5	27	
96	G5	28	J2	174	
97	J2	175	J5	78	
98	J5	79	M1	end	
99	M2	1	M5	115	
100	M5	116	M8	end	
101	M9	1	M12	150	
102	M12	151	M16	130	
103	M16	131	2	37	WASHINGTON
104	2	38	3	390	
105	3	391	4A	57	
106	4A	58	7	1319	
107	7	1320	11	2077	
108	11	2078	14	2753	
109	14	2754	14	2560	
110	17	2561	20	4366	
111	20	4367	22	5102	
112	22	5103	26	93	
113	26	94	28	858	
114	29	859	30	end	

Figure 18: On the tract book conversion chart (on back of map) volumes C 1 through C 4 will be on microfilm 92; this film will be in the microfilm room with the records of the secretary of state (RG 28)

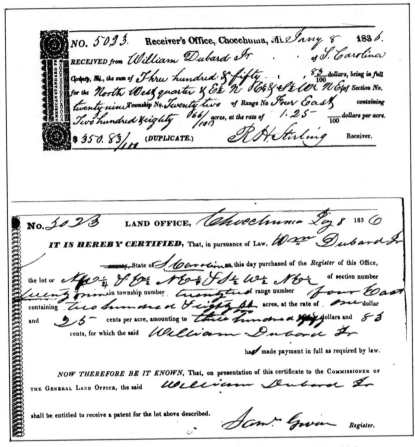

Figure 19: Land certificate of purchase from the Bureau of Land Management

government. (See appendix for the address.) The land entry file is the record of the transaction of the land passing from the federal government to an individual. Land entry files may be found at the National Archives; in fact, more information is usually available from their records. See *Guide to Genealogical Research in the National Archives* for a detailed discussion of their land records. Genealogical information will vary with each file; generally, the file will contain the name of the purchaser and his county of residence, or, perhaps, his former state of residence. It may be that there is no other new information found, but it is exciting to get a land office certificate of purchase verifying that your ancestor did indeed acquire a particular piece of land for a certain amount of money.

If you cannot locate an entry on the tract book, consider checking with the Alabama Archives (see appendix for address) for if your ancestor completed his entry in the St. Stephens or Huntsville land offices, his file would be there. Additionally, there are miscellaneous papers from these two land offices, and from the Washington office, on roll 88 of RG 28 SG 1. The records are not indexed, but they are arranged by land office and include the name of the individual buying land and the land description. If you have this information, you can query the National Archives or the Bureau of Land Management to determine if a file is available on the purchase.

FEDERAL LAND OFFICES

According to Clarence E. Carter's *The Territorial Papers of the United States*, there were three land offices in the Mississippi Territory. One was at Washington (Adams County, Mississippi) for the District West of the Pearl River, one at St. Stephens (in present day Alabama) for the District East of the Pearl River, and one in Huntsville in Madison County (now Alabama). The first step in the administration of federal land disposal was the survey. Once that had been accomplished, more land offices were opened to handle the influx of settlers. Later land offices were opened at Paulding, Columbus, Mount Salus, Jackson, Chocchuma, Grenada, and Pontotoc. (The records of these land offices are normally found at the National Archives in Washington, D. C.) A surveyor of United States lands was appointed to survey and record carefully all purchases. A register and receiver were appointed in each district to handle the actual selling of the land. The register kept a plat book showing each tract surveyed and to whom and when it was sold. The receiver kept up with the money receipts and payments.

The records at the Department of Archives and History contain correspondence between the deputy superintendent and the surveyor of the United States, south of Tennessee, as well as individual surveys of land and monthly reports of the register, but since these records are rarely indexed they can be time-consuming to search.

As previously mentioned, these federal land office records may be your only avenue of research if the county records are nonexistent. For example, if you are seeking early land records in Pike County, you will find that because the courthouse burned in 1882 there are no early land records on file there. If the land was purchased originally by *your* ancestor through the Washington Land Office (the federal land office that disposed of land in the southeastern section of Mississippi), you would want to search the microfilm holdings of U. S. Surveyer General, South of Tennessee, land applications and entries, 1808–1818 (RG 28 SG 1 microfilm 88). If your ancestor was listed, then a file may exist on him at the Bureau of Land Management, and again, additional information may be found at the National Archives under the papers of the particular land office that recorded the information on your relative.

After land was ceded to the United States government by the various Indian nations, it was sold to individuals through federal land offices, usually for cash. The records of these sales are known as "cash entries" and are on file at the National Archives. Very few of the land entry records from Mississippi land offices have been published. The only currently known publication is for the Columbus land office which opened in July 1833. Abstracts of these cash entry files are found in the *Mississippi Genealogical Exchange*, volume 16, and continuing in subsequent volumes. The cash entry abstracts usually include date of entry, number of cash entry receipt, name and residence of purchaser, legal description of land, and remarks, if any. The cash entry receipt number and the legal description of the land may help serve as an index to patent and land entry files that are available at the Bureau of Land Management and/or National Archives (see appendix for addresses).

PLATS

When a piece of land was originally surveyed by the government, a map or plat was drawn. Most of the maps were completed between 1800 and 1840, depending on the location of the land. These plats generally show physical features, e.g., roads, streams, timber, and even houses. A few even show early land claims with the name of the settler, number of acres, name of the surveyor and the date of the survey. To gain access to the plats you would again use the legal description of the land. This plat map is available for use in the Search Room and is marked "Plats." A conversion chart is on the back of the map. The microfilm rolls that contain the plats are shelved in the microfilm room with the Secretary of State, Land Office, microfilm (RG 28 SG 1 microfilm 60–65).

INDIAN LAND CLAIMS

The most notable settlement of Indian lands in Mississippi took place under the Treaty of Dancing Rabbit Creek made with the Choctaw Nation in 1830. This treaty supposedly guaranteed land to all members of the Choctaw Nation who had settled in a designated area south of the Tombigbee River. Names and ages of the parents and children are given in the *American State Papers*, volume 7, Public Lands, pages 1–139. Land was also set aside for orphans, whose names were given and parents listed, if known (volume 7, pages 627–632). White settlers who were already on the land may also be listed in the *American State Papers*. A name index to the public land volumes is entitled *Grassroots of America*. *Grassroots* will indicate the public land volume and page where an individual is listed. The *American State Papers* are available on microfilm in the microfilm reading room. Access to the index volume *Grassroots* is through the library book catalog.

PRIVATE LAND CLAIMS

Private land claims were grants of land from foreign governments (England, France, Spain) to an individual before the United States obtained possession of the area. The majority of these claims were Spanish and only involved residents of the Natchez District, the area of the Tombigbee, and what are now the Gulf Coast counties. When the United States took over the territory, preexisting claims were honored if some proof could be provided and certain residential requirements could be met. However, private land claims could (and can!) be very confusing because of the overlapping of claims made by so many different entities. In fact, a board of commissioners was established in 1803 to hear and decide private land claims when there were conflicts and to determine who had the best title. Records relating to individual claims presented before the board of commissioners were duly reported to Congress and transcribed and published in *American State Papers: Public Lands*. As previously mentioned, a consolidated index to these records is found in the book entitled *Grassroots of America*. In addition, these have been reprinted in Walter Lowrie's *Early Settlers of Mississippi as Taken From Land Claims in the Mississippi Territory* and the *Digested Summary and Alphabetical List of Private Claims Which Have Been Presented to the House of Representatives*. . . . This latter source includes all claims presented, not just those relating to Mississippi.

If your ancestor was in the area of what is now Mississippi before 1798, he might be included in the *Index to Private Claims and Field Notes*. The first portion of the book is an alphabetical list of the claimants, with a reference to a roll number and shot number (Secretary of State, Land Office microfilm). The information given on the microfilm will usually be the name of the claimant, legal description of the land, certificate or patent number; sometimes a plat is also included. Be sure to copy everything on the line, names and numbers, especially the certificate number, for if you want to see whether more information is available, you will need to forward the number (and other information) to the Bureau of Land Management or National Archives to find out if there is a file on this claim. The private land claims do not include military grants, which are available at the National Archives.

There are several seemingly overlapping sources to examine for British land grants in addition to the *Index to Private Land Claims and Field Notes*. For example, a list of land grants under the English dominion from 1763 to 1781 was compiled by Mrs. Eron Rowland from sources in the Public Record Office of London. It was published in the *Publications of the Mississippi Historical Society*, Centenary Series, volume I (1916). The list covers only the portion of the Mississippi Territory now included in the state of Mississippi. This published work seems to correspond to papers in the English Provincial Records, Record Group 25, volume 10 (microfilm 5); additionally, another listing is found in the English Records, volume 6 (microfilm 3) of grants of British West Florida, which are not in the previous list. Another source for assistance in locating documentation of British grants is a map, the William Wilton map of 1774. Gordon Wells transcribed the entries on the map, citing name, location, number of acres, and date; this information was published in the *Journal of Mississippi History*, volume 28, 1966.

Spanish claims are also documented in the state archives. One of the most comprehensive volumes on the topic is Mae Wilson McBee's *Natchez Court Records*, 1767–1805 (see source list). As McBee states in the preface, "practically all of these British land grants in the Natchez District, as well as the transfer of them, appear in the Spanish records." The Natchez volumes cited in McBee's book have been microfilmed and are available in the microfilm reading room under Record Group 26, the Spanish Provincial Archives.

Finally, the area of British West Florida and numerous Spanish claims are also cited in the papers of one of the Spanish surveyors, Vincente Pintado. These were transcribed and typed by the Louisiana WPA and are on microfilm in RG 28 SG 1 microfilm 81–85. An index accompanies each volume of the Pintado papers on the microfilm.

Another article in the *Journal of Mississippi History* may also shed some light on Spanish grants. Mrs. W. O. Harrell (Sturdivant) published a "List of Claims on Spanish Patents in Mississippi 1806" in volume 8, 1946. Her compilation came from a secondary source, the newspaper *The Mississippi Messenger*, Natchez, Mississippi Territory, in June 1806 as claims were submitted by the board of commissioners, west of the Pearl River. Record Group 26, the Spanish Provincial Archives, also contains reproductions of land grants in deed books A, B, C, and K (1777–1819), but many have not been translated, nor are they indexed.

A final word on claims: if your ancestor is not listed as filing a claim it does not mean that this information is useless to you. If you can determine from the county deed records that an ancestor of yours purchased property from someone on the private land claims list, then that individual's claim file should be examined. Since these files were used to clear title to the land, they may contain information about families other than that of the individual making the claim. Remember, private land claims property must have been received as a grant from a colonial government (England, France, or Spain) before the United States acquired the land. If an individual's claim was rejected, the only recourse was to petition Congress with his case. These petitions were printed as congressional documents; many of the individual documents are on file at MDAH. Additionally, *The Territorial Papers of the United States*, compiled by Clarence E. Carter provides numerous petitions to Congress regarding land disposition in the Mississippi Territory (volumes 5 and 6). Names of individuals are listed in the various petitions covering the period 1798–1817. Many of these names are included in the MDAH biographical index and the volumes themselves are indexed as well. MDAH also has these volumes for other states, which could prove helpful in further research.

SIX

Researching Cemeteries and Churches

CEMETERY RECORDS

Cemetery records can be used to help establish both birth and death dates; in addition, some have epitaphs that, besides being interesting, can provide more clues. There are several different places in the Archives library to search for cemetery records. To find the cemetery records in the book collection, look in the book card/computer catalog under the subject heading CEMETERY RECORDS—MISSISSIPPI. If MDAH has a particular book on your ancestor's county of residence, it should be listed here. The majority of the Mississippi cemetery books are located in the Search Room, and this will be indicated on the catalog card with a plastic sleeve.

Mississippi Cemetery and Bible Records published by the Mississippi Genealogical Society, are also listed in the book catalog. These are tombstone inscriptions copied by MGS volunteers. The index by county, however, is in the non-book catalog. The cemeteries that have been recorded by MGS members are listed by county on 3 x 5 cards. Within the county, the name of the cemetery, the volume, and page number are cited. These volumes are located in the Search Room and are readily available.

Many patrons have volunteered their personal surveys of various cemeteries throughout the state. These records are located in the Search Room filing cabinets and are designated with the label "Cemetery Files." The file folders are in alphabetical order by county.

Another place to check for cemetery files is the uncataloged set of Mississippi DAR genealogy books (see source list), also located in the Search Room. Volumes received before 1986 have been indexed by cemetery name as well as by county. The index volume will be found at the end of the shelf of DAR books.

The Works Progress Administration workers helped genealogical researchers by documenting the location of various cemeteries throughout the state. These workers made a county-by-county search of the cemeteries that could be found as of the late 1930s. The list they produced can be found in the subject file and in a folder behind the reference desk. Under each county name, the cemeteries are listed in alphabetical order with a designation indicating which are black and which are white, as well as the coordinates, i.e., township, range, and section, should you want to plot one on the map. The WPA also compiled the grave registrations of Mississippi soldiers. If your ancestor was a soldier in the Revolutionary War, the War of 1812, Indian Wars, Mexican War, Civil War, Spanish-American War or World War I and was buried in Mississippi, check the grave registrations in the microfilm room. These card files are on microfilm arranged by war and then alphabetically by the name of the individual. As mentioned previously, the Confederate grave records, indexed by Betty Wiltshire, are found in the Search Room.

Finally, check the *Cemetery Record Compendium* (see source list) to see if the Mississippi cemetery record you need has been published in a genealogical periodical. While this information may not be current, it is a reminder that the card/computer catalog should be checked in case a genealogical society in a particular county is publishing local records, such as cemetery listings.

A word of caution regarding tombstone inscriptions—do not automatically accept the accuracy of the dates recorded! Relatives may have placed a tombstone at the grave site many years after the individual died.

Records will often be available at the individual cemetery offices. Usually the name of the purchaser of the lot is given as well as the location and perhaps even some documentation relating to the payment on the upkeep of the lot. This latter information could possibly lead to another relative of interest. Additionally, the office usually maintains a complete list of burials. Since tombstones may be broken or even missing, this burial list can be very important.

```
        MS Dept. of Archives & History              MS Dept. of Archives & History
              Subject Files                                Subject Files
May 18 1993                              Tue May 18 1993
)
   CHRISTIAN, THOMAS H.                        LAUDERDALE COUNTY HISTORY
   CHRISTIANS IN ACTION INC.                   LAUDERDALE COUNTY POST OFFICES
   CHRISTIE, WILLIAM                           LAUDERDALE COUNTY TAXES
   CHRISTMAS                                   LAUDERDALE SPRINGS
   CHRISTMAS CARDS                             LAUDERDALE, HUGH R.
   CHRISTMAS CAROLS                            LAUDERDALE, JOHN C.
   CHRISTMAS CROSSING                          LAUDERDALE, SAMUEL MORTIMER
   CHRISTMAS, ANNIE                            LAUDERDALE, WILLIAM M.
   CHRISTMAS, HENRY                            LAUGHLIN
   CHRITTON                                    LAUGHLIN, JEFFERSON DAVIS
   CHROMCRAFT FURNITURE SENATOBIA              LAUNDRY AND CLEANING ASSOCIATION
   CHRYSALIS BALLET COMPANY                    LAUREL
   CHULAHOMA                            *      LAUREL CHURCHES
   CHUNKEY GAME                                LAUREL COMMERCE AND INDUSTRY
   CHUNKY                                      LAUREL COTTON MILL
   CHUNKY SHOALS                               LAUREL EDUCATION
   CHUNKYVILLE                                 LAUREL HILL
   CHURCH FOR THE DEAF                         LAUREL HILL NEAR NATCHEZ
   CHURCH HILL                                 LAUREL HILL NEAR RODNEY
   CHURCH HISTORY                              LAUREL HISTORIC DISTRICT
   CHURCH OF CHRIST                            LAUREL HISTORIC HOMES
   CHURCH OF CHRIST HOLINESS                   LAUREL HISTORICAL PLACES
   CHURCH OF GOD                               LAUREL HISTORICAL SKETCHES
   CHURCH OF JESUS CHRIST OF THE LATTER DAY SAINTS   LAUREL LAUREN ROGERS LIBRARY AND MUSEUM OF ART
) CHURCH OF THE GOOD SHEPHERD                  LAUREL POLITICS
   CHURCH OF THE NATIVITY     BILOXI           LAUREL PROMINENT PERSONS
   CHURCH OF THE REDEEMER    BILOXI            LAURENCE, FRANK M.
   CHURCH SCHOOLS                              LAURENCE, JOHN
   CHURCH STATISTICS                           LAURO, JAMES THOMAS JIM
   CHURCH WOMEN UNITED CWU, EPISCOPAL CHURCH   LAVAIL, MAT
   CHURCHES                                    LAVALLEE, LAWRENCE RAYMOND
        SEE ALSO:[ NAMES OF INDIVIDUAL CHURCHES ]   LAVELL SITE
   CHURCHES AFRO-AMERICAN                      LAW DAY
        SEE :[ AFRO-AMERICAN CHURCHES ]        LAW ENFORCEMENT ASSISTANCE COMMISSION
   CHURCHES EPISCOPAL                          LAW ENFORCEMENT ASSISTANCE, DIVISION OF
   CHURCHES HISTORIC MS                        LAW ENFORCEMENT DAY
   CHURCHES METHODIST                          LAW ENFORCEMENT LEAGUE
   CHURCHES PRESBYTERIAN                       LAW ENFORCEMENT MEMORAIL ASSOC.
   CHURCHES ROMAN CATHOLIC                     LAW ENFORCEMENT MS
   CHURCHWELL, WYATT C.                        LAW ENFORCEMENT OFFICERS' TRAINING ACADEMY
   CIRCLE EIGHT SQUARE DANCE CLUB              LAW ENFORCEMENT SEMINARS MS
   CIRCUIT CLERKS                              LAW RESEARCH SEVICE OF MS
   CIRCUSES                                    LAW'S HILL
   CIRCUSES 1839-1849                          LAW, BERNARD F.
   CIRCUSES 1850-1859                          LAW, JAMES H.
   CIRCUSES 1860-1869                          LAW, JOHN
   CIRCUSES 1870-1879                          LAWRENCE
   CISTERCIAN MONASTERY                        LAWRENCE COUNTY
   CITIES MS RATING                            LAWRENCE COUNTY CENSUS
) CITIZEN'S ARREST                      *      LAWRENCE COUNTY CHURCHES
   CITIZENS AGAINST NUCLEAR DISPOSAL           LAWRENCE COUNTY HISTORICAL RESOURCES
   CITIZENS AGAINST THE REGISTRATION & DRAFT   LAWRENCE COUNTY HISTORICAL SOCIETY
   CITIZENS BAND RADIOS                        LAWRENCE COUNTY HOMES
   CITIZENS COMMITTEE FOR FAIR REAPPORTIONMENT LAWRENCE, J. BENJAMIN
   CITIZENS COMMITTEE FOR THE HOOVER REPORT    LAWRENCE, JANICE
```

Figure 20: Notice the various church related headings as found in these samples from the subject file master list

CHURCH RECORDS

Several years ago, MDAH staff member Donna Pannell created a very helpful finding aid to all of the church records. This guide is cataloged and located at the reference desk, where it is easily accessible to all interested patrons. The guide is indexed by county, church name, and denomination. The materials cited are from both the book collection and the private manuscript collection. The call number, as well as the scope of record, is included.

Brief church histories may also be found in the subject files or Record Group 60 (WPA). The subject file index (fig. 20) may have a separate entry for a particular church or information may be found by searching the heading, e.g., name of town—churches or religion, or the name of the county—churches or religion.

The WPA county historical source material (RG 60) is always a good place to search for information on early churches in a county. In many instances, this is the only existing history of the church.

One of the original goals of the WPA's Historical Records Survey program was to inventory state, county, and municipal archives and private manuscript collections and *church records*. The original plan was to make an inventory of and publish volumes for each denomination. Separate volumes were compiled for the Protestant Episcopal Church and for the Jewish congregations before a decision was made to cease the individual publications. The remaining churches were published in *Guide to Vital Statistics, Volume II, Church Archives* (see source list). The primary purpose of the publication was to document the location of existing material relating to births, marriages, deaths and divorces. The volume is arranged alphabetically by county, then by city or town, and finally, alphabetically by denomination within each town. The name of the church plus a brief statement regarding the dates and types of vital records in its possession is given. The drawback here is the date of compilation—where are these records now? Do they still exist?

Finally, if your ancestor was a preacher or an active layman, remember to examine the denomination's annual conference proceedings, which sometimes provide lengthy death notices. The denomination newspaper is also a source to consider. The Archives does have some of these proceedings and newspapers, but you will need to examine the catalogs to find them. If you do not locate the Baptist or Methodist records you are seeking, you should search the library at Mississippi College in Clinton (Baptist) and Millsaps College in Jackson (Methodist) (see appendix for addresses). The Catholic Archives is located at 237 E. Amite Street, Jackson, MS 39201.

SEVEN

Resources for Minority Groups

African-Americans

African-Americans and other minorities generally use the same records as white Americans to trace their ancestry back to the reconstruction period. While this chapter targets some sources that are specifically for minority groups, the sources previously mentioned should also be used with diligence. Just as in any family research, you will want to start with yourself and work back through the generations. Oral history has traditionally been strong in black families; this could prove to be a vital component in your search for your family history. Do not delay interviewing older family members and friends; as each relative goes, a chapter of your family history is lost! You would normally start a census search with the 1920 census (or whenever you know your relatives were in Mississippi) and work your way back census by census as we have previously discussed.

The 1870 federal census is the first one to list all of the black population by name. Before that, only the free blacks were included, since they were the only ones listed in vital, land, military and other pre-Civil War records. Many researchers want to use the slave census, thinking that their slave ancestor will be named there. MDAH has the Mississippi slave schedules for 1850 and 1860; they are arranged by county, and within the county each slaveholder is listed with the age and sex of all of his slaves indicated. *The slaves are not listed by name in this record!* The slave schedule can be useful

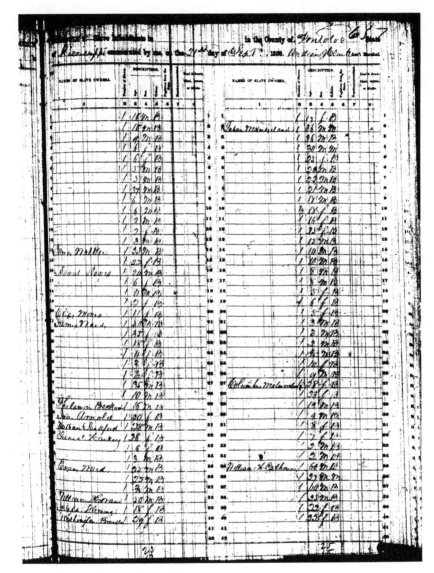

Figure 21: Slave schedule; only the owners are listed by name

as circumstantial evidence, however, to prove that a slave of a certain age and sex was the property of a particular owner (fig. 21).

One federal record that is frequently overlooked by black genealogists is the mortality schedule. The mortality schedules for 1850 and 1860 list deaths of slaves as well as free men and also gives their place of birth. The indexes do not always indicate the race of the deceased; examine the microfilm for your county of interest to be certain you have not overlooked a vital clue.

The Freedmen's Bureau was created by Congress in 1865 to help the newly freed slaves assimilate and become useful and productive citizens. It established schools and banks and also helped blacks negotiate for just and fair wages for their labor. The Mississippi Freedmen's Bureau records are on fifty rolls of microfilm, the majority of which is unindexed.

The Freedmen's Bureau labor contracts (rolls 43–50) have been indexed by MDAH. Some thirty-six thousand former slaves in Mississippi are listed on the contracts, in which they agreed to work for a planter, possibly their former master, for a fee, plus medical care, housing, and sometimes a share of the crop. These records contain information such as county of residence, name of planter, name of plantation (if given), name of freedman (frequently only a given name), age (if given), and the terms of the contract. Sometimes even family units and relationships are indicated on the contracts. The index, which is on microfiche, allows you to search by the name of the freedman, the name of the planter, or the name of the plantation. If you locate your relative on one of these index guides, it will refer you to another fiche which is arranged by the roll number and contract number. Notice in figure 22 that several freedmen by the name of Donaldson resided in Attala County and all agreed to work for the same person (the contract number is the same for all of them.). The contract number is 46–294, so you would next examine the fiche cards arranged by contract number (fig. 23). Contract 46–294 indicates that the planter (and possibly former owner) was N. M. Donaldson, the plantation was called Pleasant Hill, and the contract was signed 8/7/1865. The names and ages of the former slaves are listed in the bottom portion of the chart. The "F" and "D" category indicates "freedmen" or "dependent." A "dependent" was usually a small child, an elderly person, a disabled individual, or one who would not be working for a wage.

Should you want to see a copy of the actual contract on film, you will find it filed in the microfilm room in a file drawer labelled "Freedmen's

Dolly	rence	45-324
Dolly	Lowndes	45-408

FREEDMANS NAME	COUNTY NAME	CONTR#
Dolly	Lowndes	45-447
Dolly	Lowndes	47-084
Dolly	Madison	44-188
Dolly	Madison	46-113
Dolly	Madison	46-118
Dolly	Noxubee	43-056
Dolly	Oktibbeha	43-070
Dolly	Oktibbeha	45-212
Dolly	Oktibbeha	46-037
Dolly	Oktibbeha	47-270
Dolly	Oktibbeha	47-325
Dolly	Simpson	43-007
Dolly	Yazoo	43-354
Dolly	Yazoo	50-142
Dolly	not given	43-033
Dolly Ann	Chickasaw	48-104
Dolphin	Attala	46-284
Dolphus	Lauderdale	47-123
Dolt	Lauderdale	44-072
Don	Lowndes	45-369
Don	Pontotoc	47-007
Donalason, Bitsy	Madison	44-207
Donalason, Gabriel	Madison	44-207
Donald, M.	Lauderdale	45-178
Donaldson, Charles	Madison	44-175
Donaldson, Cornelia	Attala	46-294
Donaldson, David	Attala	46-294
Donaldson, George	Attala	46-294
Donaldson, Hannah	Attala	46-294
Donaldson, Harriet	Attala	46-294
Donaldson, Joseph	Attala	46-294
Donaldson, Lucy	Attala	46-294
Donaldson, Richard	Attala	46-294
Donaldson, Sarah Ann	Attala	46-294
Donaldson, Thomas	Attala	46-294
Done, Benjamine	Hinds	47-036
Donja	Oktibbeha	46-029
Donling, Martha	Noxubee	50-224
Donnald, Drew	Yazoo	43-362
Donnell, Harriet	DeSoto	48-144
Donnell, William	DeSoto	48-144
Doodle	Marion	43-104
Dook	Winston	44-299
Doora	Noxubee	46-380
Dora	Attala	45-481
Dora	Attala	46-409
Dora	Calhoun	46-277
Dora	Clarke - Enterprise	44-298
Dora	Franklin	47-407
Dora	Hinds	43-277
Dora	Lowndes	44-281
Dora	Lowndes	49-395
Dora	Madison	47-374
Dora	Oktibbeha	45-216
Dora	Oktibbeha	47-301
Dora	not given	43-033
Dora	not given	44-342
Dorah	Itawamba	46-251
Dorah	Lowndes	43-042
Dorah	Oktibbeha	46-029

FREEDMANS NAME	COUNTY NAME	CONTR#

Figure 22: Labor contract index by freedman's man; gives name, county and contract number

```
CONTRA               FREEDMANS LABOR CONTRACT DATA MASTER FILE
--------------------------------------------------------------------
                Robert                5      D
                Victoria             25      F
46-294  -*-*-*-*-*-*-*-*-*-*-*-*-*-*-*-*-*-*-*-*-*-*-*-*-*-*-*-*-*-*-*-
        Planter    : Donaldson, N. M.
        Plantation: Pleasant Hill
        County     : Attala
        Date       : 08/07/1865
                                     Age    Status    Remarks
        *-*-*-*-*-*-*-*-*-*-*-*-*-*-*-*-*-*-*-*-*-*-*-*-*-*-*-*-*-*
        Donaldson, Cornelia   29      F
        Donaldson, David       3      D
        Donaldson, George     17      F
        Donaldson, Hannah     35      F
        Donaldson, Harriet    27      D      pregnant
        Donaldson, Joseph      5      D
        Donaldson, Lucy       30      F
        Donaldson, Richard    13      D
        Donaldson, Sarah Ann   9      D
        Donaldson, Thomas     29      F
        illegible             29      F

46-295  -*-*-*-*-*-*-*-*-*-*-*-*-*-*-*-*-*-*-*-*-*-*-*-*-*-*-*-*-*-*-
        Planter    : Winters, John
        Plantation:
        County     : Attala
        Date       : 08/07/1865
                                     Age    Status    Remarks
        *-*-*-*-*-*-*-*-*-*-*-*-*-*-*-*-*-*-*-*-*-*-*-*-*-*-*-*-*-*
        Aaron                 22      F
        Addam                 22      F
        Alex?                  7      D
        Andrew                28      F
        Ann                   13      F
        George                 9      D
        Isaac                 14      F
        James                 36      F
        Jane                  49      :
        Jane                  17      F
        Joseph                 3      D
        Laswell               29      F
        Levi                   5      D
        Lida                  25      F
        Mary                  23      F
        Nancy                  3      D
        Nuton                 26      F
        Rachel                45      F
        Robert                16      F
        Sarah                 70      D
        Stephen               37      F

46-296  -*-*-*-*-*-*-*-*-*-*-*-*-*-*-*-*-*-*-*-*-*-*-*-*-*-*-*-*-*-*-
        Planter    : Rimmer, J. D.
        Plantation:
        County     : Attala
        Date       : 08/08/1865
                                     Age    Status    Remarks
        *-*-*-*-*-*-*-*-*-*-*-*-*-*-*-*-*-*-*-*-*-*-*-*-*-*-*-*-*-*
        Amos                  10      D
        Anna                   3      D
```

Figure 23: Personal information as found in the labor contracts; arranged by contract number

Bureau." This particular contract would be the 294th contract on microfilm roll 46 (fig. 24a,b).

Since the Mississippi labor contracts cover the years 1865 and 1866, this is in many respects the first "census" many blacks appear in. If you do not find a contract for your ancestor, remember that these contracts were not mandatory and many former slaves did not enter into formal agreements; as mentioned, only some thirty-six thousand freedmen were listed in the Mississippi labor contracts, and, according to the 1860 census figures, there were over three hundred thousand slaves in the state at that time. However, this source does provide researchers with many names that were not available previously.

The mortgage or deed records found in the county records frequently are similiar to the Freedmen's Bureau labor contracts in that the freedmen agreed to work in exchange for food and clothing.

The Freedman's Savings and Trust Company was established by Congress as a banking institution for the benefit of the newly freed slaves. *The Register of Signatures of Depositions* contains signatures and personal information about the depositors. Evidently, there were banks at Natchez, Vicksburg, and Columbus, as these are the only Mississippi registers on the National Archives microfilm. The Mississippi registers are alphabetical by city and then by account number. In addition to the name of the depositor, the register often includes age, place of birth, residence, occupation, names of parents, wife, and names of children. Some of the applications even contain the names of the former owner.

The *Index to the Deposit Ledgers* includes the depositor's name and account number. This index can be a useful aid in locating information in the *Register of Signatures*, which is not indexed. MDAH has roll 3 of the ledger indexes, as this is the only roll that has Mississippi cities on it. However, only Natchez and Vicksburg are included; the index for the Columbus office is missing from the National Archives, as it is not available.

On roll 42 of the Mississippi Freedmen's Bureau records, you will find marriage records kept by the bureau. This roll provides more information than just the name and residence of the bride and groom and the name of the minister; it also tells the couple's ages, whether they had lived with another and for how long, number of children, how separated (by force or death or consent), and number of children unitedly. A cursory examination of this roll shows the majority of the marriages to be from the Vicksburg area. An index to the marriages on this roll is being prepared and should soon be available for researchers. This is by no means the only record of freedmen marriages. The individual county marriage records (listed in the non-book catalog) should also be examined, as marriage rolls for blacks are clearly marked with the dates of the marriages and the indication freedmen (fig. 25).

Many other Freedmen's Bureau records may contain information that would be of value to the family historian, but the way in which the records are organized and microfilmed makes them difficult to use.

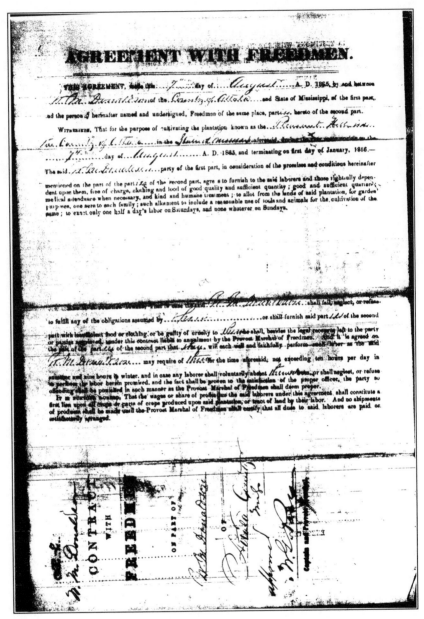

Figure 24: Actual labor contract 46–294 as found on roll 46 of the National Archives microfilm (facing pages)

IN TESTIMONY WHEREOF, The said parties have affixed their names to this agreement, at _A Committee_ .... County, State of Mississippi, on the day and date aforesaid.

NAMES.	AGE.	SEX.	MONTHLY RATE OF WAGES.	INTEREST IN PROFITS
Thomas Donaldson	29	Male		
George Donaldson	11	"		
Hannah Donaldson	55	Female		
do	29	"		
Cornelia Donaldson	29	"		
Lucy Donaldson	31	"		
H				

DEPENDENTS.

NAMES.	AGE.	SEX.	NAMES.	AGE.	SEX.
Frances Donaldson	27	Female	Harriett is an infant only		
Sarah Ann Donaldson	9	"	any about six months		
Jos. Donaldson	8	Male	and will be of no		
David Donaldson	3	"	service for the balance		
Richard Donaldson	13	"	of the term —		
			Wm. H. Donaldson		

EXECUTED IN PRESENCE OF—— _Wm. Alex___
W. W. Son

```
Film
      Noxubee Co., Mississippi...
 48   Marriage records (B)      v. D        1869-1870
       "         "   (Freemen)     E        1865-1871
 49    "         "                 1-2      1870-1874
 50    "         "                 3        1874-1876
 51    "         "   (p. 1-449)    4        1876-1877
  1    "         "   (p. 440-603)  4        1877-1878
  2    "         "                 W-X      1877-1879
  3    "         "                 1-2      1879-1884
  4    "         "                 3-4      1884-1888
  5    "         "                 5-6      1887-1891
  6    "         "                 7-8      1891-1895

                                        Card 2 of 3




Film
      Clarke Co., Mississippi.  ...
 47      Marriage records, white, v. 3    1914-1920
 48         "          "   freedman, colored,
                v. A-B  1865-1873
 49              C-D    1873-1888
 50              E-F    1888-1898
 51              G      1898-1904
 52              1      1904-1909
 53              2      1909-1914
 54              3      1914-1919
```

Figure 25: Freedmen marriages found in the county record microfilm in the non-book catalog

In November 1865 the Mississippi legislature passed a law ordering the clerks of the various probate courts to apprentice "all freedmen, free negroes and mulattoes, under the age of eighteen . . . who are orphans, or whose parent or parents have not the means, or who refuse to provide for and support said minors" . . . to a competent person who would have charge of that individual. Male apprentices would be indentured until the age of twenty-one, and females until they were eighteen (*Laws of Mississippi*

1865). Sometimes the orphan or freedman was apprenticed to his or her former master as seen in figure 26. MDAH has apprentice records for Amite, Issaquena and Panola counties. (Remember to always double check the MDAH holdings of county microfilm for new rolls are constantly being added.)

One of the more progressive (for its time) projects of the Works Progress Administration was the interviewing of former slaves. These slave narratives are found at MDAH in Record Group 60, with the other WPA material; they have also been published as part of a series of narratives entitled *The American Slave: A Composite Autobiography*, by George P. Rawick (see source list). In addition to descriptions of living conditions and work habits, these narratives frequently include the names of other slaves and their masters. MDAH has the Mississippi narratives only.

Another source that might prove helpful is the Enrollment Cards of the Five Civilized Tribes, 1898–1914. African-Americans who were slaves of Indians and were later freed and admitted to tribal citizenship were enrolled as a separate group. MDAH, at present, has only the Choctaw Freedmen rolls (fig. 27), but there are similiar records available for the Chickasaw Freedmen. A detailed explanation of how to get to these documents will be given in the Indian records section of this chapter.

Another record useful to a few black genealogists is the Confederate pension file. Some slaves who accompanied their masters to the war were eligible to receive Confederate pensions. These are filmed in alphabetical order on the pensions microfilm located in the microfilm reading room. They could prove helpful in determining the location of an individual and possibly his death date when the payment ceased. Pension files for service with the United States forces would also be helpful, of course, but these records are at the National Archives, not at MDAH.

If you are able to determine a possible slave owner or planter, you can then focus your research on that family and plantation or look for public records that may pertain to them. By searching for the slaveholder's surname in the index to county wills or deeds before 1865, you may find a listing of slaves as property in these records. Also, if the slave owner died in debt, his property was often sold to pay his debts. Court records, especially probate court records, frequently contain bills of sale that list the name and value of the slave as well as the name of the buyer. Most of these miscellaneous probate records are still on file in the county, but since records are being filmed all the time, be sure to examine the MDAH county holdings file for the county of interest in your research. There are several indexes to court cases in the book collection. Many of these court cases do contain wills or inventories of estates in which slaves may be mentioned. Court cases from 1799 to 1859 that were considered to have information of a genealogical nature were indexed in *Mississippi Court Records from the Files of the High Court of Errors and Appeals 1799–1859* by Mary Louise Flowers Hendrix. Additionally, the *Natchez Court Records 1767–1805* by Mae Wilson McBee contains a large number of slave sales with the slave being named and his homeland being given. Regretfully, the names of the slaves are not included in the index, only the buyer and the seller.

If the name of a slaveholder can be established, you will want to see if plantation records have survived. Some plantation journals are in the private manuscripts collections at the state archives, but the majority of them are still in private hands, either still in the house where they were written, or in the possession of family members elsewhere. The private manuscript holdings at MDAH are usually listed by the planter's name or the name of the plantation. If you are still unsure of the family or plantation name but know the county, a "key word" computer search of the manuscript holdings relating to that particular county may be requested. Plantation journals usually contain information about weather conditions, the names of the slaves, how much work was accomplished by each slave, and other daily working activities on the plantation. For an example of the type of information found in a plantation journal, see the Charles Clark family papers (Bolivar County) or the Surget papers (Adams County).

A very few lists of slave sales are in the official records collections at the Archives, and some early ones, e.g., 1820s and 1830s, can be found in the Adams County microfilm records; additionally, some may be scattered in the private manuscript collections.

Manumission records are not numerous at the Archives; there are a very few "certificates of freedom" in the Adams County records. These were also transcribed in the Adams County WPA records. If other counties had them, and if they still exist, they must still be in the county courthouses. Newspapers may also be examined by African-American genealogists for notices of runaway slaves or slave sales. In the antebellum period, you will find many advertisements for slave sales as well as "want ads" for information pertaining to runaway slaves. These ads usually have detailed descriptions. However, since the newspapers are not indexed, unless you know when and where the name of your relative might have appeared in the paper, this could be an unproductive search.

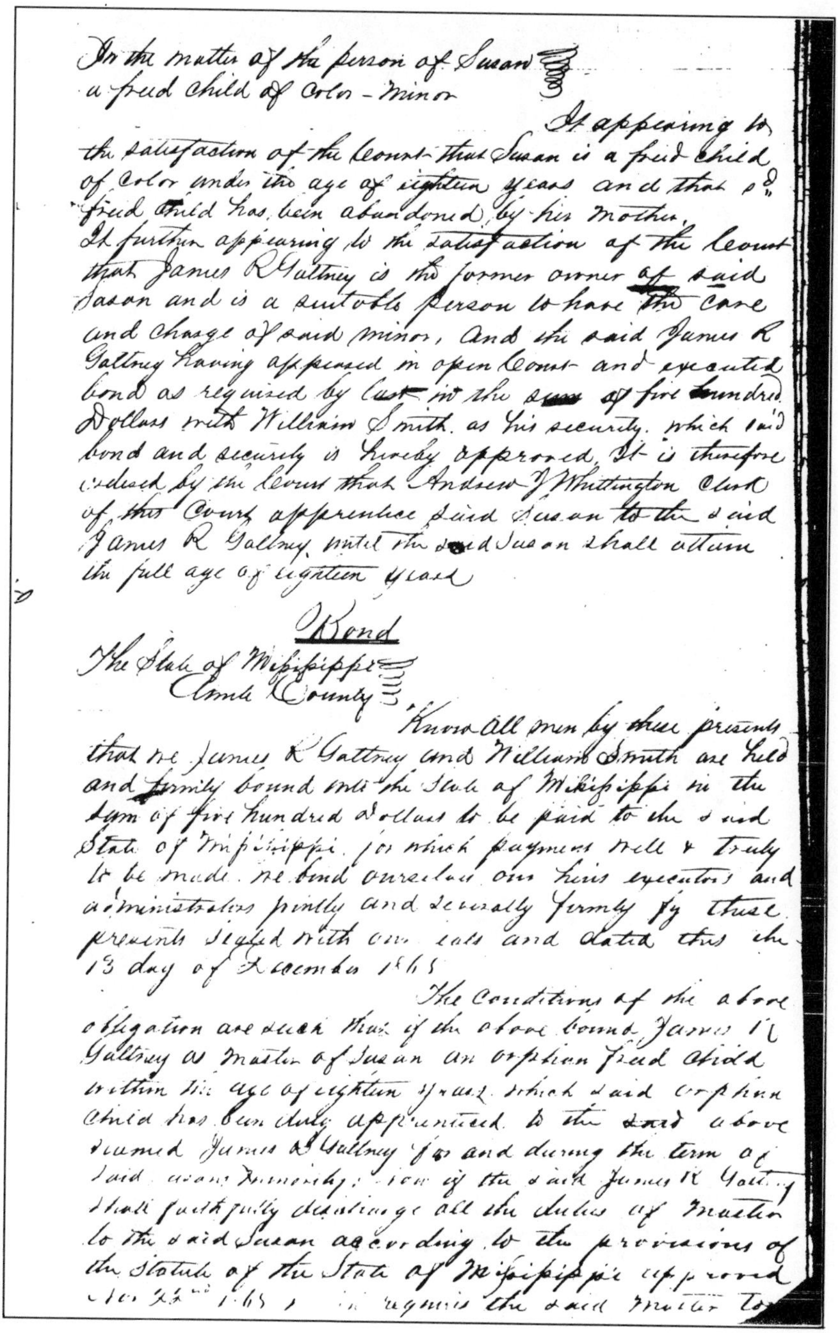

In the matter of the person of Susan
a freed child of Color – minor

It appearing to
the satisfaction of the Court that Susan is a freed child
of Color under the age of eighteen years and that s'd
freed child has been abandoned by his mother,
It further appearing to the satisfaction of the Court
that James R Gattney is the former owner of said
Susan and is a suitable person to have the care
and charge of said minor, And the said James R
Gattney having appeared in open Court and executed
bond as required by law in the sum of five hundred
Dollars with William Smith as his security. which said
bond and security is hereby approved, It is therefore
ordered by the Court that Andrew J Whittington Clerk
of this Court apprentice said Susan to the said
James R Gattney until the said Susan shall attain
the full age of eighteen years

Bond

The State of Mississippi
Amite County

Know all men by these presents
that we James R Gattney and William Smith are held
and firmly bound unto the State of Mississippi in the
sum of five hundred dollars to be paid to the said
State of Mississippi for which payment well & truly
to be made we bind ourselves our heirs executors and
administrators jointly and severally firmly by these
presents sealed with our seals and dated this the
13 day of December 1865

The Conditions of the above
obligation are such that if the above bound James R
Gattney as master of Susan an orphan freed child
within the age of eighteen years which said orphan
child has been duly apprenticed to the said above
named James R Gattney for and during the term of
said orphan's minority. Now if the said James R Gattney
shall faithfully discharge all the duties of master
to the said Susan according to the provisions of
the Statute of the State of Mississippi approved
Nov 22nd 1865, and requires the said master to

Figure 26: Apprentice record from Amite County; child Susan being apprenticed to former owner

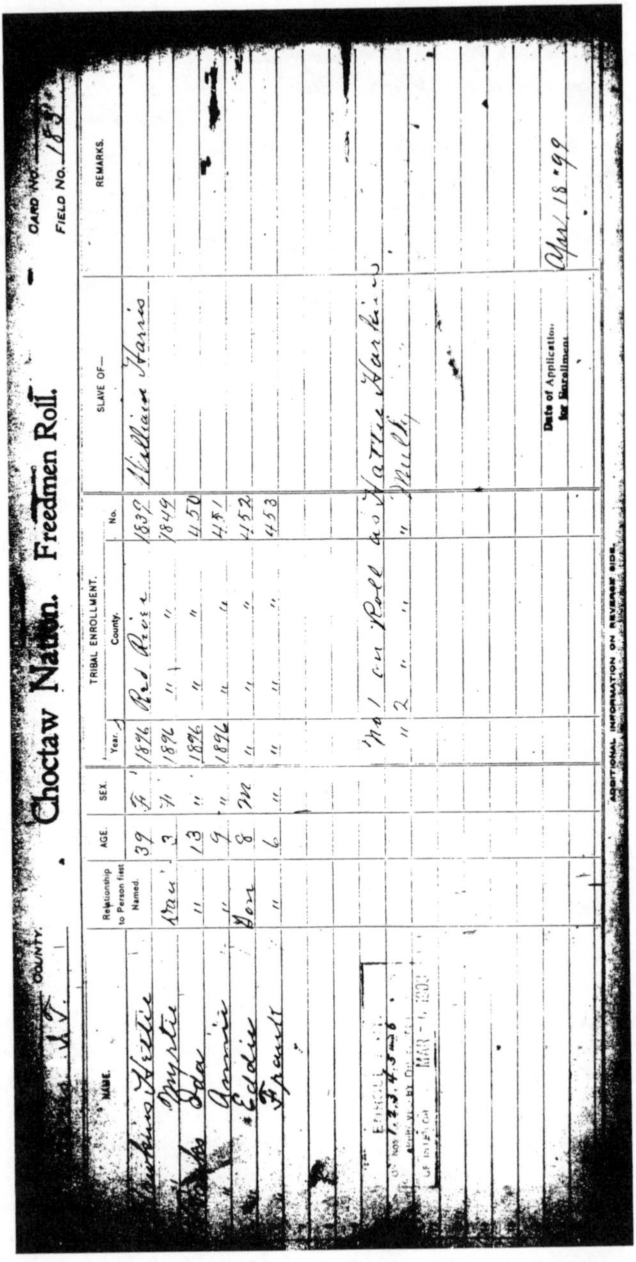

Choctaw Nation. Freedmen Roll.

COUNTY. I.T. CARD NO. FIELD NO. 18

NAME	Relationship to Person first Named	AGE	SEX	TRIBAL ENROLLMENT Year	County	No.	SLAVE OF—	REMARKS
Harkins Hettie		39	F	1896	Red River	1837	William Harris	
Myrtie	Dau	3	"	1896	"	1849		
Ida	"	13	"	1896	"	450		
Annie	"	9	"	1896	"	451		
Eddie	Son	8	M	"	"	452		
Frank	"	6	"	"	"	453		

No 1 on Roll as Hattie Harkins

No 2 " " Mirtle

Enrollment of Nos 1, 2, 3, 4, 5 and 6 ... MAR -1 1903

Date of Application for Enrollment: Apr. 18 '99

ADDITIONAL INFORMATION ON REVERSE SIDE.

Figure 27: Choctaw freedman card with former owner listed

Many of the records available in the Archives could help to document the history of African-American presence in Mississippi but have only marginal value for genealogical research as they do not provide names of individuals. Although, regretfully, this is also true of records in the National Archives, that library does present more possibilities. A good indication of their holdings that would be helpful to the black family historian is given in *Guide to Genealogical Research in the National Archives* (see source list).

The private manuscripts collection is an assortment of diaries, business journals, letters and even some church registers. The papers range in time from the 1700s to the latter part of the twentieth century. The antebellum church records, especially, should be examined, for many have membership lists for blacks and whites as well as notices of baptisms and funerals. As previously mentioned, the private manuscripts collection also has many plantation journals that document the everyday life on a particular plantation.

NATIVE AMERICANS

An Indian historian recently said that is is impossible to document Native American genealogy in Mississippi. To a point he is correct, since the years of available records do not connect. For instance, the 1870 and 1880 census schedules included only those Indians living off the reservation, and the 1860 federal census included only Indians living with non-Indian heads of households. Thus there are large gaps between the available census schedules that record Native Americans. Putting the pieces together on this puzzle could be a lifelong challenge!

Persons researching their Indian ancestry will also use the same basic sources (census, county records, etc.) as the white family historian. However, researchers seeking information on Native American ancestors have an additional series of census records to consult before examining the 1920 federal population census. The Mississippi Archives has Choctaw census records for 1926–1939, with names in alphabetical order. For 1926–1927, only name, sex and age are provided, with no relationships indicated. Beginning in 1928 questions regarding the percent of Indian blood were added, and by 1929 relationship to head of household was included. The data on the rolls vary to some extent but basically give Anglo or Indian name, Indian roll number, age, sex, relationship to head of household, marital status, residence and degree of Indian blood. As was mentioned in chapter 2, there are several birth and death rolls scattered among these later Indian census records so be sure to search the microfilm carefully. The limitation in this information is that only persons who remained on the reservation are on these rolls. There is no master index by Indian or Anglo name to these census records.

After examining these special Choctaw census records, researchers should proceed to the 1920 federal population census. Since Indians on reservations were not considered citizens until 1924, census takers in the nineteenth and early twentieth centuries did not count them; instead, they were included on a special census taken by the government. This special census of the reservation usually follows the regular population schedule on the microfilm of the county where the reservation is located. The Indian census asks for more detailed information than usual (name, age, and place of birth); this census also included name of tribe, tribe of father, tribe of mother, and percent of Indian blood. When searching for an Indian ancestor on the Soundex (see chapter 2 for an explanation), remember that Indians with only given names are on the index but usually follow all of the entries that include surnames. In accordance with previous instructions, you should use the Soundex to determine the county, enumeration district, and page where your ancestor can be found. If you cannot locate the ancestor on the Soundex, read the special Indian census for the county where the reservation was located.

Between 1898 and 1914 there was a count taken to get an accurate number of persons claiming Indian ancestry, including those of full blood, freedmen (former black slaves of Indians who were freed and taken into the tribe), citizens by marriage, and those with a percentage of Indian blood. These Indian enrollment cards of the Five Civilized Tribes (often called the Dawes Rolls) are on microfilm in the reading room. At present, MDAH has primarily those rolls relating to the Choctaw Tribe. Gaining access to these records can be confusing. It is a three step process: 1) index, 2) final roll, and 3) enrollment/census card. The index is on roll 1 of the set and lists the Indians by category (Choctaw by marriage, by blood, etc.). The index and final roll includes all five tribes (Choctaw, Chickasaw, Cherokee, Creek, and Seminole) but the Archives does not have the enrollment cards for tribes other than the Choctaw. Within each category, the names are somewhat alphabetical with a roll number given to the side. (In figure 28, see Marie Jane Ady; her final roll number is 675.) The final rolls are also arranged by category and then by roll number. In the "Choctaws by Blood" category, number 675 lists Ady, Marie Jane, with her age, sex, percent of Indian blood, and her enrollment or census card number (fig. 29). With the census card number in hand, pull the enrollment cards' microfilm, which will be arranged first by category, in this case, "Choctaws by Blood" and then by the census card number or field number, e.g., 325 for Marie Jane Ady (fig.30). The information given on the enrollment card usually includes roll number, name, age, sex, degree of Indian blood, relation to head of household, and names of parents. Frequently information about births, marriages, and deaths within the family is also noted at the bottom of the cards. The cards are arranged in numerical order by the census card number or field number.

Persons whose claim to Indian ancestry was rejected or denied are not on the index; in fact, they are not indexed at all. To find such persons one would need to read the microfilm rolls marked "R" and/or "D." The actual testimony files recorded for the enrollment cards are housed at the National Archives, Southwest Region, in Fort Worth, Texas (see appendix for address). If you find an enrollment card for your ancestor, contact this agency to determine whether a visit or photocopy request is warranted.

In addition to the enrollment cards, Mississippi has several early Indian census schedules. In 1855 a census of the eastern Choctaws in the Indian Territory was completed. The majority of the names are not Anglicized but remain in the native form; a typed index accompanies this census. It resembles the early federal population census in that only the head of the household is listed by name, with a numerical breakdown of the members of the household and the county of residence; in the remarks column, frequently a designation of "clan" is added. This census basically includes Choctaw families residing east of the Mississippi River and in the states of Mississippi, Louisiana, and Alabama.

The 1837 and 1839 rolls of Chickasaws who migrated west are also similar in context to the early federal census. The names, however, are in no discernible order. The information includes name of head of household, number of males under the age of ten, number over ten and under twenty, those over twenty and under fifty, and number over fifty. The women of the household were counted in the same manner, and the total number of slaves was also included.

In 1831 and 1832, the government registered the Choctaw Indians who had emigrated to their land west of the Mississippi; some 4,293 are listed in this register. Individual family groups seem to be listed together, with the head of the household being underlined. Most are listed only by given (or one) name. In addition to the name, age, and sex, the height of the individual is also documented, as well as whether or not the person possessed

FINAL ROLL CHOCTAWS BY BLOOD

Name.	Roll No.	Name.	Roll No.
Aaron, Sallie	1230	Adams, Arabella F.	13796
Aaron, Jim	3420	Adams, Nanava M.	13797
Aaron, Johnson	3451	Adams, Jincy	14119
Aaron, Sarah	3452	Adams, John S.	15532
Aaron, Moses	3453	Aduddell, Carl	12499
Aaron, Annie	3454	Agent, Annie G.	14464
Aaron, Selina	3502	Agent, Ruby G.	14465
Aaron, Nebus	3522	Agent, Charles C.	14466
Aaron, Austin	3537	Agee, Florence	15275
Aaron, Elsie	3538	Agee, Obera	15276
Aaron, William	3677	Agee, Zora	15277
Aaron, Lucy	3678	Agee, Hester Lee	15278
Aaron, Elsie	3679	Agee, Pearl	15279
Aaron, Denison	3680	Ahekatubby, John	1544
Aaron, Bekinsie	3681	Ahekatubby, Simeon	1545
Aaron, Louina	3682	Ahekatubby, Emma	4556
Aaron, Mary	3683	Ahekatubby, Daniel	4557
Aaron, Alex	3684	Ahayotubbe, Leson	3540
Aaron, Leana	3685	Ahayotubbe, Betsy	3541
Aaron, Selea	3686	Ahotubbi,	9926
Aaron, John	3714	Ahotubbi, Winnie	9927
Aaron, Sealy	3715	Airington, Jackson	550
Aaron, Tama	3716	Airington, Mary Eliza-	
Aaron, Emma	12107	-beth	551
Aaron, Frances	14653	Airington, Rosa Valen-	
Abels, Henrietta E.	4477	tine	552
Abels, Margaret L.	4478	Airington, Lilly Ann	553
Abels, Edward M.	4479	Airington, Andrew Jack-	
Abels, Lucile Belvin	4480	son	554
Able, Etta M.	15458	Airington, Arthur Garvin	555
Able, Maggie	15459	Airington, John L.	556
Able, Enos O.	15460	Airington, Jesse	557
Able, Amos	15461	Airington, Charlie Jack-	
Achukmatema	9889	son	558
Adkins, Tobitha	384	Airington, Monroe	559
Adkins, Hugh L.	385	Airington, Luther	560
Adkins, Lena	386	Airington, Benjamin F.	9998
Adkins, Sarah Jane	387	Airington, William	9999
Adkins, Louis Floyd	388	Airington, James	10000
Adkins, Stella	389	Airington, Walter	10001
Adkins, Wm. McKinley	390	Airington, Lennie	10002
Adkins, Vivian	391	Airington, Claude	10003
Adkins, Bettie	392	Airington, Levi	10155
Ady, Marie Jane	675	Airington, Jesse E.	10156
Adams, Margaret	7888	Airington, Eddie A.	10157
Adams, C. H.	7889	Airington, Aldine V.	10158
Adams, James	8505	Airington, Ida A.	10159
Adams, Reuben	8507	Airington, Minhie B.	10160
Adams, Louina	8508	Airington, Andie E.	10161
Adams, Selin	8509	Airington, Rufus	10266
Adams, Jonas	8510	Airington, Pearl	10267
Adams, Rhoda	8511	Airington, Fred J.	10268
Adams, Davis	8512	Airington, Dora	10269
Adams, Abel	8706	Airington, William Flor-	
Adams, James	8811	ence	10270
Adams, Sallie	8812	Airington, William	11029
Adams, Sarah	8834	Airington, Leroy	11030
Adams, Willy	8882	Airington, Noah	13575
Adams, Thomas	8909	Airington, Willie Polee	13575
Adams, Wilburn	9134	Airington, Willie Rap	13576
Adams, Melvina	9477	Ainsworth, Martha B.	7323
Adams, Katie E.	11052	Ainsworth, James C.	7324
Adams, Willie	11072	Ainsworth, Thomas D.	7791
Adams, Anna	11075	Ainsworth, Thomas G.	7792
Adams, Edward B.	12166		

Figure 28: Index to the Five Civilized Tribes "Choctaw by Blood" category; note Ady, Marie Jane, roll no. 675

No.	Name	Age	Sex	Blood	Census Card No
631	Moore, Mary Cordelia	15	F	1-32	294
632	Moore, Martha Ann	14	F	1-32	294
633	Moore, Janie Lizzie	12	F	1-32	294
634	Moore, Onie Hester	9	F	1-32	294
635	Moore, William Lyles	5	M	1-32	294
636	Moore, Olley Robert	3	M	1-32	294
637	Moore, Ira Tabitha	1	F	1-32	294
638	Spicer, Julia Ann Margaret	26	F	3-8	296
639	Spicer, Nancy Belle	8	F	3-16	296
640	Spicer, Harmon Custer	5	M	3-16	296
641	Spicer, Joseph C.	3	M	3-16	296
642	James, Silas	60	M	1-2	297
643	James, Orina	5	F	1-4	297
644	James, Silas Jackson	2	M	1-4	297
645	Holson, John B.	10	M	Full	300
646	Moore, Preston	2	M	1-2	300
647	Muldrow, Mary Daisy	26	F	3-16	308
648	Fisher, Blanche	17	F	3-16	308
649	Muldrow, Osborn Fisher	3	M	3-32	308
650	Spain, Granger	27	M	1-32	309
651	Spain, Annie M.	7	F	1-64	309
652	Spain, Agnes	2	F	1-64	309
653	Taylor, Lousina J.	56	F	1-16	310
654	Taylor, Ruel Fenton	19	M	1-32	310
655	Taylor, Sallie	15	F	1-32	310
656	Taylor, Lurel E.	13	M	1-32	310
657	Taylor, Carrie D.	10	F	1-32	310
658	Taylor, Wayne Oscar	8	M	1-32	310
659	Impson, Isaac	36	M	Full	313
660	Quincy, Melvina	46	F	Full	314
661	Quincy, Jerome Ervin	25	M	1-2	314
662	Quincy, Magdelene	23	F	1-2	314
663	Quincy, Martha	21	F	1-2	314
664	Quincy, Erasmus	15	M	1-2	314
665	Quincy, Vada	12	F	1-2	314
666	Quincy, Alice	10	F	1-2	314
667	Quincy, Julia	8	F	1-2	314
668	Quincy, Wm. Warren	5	M	3-4	314
669	Gates, Gaines	22	M	Full	315
670	Billis, Jackson	49	M	Full	316
671	Cealey, Susan	27	F	Full	318
672	Thornton, Sylvia	30	F	3-4	319
673	Goforth, Andrew	4	M	7-8	319
674	Thornton, Luther	2	M	7-8	319
675	Ady, Marie Jane	49	F	1-4	325
676	Johnson, Maude L.	22	F	1-8	325
677	Johnson, Victor M.	25	M	1-8	325
678	Johnson, Tennie	2	F	1-16	325
679	Sheegog, Myrtie	22	F	1-4	328
680	Sheegog, May Eula	4	F	1-8	328
681	Sheegog, James Bland	2	M	1-8	328
682	Sheegog, Maggie Lillie	1	F	1-8	328
683	Stricken from roll.				
684	Goldston, Estella	20	F	1-8	339
685	Scott, Phoebe Ethel	18	F	1-8	339
686	Mayo, James L.	13	M	1-8	339
687	Mayo, Ida Preston	11	M	1-8	339
688	Mayo, John Edward	8	M	1-8	339
689	Mayo, William Phillip	6	M	1-8	339
690	Scott, Lorena	1	F	1-16	339
691	Peter, Stephen	49	M	Full	340
692	McDonald, Lucy E.	20	F	1-16	346
693	Moore, Thomas	38	M	1-16	347
694	Moore, Mary J.	15	F	1-32	347
695	Moore, Elizabeth	13	F	1-32	347
696	Moore, Robert Thomas	10	M	1-32	347
697	Moore, Benjamin O.	7	M	1-32	347
698	Moore, Henrietta	3	F	1-32	347
699	Mouser, Robert B.	24	M	1-4	350
700	Finch, Iola	11	F	1-8	351
701	Finch, Burton	9	M	1-8	351
702	Turnbull, Emma	18	F	3-4	353
703	Anderson, Amanda	29	F	Full	357
704	Anderson, Luella	13	F	3-4	357
705	Anderson, Wilson	11	M	3-4	357
706	Anderson, Minnie	9	F	3-4	357
707	Anderson, Ainie	6	F	3-4	357

No.	Name	Age	Sex	Blood	Census Card No
714	Carney, Caroline	6	F	3-4	365
715	Gardner, Robert	25	M	1-4	366
716	Gardner, William Dempsey	20	M	1-4	366
717	Moore, Lily	30	F	Full	367
718	Stricken from roll.				
719	Carnes, Julius V.	20	M	Full	368
720	Carnes, Molsie	15	F	Full	368
721	Carnes, Evangeline	9	F	Full	368
722	Carnes, Elsie	18	F	Full	368
723	Thompson, Lucy	23	F	Full	369
724	Stricken from roll.				
725	Anderson, Andel	49	M	Full	370
726	Stricken from roll.				
727	Anderson, Laura	12	F	Full	370
728	Anderson, Minnie	18	F	Full	370
729	Stricken from roll.				
730	Folsom, Alfred Wright	62	M	Full	374
731	Summer, Amanda L. M.	24	F	1-32	375
732	Summer, Minnie	7	F	1-64	375
733	Turnbull, Sam	15	M	1-4	378
734	Moore, Mary	26	F	Full	380
735	Moore, Dora	8	F	1-2	380
736	Carney, Malinda	11	F	1-2	380
737	Moore, Sampson	5	M	1-2	380
738	Culberson, Eliza	21	F	Full	381
739	Stricken from roll.				
740	Stricken from roll.				
741	Stricken from roll.				
742	Pickens, Isom	29	M	Full	384
743	Robinson, Emeline E.	62	F	1-2	385
744	Roberts, Myrtle	11	F	3-16	386
745	Roberts, Maud	9	F	3-16	386
746	Roberts, Minnie	7	F	3-16	386
747	Roberts, Mamie	5	F	3-16	386
748	White, Eddie	17	M	3-16	386
749	White, Willie	15	M	3-16	386
750	Roberts, Ethel	2	F	3-16	386
751	Roberts, Mildred	1	F	3-16	386
752	Gardner, Mary	10	F	1-8	387
753	Gardner, Margaret Frances	8	F	1-8	387
754	Gardner, Roy	6	M	1-8	387
755	James, Walton	17	M	1-2	390
756	Stricken from roll.				
757	Sexton, Emmerson	34	M	Full	391
758	Colbert, Martha	65	F	Full	392
759	Colbert, John	14	M	1-2	392
760	Bohanon, Robert	32	M	1-2	393
761	Colbert, Alexander	27	M	1-2	395
762	Stricken from roll.				
763	Stricken from roll.				
764	McGee, David	16	M	1-2	399
765	Anderson, Buster	11	M	1-2	399
766	McGee, Sophia	4	F	1-2	399
767	Folsom, Alfred Emerson	58	M	3-8	400
768	Folsom, Ollie	38	F	1-16	400
769	Folsom, Emis	10	F	7-32	400
770	Morris, Joel	41	M	Full	402
771	Byington, Emma	26	F	Full	403
772	Byington, Emmerson	16	M	1-2	403
773	Byington, Malissa	13	F	1-2	403
774	Byington, Winnie	8	F	1-2	403
775	Byington, Lutie	5	F	1-2	403
776	Wyatt, Ed. J.	40	M	1-4	404
777	Wyatt, Roxsie	10	F	1-8	404
778	Wyatt, Ed J., Jr.	8	M	1-8	404
779	Wyatt, Mary	4	F	1-8	404
780	Wyatt, Ernest Montgomery	1	M	1-8	404
781	Moss, Lurinda	25	F	1-2	405
782	Moss, Dora May	4	F	1-4	405
783	McCurtain, Allen C.	29	M	Full	407
784	McCurtain, Rebecca	33	F	Full	407
785	Harrison, Lewis H.	36	M	3-4	411
786	Harrison, Emmet E.	10	M	3-8	411
787	Harrison, Cassie M.	8	F	3-8	411
788	Harrison, William Doyle	6	M	3-8	411
789	Harrison, Cevera L.	4	M	3-8	411

Figure 29: Final rolls are arranged by number. 675 lists Ady, Marie Jane with the census card number 325

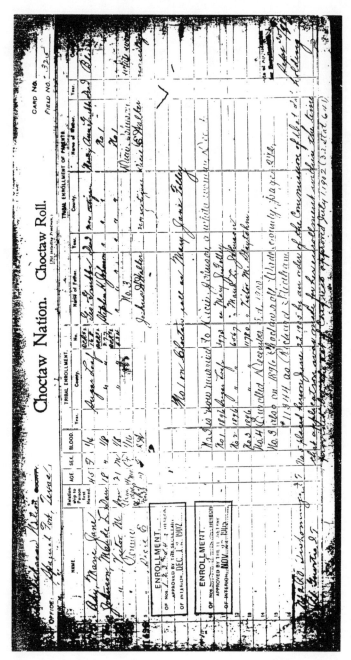

Figure 30: Census cards are arranged first by category "Choctaw by Blood," and then by census card number. Ady, Marie Jane is on card 325 with other family members

any slaves. Additionally, the deaths of individuals who died in the second year were noted in the remarks column.

All three of these "extra" lists (1831/1832, 1837/1839, and 1855) are on one roll of microfilm at the state archives. It is negative film and for the most part is very difficult to read.

After the Treaty of Dancing Rabbit Creek was signed in 1830, a register of the Indians (and whites too, for that matter) who stayed and claimed land was filed. This register, known as the Armstrong Roll, is found in the *American State Papers, Public Lands*, volume 7, beginning with page 70. The Armstrong Roll has also been indexed and published in three volumes by Larry S. Watson. The information given is primarily related to the land the Indians were claiming, but sometimes family information appears such as number of persons over the age of twenty-one, number of whites in the family, and number of slaves. If nothing else, this register documents where a particular person was in 1830. (Additionally, this record can sometimes provide the proof of a marriage between a white and an Indian.)

A final source that may be helpful in establishing the residence of an Indian or early settler in the territory is the *Papers of the Panton Leslie Company*. This was an early trading company operating throughout the southeast; records survive relating to letters concerning supplies to the traders and Indians and to settlers doing business with the company. These papers are on microfilm, and a published guide to using the collection is shelved in the microfilm room for easy access.

EIGHT

Place Names

Coming to the point of needing information from a lost cemetery or an extinct town can be a major frustration in genealogical research. To assist you in locating "lost" communities or sites, MDAH has several helpful sources. The book *Hometown, Mississippi* by James Brieger (see source list) is extremely helpful in documenting the location of currently existing as well as extinct towns. The entries are arranged by county and then alphabetically by town. The information given usually includes the location and a very brief undocumented history. The main thing to remember about this book is that there are two indexes at the beginning. The first index is a typical one, an alphabetical list of towns and the page number where information on that town can be found. The second index is an alphabetical list of towns whose names have changed; it gives the old name and then the new one. To locate information on the old town, you would then look in the first index under the new town name.

The subject file, as previously mentioned, contains information on churches, counties, and towns, extinct as well as existing. A computer printout next to the reference desk lists all of the subject files that are available for research. Remember, these are clippings, pamphlets, and other ephemeral material, and while one file may have a wealth of helpful information, another may not. (A call slip is required for an MDAH staff member to retrieve these files.)

The U. S. Geological Survey publishes *The Mississippi Geographic Names Information System Alphabetical List* (see source list), which lists numerous towns, churches, cemeteries, schools, and other cultural entities that have appeared on their quad maps. This index refers you to a particular map that locates the site. These quad maps are located in the Search Room for easy access. Coordinates are not given in the index, so a close examination of the map is usually needed. The quad maps may not be photocopied; copies are available at a nominal fee from the Department of Environmental Quality, Geology Office (see appendix for address).

Maps, both old and current, can be helpful in locating places. The map collection at MDAH consists of originals, facsimiles, and photocopies from the 1770s to the present. For most of the genealogical patrons, the most useful access is by subject or period of Mississippi history, for example: "MISSISSIPPI TERRITORY" or "HOLMES COUNTY" or "RAILROADS." Maps are also cataloged by the cartographer (when identifiable) and by chronological date. Many of the maps in the collection are too large or fragile for photocopying, but smaller maps may usually be photocopied. (A special order for duplications of maps can be placed for items too large for photocopying.) One of the most useful maps for documenting locations is an 1883 postal service map of Mississippi and Alabama. Although it is quite large and cannot be photocopied, it is a gem documenting places for genealogists!

Towns, lakes, plantations, and other locations in Goodspeed's *Biographical and Historical Memoirs of Mississippi* were indexed by the MDAH staff many years ago. Each place name mentioned is listed on 3 x 5 cards, along with the page number in Goodspeed's where the citation is found. (These cards are filed in the non-book catalog in the Search Room.) This source rarely gives any history, but it does document the place's existence and locate it in a county.

NINE

Newspapers and Periodicals

The Mississippi Department of Archives and History has the largest collection of Mississippi newspapers in the state. These papers are on microfilm. In 1993, all newspapers at MDAH are accessible through the non-book catalog under the name of the town where the newspaper was published. The cards provide the dates that are available in the department's holdings. As with the other collections, as each town's newspapers are examined thoroughly, the card files are being replaced by a computer printout providing the most complete inventory of the newspaper holdings. The lists for the towns Aberdeen through Jackson, and for Natchez, are available for patron use. A chronological list of newspapers as well as a listing by town and/or county can now be generated. The earliest known newspaper in the collection is a Natchez publication of 1801. The early newspapers are indexed (marriages and deaths) in several places. The marriage announcements and death notices found in early Jackson, Natchez, and Holly Springs newspapers are recorded in the biographical index.

The subject file is primarily a clipping file about people and events found in newspaper accounts from territorial days to the present; many obituaries may be found there. *Newspaper Notices of Mississippians 1820–1860* (see source list) indexes marriages and obituaries found in the newspapers during that period, and a compilation of many marriage and death notices is also found in *Marriages and Deaths from Mississippi Newspapers* (see source list). Persons interested primarily in Vicksburg should consult Mary Lois S.

Ragland's *Spreading the Word: Mississippi Newspaper Abstracts of Genealogical Interest, 1825–1935* (see source list). As a general rule, the early newspapers did not give the lengthy accounts of marriages and deaths that are found in today's newspapers, so do not be surprised at a one or two sentence obituary.

If no newspaper exists for the town where your ancestor lived, be sure to check for other papers published in that county or neighboring county papers. You may not find a death notice, but perhaps there will be a notice of the estate settlement. Remember too that if your ancestor was a clergyman or an active layman, an obituary may well have appeared in his denomination's newspaper.

Current newspapers may also provide assistance to the genealogist since many now run genealogical query columns. Three such columns are "Family Trees," by Billie Parkes, which appears in the Jackson *Clarion Ledger*, "Branches and Twigs," by Regina Hines, which appears in the Pascagoula *Mississippi Press* and "Roots n' Records," by Joyce Shannon Bridges, which runs in the *Magee Courier*.

MDAH has numerous runs of periodicals relating to Mississippi and the South. The ones that come on a regular basis are usually cataloged in the book card/computer catalog under the name of the periodical as well as the subject. Many of the historical and genealogical societies of Mississippi publish periodicals indexing local sources, e.g., *Pontotoc Pioneers, Itawamba Settlers*, etc. (see source list under the county name). These are also found listed in the book card/computer catalog under the society's name, as well as under the counties of primary interest and the name of the periodical. Remember always to check journals of professional organizations, as they usually contain in-depth biographical data about members who have died. Although the Mississippi Department of Archives and History does not have these journals for every professional organization in the state, those that are on file should not be overlooked.

TEN

Miscellaneous Sources

DOCTOR FILES

One of the department's most useful "special" sources is a file of Mississippi doctors. This card index, which has been microfiched, was compiled by the late Dr. J. A. Milne. He read through the 1850 and 1860 federal population census schedules noting any person listing "physician" as his occupation. Milne also gathered from physicians' directories and newspaper citations data such as medical school, place and years of practice, spouse, children, date and place of death. This fiche is arranged alphabetically by the name of the physician. If you do not find your relative listed here, you can check with the American Medical Association (see appendix for address) to see if there is a file on him in its "Deceased Physician's Masterfile." Information on physicians who were alive after 1878 may be requested for a small fee from the American Medical Association Library and Archives, P. O. Box 10623, Chicago, Illinois 60610. The files usually show the date and place of birth and death, the medical school and the place of practice.

NATURALIZATION RECORDS

The naturalization records at the Archives can be found in several different places. In the 1930s the Historical Records Survey program of the WPA produced an index to the naturalization records they were able to locate in the various courthouses around the state. This index, the *Index to Naturalization Records Mississippi Courts 1798–1906* (see source list), lists all aliens applying for and/or obtaining citizenship as found in the courthouse/archives records. The book is arranged by county, and within the county the names of the aliens and the source of documentation is given. There is a name index in the book, but it is not complete, so if you think you know the county where your ancestor resided in his early years in Mississippi, check by the county listing as well. From this book you will learn which (few) naturalization records are actually in the Archives collection and which remain in the county courthouses. Many of the WPA workers' note cards ("take-off" cards) are found at MDAH in WPA Record Group 60. The cards are arranged by county, but again, the holdings lists are not complete. These note cards provide information such as date of arrival, port of entry, country of birth, etc.

Various petitions for naturalization filed in Warren and Lauderdale counties from 1907–1919 have been made available for research by the United States district court (fig. 31). (These petitions are on microfilm in the drawer labelled "Federal Archives" in the microfilm room.) The information given includes name of petitioner, residence, occupation, date and place of birth, date of immigration, and port of entry. Declarations of intention and other loose papers attesting to an individual's allegiance to the United States are also filmed with these petitions. Additionally, one volume that has been filmed contains declarations of intention filed in the Office of the Circuit Clerk of Warren County for the period 1921–1928. The declarations include name, age, occupation, physical description, date and place of birth, date of immigration, and port of entry. The name of the spouse and his or her place of birth is also provided. All three of the microfilm rolls are indexed by the name of the immigrant. A final place to check for naturalization records is in the county records. As new county material is filmed by the Church of Jesus Christ of Latter-day Saints, it is added to MDAH's holdings list.

PASSPORTS

The most complete listing of passports for the southeastern United States is *Passports of Southeastern Pioneers, 1770–1823* by Dorothy Williams Potter (see source list). The majority of the passports authorize passage through Indian or Spanish-held lands east of the Mississippi River. Many of the early

No. 2

ORIGINAL

UNITED STATES OF AMERICA

Department of Commerce and Labor
BUREAU OF IMMIGRATION AND NATURALIZATION
DIVISION OF NATURALIZATION

PETITION FOR NATURALIZATION

Circuit Court of United States

In the matter of the petition of *William Schlesinger* to be admitted a citizen of the United States of America.

To the *Circuit* Court of *United States*

The petition of *William Schlesinger* respectfully shows:

First: My full name is *William Schlesinger*

Second: My place of residence is number *226 N Washington* street, city of *Vicksburg*, State *Mississippi*

Third: My occupation is *Dry Goods Merchant*

Fourth: I was born on the *18* day of *July*, anno Domini 1870, at *Brest Russia*

Fifth: I emigrated to the United States from *Brest Russia*, on or about the *___* day of *July*, anno Domini 1889, and arrived at the port of *New York*, in the United States, on the vessel *don't know name*

Sixth: I declared my intention to become a citizen of the United States on the *10* day of *April*, anno Domini 1903, at *Vicksburg*, in the *Circuit* Court of *Warren County, Miss.*

Seventh: I am married. My wife's name is *Jennie*. She was born in *Brest Russia*, and now resides at *Vicksburg Miss*. I have *4* children, and the name, date and place of birth, and place of residence of each of said children is as follows: *Tillie born May 1892 - Sadie born July 1895 - Joseph born May 1899 Lipman born March 1900 all born in Brest Russia all reside at Vicksburg Miss*

Eighth: I am not a disbeliever in or opposed to organized government or a member of or affiliated with any organization or body of persons teaching disbelief in organized government. I am not a polygamist nor a believer in the practice of polygamy. I am attached to the principles of the Constitution of the United States, and it is my intention to become a citizen of the United States and to renounce absolutely and forever all allegiance and fidelity to any foreign prince, potentate, state, or sovereignty, and particularly to *Nicholas II Emperor of Russia* of which at this time I am a subject, and it is my intention to reside permanently in the United States.

Ninth: I am able to speak the English language.

Tenth: I have resided continuously in the United States of America for a term of five years at least immediately preceding the date of this petition, to wit, since the *17* day of *July*, anno Domini 1889, and in the State of *Mississippi* for one year at least next preceding the date of this petition, to wit, since the *7th* day of *July*, anno Domini 1901.

Eleventh: I have not heretofore made petition for citizenship to any court. _____ Court of _____ at _____, on the _____ day of _____, anno Domini 1 _____, and the said petition was denied by the said Court for the following reasons and causes, to wit, _____

Attached hereto and made a part of this petition are my declaration of intention to become a citizen of the United States and the certificate from the Department of Commerce and Labor required by law. Wherefore your petitioner prays that he may be admitted a citizen of the United States of America.

Dated *Oct 3*, 190 7

William Schlesinger
(Signature of petitioner.)

Western Division of Southern
District of Mississippi ss:

William Schlesinger, being duly sworn, deposes and says that he is the petitioner in the above-entitled proceeding; that he has read the foregoing petition and knows the contents thereof; that the same is true of his own knowledge, except as to matters therein stated to be alleged upon information and belief, and that as to those matters he believes it to be true.

Subscribed and sworn to before me this *3* day of *Oct* anno Domini 19 07

[SEAL]

B Mosely Clerk.
By *J F Short* Deputy Clerk.

* If the alien arrived otherwise than by vessel, the character of conveyance or name of transportation company should be given.

Declaration of Intention and Certificate of Landing from Department of Commerce and Labor filed this *3* day of *Oct* 190 7

L B Mosely Clerk.
By *J F Short* Deputy Clerk.

AFFIDAVIT OF WITNESSES

Circuit Court of US

In the matter of the petition of *William Schlesinger* to be admitted a citizen of the United States of America.

Western Division of Southern
District of Mississippi

Nathan Zebulsky, occupation *Dry Goods Merchant*, residing at *Vicksburg, Miss.*
and *___*, occupation *___*, residing at *Vicksburg, Miss.*

Schlesinger, each being severally, duly, and respectively sworn, deposes and says that he is a citizen of the United States of America; that he has personally known *William*, the petitioner above mentioned, to be a resident of the United States for a period of at least five years continuously immediately preceding the date of filing his petition, and of the State in which the above-entitled application is made for a period of *___* years immediately preceding the date of filing his petition; and that he has personal knowledge that the said petitioner is a person of good moral character, attached to the principles of the Constitution of the United States, and that he is in every way qualified, in his opinion, to be admitted a citizen of the United States.

[SEAL]

Subscribed and sworn to before me this *3* day of *Oct* 190 7

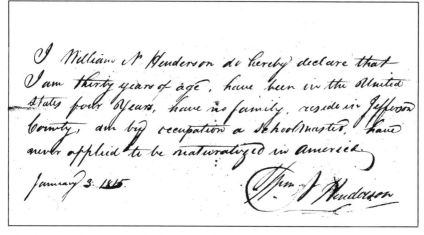

Figure 32: Alien enemy declaration of William Henderson

Indian treaties specified that no inhabitant of the United States was to cross Indian lands without a passport. According to Potter, "the earliest passports were given to persons entering the Indian nations to trade, collect debts, recover stolen horses and slaves, remove property of white intruders, or just to pass through." The volume is indexed by personal name, and each entry is documented. By the alien enemies act of 1812, all British subjects were required by the department of state to register in the respective territories of their residence. The information required included name, age, length of time in United States, and place of residence (fig.32). The Mississippi passports and alien enemies documents can be found at MDAH in Record Group 2, Papers of the Territorial Governor, volume 4.

NEW ORLEANS PASSENGER LISTS

The state archives has a largely untapped collection of abstracts of passenger lists from ships arriving in New Orleans from January 1820–July 1875. Although the abstracts have valuable information, you have to know approximately when your ancestor arrived to use them! These seventeen rolls of microfilm are arranged chronologically by the date of arrival of the ship. The usual information provided includes name of vessel, arrival date, port of embarkation, name of passenger, age, sex, occupation, homeland, and the country (or city, if known) where he intended to reside (fig.33).

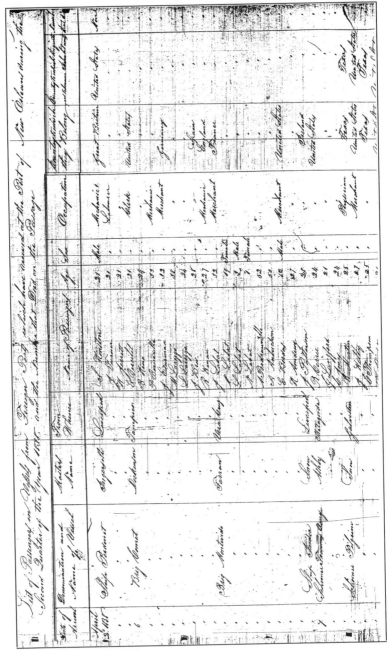

Figure 33: List of passengers arriving in New Orleans in 1838

Municipal Archives

These index cards are arranged in alphabetical order by the name of the town. Available information ranges from municipal minutes taken in Bay St. Louis in 1858 to records of Jackson cemetery interments to Natchez minute books and harbor master reports. (These archival records, listed in the non-book catalog are housed in the closed stack area and require a call slip.)

Court Records

Court records are available in Mississippi for research from 1781 to 1966. The Spanish court records that have been indexed will be found in *Natchez Court Records, 1767–1805* (see source list). This index, for the most part, refers to material in Record Group 26, Spanish Provincial Archives. This volume includes many abstracts of cases relating to slaves, disposition of estates and land transactions. The territorial court records that survive are listed in Record Group 6, Territorial Court. The individuals involved in the court action are listed by name in the finding aid. *Mississippi Court Records from the Files of the High Court of Errors and Appeals, 1799–1859*, by Mary Flowers Hendrix has proved to be a lifesaver for many researchers. Hendrix indexed court cases that she felt had genealogical value. If the county courthouse burned, these files may be the only surviving records of the county for a certain time period. The High Court of Errors and Appeals and the Supreme Court records from 1859 to the late 1890s are accessible through a computer search. These Mississippi court cases are indexed by the names of the parties and the county where the action occurred. Twentieth-century cases have not yet been indexed other than through the docket books. (The docket books are presently in the office of the clerk of the Supreme Court.)

Private Manuscripts

The manuscript collection and its varied contents have been mentioned previously. Since all of the manuscript descriptions have been placed in the computer, MDAH is now able to conduct "key word" searches of the manuscript holdings. For example, should you need a list of the manuscript collections relating to Vicksburg, you could request a computer search for that term.

When the search is completed, you have the option of reading the cited information from the terminal screen or from printed list. (There is a "by page" charge for the printout.) The printout would give only the line from the description where the "key word" appeared and the "Z" number (call number). The result of the "key word" search can only be as good as the initial description of the collection, since the search is based totally on the manuscript descriptions.

Manuscript material *must* be checked for restrictions prior to any photocopying. Restrictions may have to do with the condition of the material in question or with the personal wishes of the donor of the collection. If there are no restrictions and the material is in good condition, manuscript papers may be photocopied.

LEON HOLLINGSWORTH GENEALOGICAL CARD FILE

Leon Hollingsworth was one of Georgia's preeminent professional genealogists. In the process of his research, over some thirty years, he compiled a card file of information on individuals and families throughout the Southeast. This file is available on microfilm and is arranged in alphabetical order, giving an individual's name and the source of the information.

EDUCATIONAL INSTITUTIONS

In the nineteenth century, many academies and other educational institutions produced catalogs that listed not only the courses offered but the names of the students and faculty. MDAH has many of these school catalogs available in microfiche format; additionally, papers from some of these institutions, such as Jefferson College and Oakland, can be found in the private manuscripts collection. Finally, while the archives does not maintain complete runs, it does have the annual yearbooks of many of the state colleges, both public and private.

OTHER INSTITUTIONS

Sometimes unexpected sources can produce genealogical information. One example is the *Annual Report of the Superintendent of the Penitentiary, 1875–1905*. These volumes list the convicts by name, showing the county of residence, race, crime, date of sentence, term, expiration of sentence, place of birth, age, and sex. These are published reports and may be found through the book card catalog. If a convict died or was pardoned during those years, that is also noted. Other types of institutional reports in the MDAH collections that might prove helpful to genealogists include *Annual Report to the Trustees of the Mississippi State Institution for the Education of the Blind, Annual Report of the Officers of the Deaf and Dumb Institute to the Legislature of Mississippi, and Biennial Report of the Directors of the Jefferson Davis Beauvoir Memorial Home.* Hospital records found at the Archives are another matter altogether. If an individual is seeking information on himself, i.e., his own birth, he *must* have good documentation of his identity in order to see his own record. Good documentation would be a driver's license with photo and a social security card or, for a mail request, a notarized statement verifying an individual's identity. If you need to examine an ancestor's hospital record, you must provide MDAH with a court order.

WPA County Histories (Record Group 60)

The Works Progress Administration county history files have been mentioned in regard to the listings of veterans and church histories, but they also contain much other information. Once you determine your ancestor's county of residence, you should read through all of the county history material, for in addition to having files on early schools and churches, the WPA histories invariably have files on prominent lawyers, physicians, Negroes, early settlers, and pioneer families. This material is on poor-quality paper and is not always easy to read (many have edited comments written over them), but it is a gold mine of information and should not be overlooked. For many counties, this is the only history available.

Surname Register

The surname cards are found in the non-book catalog and are filed in alphabetical order by the family name. These cards list a particular family or person being researched and the name and address of an individual who would like to share information. Blank cards are available for patrons at the reception desk should you want to add your name to the file.

Genealogical Files

These are family information files that have been compiled by MDAH patrons. The material may consist of large quantities of documented records or simply be a photocopy of birth and death information from an old family Bible. (The files are in alphabetical order by surname in the Search Room's filing cabinets.)

II

DESCRIPTIVE PROFILES OF PRINTED SOURCES

The purpose of this source guide is to identify useful printed materials found in the Mississippi Department of Archives and History. While the Archives does not lend any of its collection, many of the sources included in this listing are also available in other libraries and can be borrowed from them. Typically both public and academic libraries participate in interlibrary loan and can be helpful in both locating and borrowing a source. An asterisk (*) before a source title indicates that it is found only at MDAH.

The arrangement of listings is as follows: (1) General Sources arranged alphabetically by title, (2) Census and Mortality Schedules arranged alphabetically by title, (3) County Sources arranged alphabetically by county and then by title under each county.

Some points to remember:

1. Bibliographic entries include title, author, publisher, place of publication, copyright date, and number of pages, when shown. Reprints and editions are noted when possible.

2. Information given in the title is not repeated in the annotation. The annotation is a summary of the data and should not be deemed a critique. We have also tried to indicate whether the listing comes from primary or secondary sources.

3. Unpublished and ephemeral materials are also included. However, sources appearing on microform are excluded.

4. Some periodicals of genealogical interest have been included, as well as some church newspapers. Although MDAH contains the largest newspaper collection in the state, local and state newspapers have not been included in this listing.

We know that some sources that exist in MDAH are not included, and we make no claim as to the completeness of this listing. Many county sources are available in the Archives because of the generosity of local historical or genealogical societies. We chose not to include biographies, church histories, or individual family histories. We do hope that this guide will offer you a means to get the most profit from your expenditure of time and energy.

ONE

General Sources

Abstradex of Annual Returns, Mississippi Free and Accepted Masons (with 1801, 1816, and 1817 petitioners and first returns through 1851). 1819–1849. Jeanne Hand Henry. New Market, AL: Southern Genealogical Services, 1969. 456 pp.

Abstracts Masonic records giving name and town of residence. Arranged by lodge and then alphabetically by name. Indexed.

The American Slave: A Composite Autobiography. George P. Rawick, ed. Westport, CT: Greenwood Press, 1977. 331 pp.

A well-known and worthwhile publication of narratives taken from unpublished interviews of ex-slaves. Interviews provide valuable historical information as well as references to family relationships. This material was originally gathered by the WPA Federal Writers' Project and is arranged alphabetically by name. MDAH has the Mississippi narratives only.

Anglo-Americans in Spanish Archives. Lists of Anglo-American Settlers in Spanish Colonies of America: A Finding Aid. Lawrence H. Feldman. Baltimore: Genealogical Publishing Co., Inc., 1991. 349 pp.

A significant guidebook for researchers delving into colonial Spanish family records. Each name listed comes from a primary source. Those records searched include all census manuscripts for Louisiana and the Floridas, oaths of allegiance to the Spanish crown along with lists of rebels, slave owners, land owners, surrender lists, militia rolls, tobacco growers, contributors, and signers of petitions and letters. References cited pertain to location and date that leads the researcher to box and folio in the Spanish Archives. Designed to abstract information for those seeking family data from the papers of colonial America.

The Bench and Bar of Mississippi. James D. Lynch. New York, NY: E.J. Hale & Son, Publishers, 1881. 539 pp.

Descriptive information about lawyers in Mississippi who were no longer living at the time of this 1881 publication. Has its own index and is also included in the MDAH biographical index.

A Bibliography of American County Histories. P. William Filby. Baltimore: Genealogical Publishing Co., Inc., 1985. 449 pp.

A standard genealogical resource that provides a bibliography of selected county histories throughout the United States. Arranged alphabetically by state and then by county. Although most of the titles were taken from secondary sources, this is still considered a reliable work. No county histories are included after the year 1984.

Biographical and Historical Memoirs of Mississippi: Embracing an Authentic and Comprehensive Account of the Chief Events in the History of the State, and a Record of the Lives of Many of the Most Worthy and Illustrious Families and Individuals. Spartanburg, SC: The Reprint Company Publishers, 1978. Chicago: Goodspeed Publishing Company, 1891. 2 vols.

Albeit a publication of historical intent, these volumes (commonly known as "Goodspeed's") are rich in names for the genealogist. Originally published in the latter part of the nineteenth century, this work is a historical and biographical compilation of information about Mississippi and Mississippians. Even though the information gathered here was taken from a variety of sources that were not always verified, the researcher will find valuable material. Items of particular genealogical interest include personal memoirs that give details concerning education, occupations, and religion. The text reads much as an oral history recalled by hometown citizenry. Both volumes are included in the MDAH biographical index. A separately bound name index is also available.

Black Genesis. James Rose and Alice Eichholz. Detroit, MI: Gale Research Company, 1978. 326 pp.

A good introduction to the use of sources for the researcher interested in black family ancestry. Offers a resource listing along with selected published sources by state. The bibliographic entries for Mississippi are worth noting and can provide a practical starting point for black genealogical research. General index included.

The Black Press in Mississippi, 1865–1985: A Directory. Julius E. Thompson. West Cornwall, CT: Locust Hill Press, 1988. 164 pp.

A directory of newspapers, magazines, and newsletters created by blacks in Mississippi. Entries cover the years 1865 to 1985 and are arranged alphabetically by county.

The Cemetery Record Compendium: Comprising a Directory of Cemetery Records and Where They May Be Located. Logan, UT: The Everton Publishers, Inc., 1979. 261 pp.

A helpful directory of cemetery record information that has been published in a genealogical magazine or journal. Abbreviated entries are arranged alphabetically by state and then by county and city. Includes bibliography.

Choctaw Mixed Bloods and the Advent of Removal. Samuel James Wells. University of Southern Mississippi, 1987. 287 pp.

A master's thesis that offers valuable listings of Choctaw names dating from the early 1800s. The table of contents and listing of charts give some access assistance.

*Church Records in Mississippi Department of Archives and History. Donna Pannell. Privately printed, 1986. 3 parts.

An unpublished guide to Mississippi church records that is arranged in three parts by name of church, county, and denomination. Data include name of church, town, denomination, publication title, and call number assigned by MDAH. A single source that directs the researcher at MDAH to genealogical information found in church records for both primary and secondary material.

Civil War Claims in the South: Damage Claims Filed Before the Southern Claims Commission, 1871–1880. Gary B. Mills. Laguna Hills, CA: Aegean Park Press, 1980. 147 pp.

A publication that makes available a vast amount of biographical data by indexing the Civil War damage claims. The documentation of these claims created files that contain wills, birth records, military records, family letters, and travel logs as well as detailed personal descriptions and other types of family-related narrative. This book directs the researcher to the complete files found in the National Archives and explains how to find the information. In addition, claims filed by ex-slaves are included.

Clarion-Ledger Index September 1985-December 1991. Gordon Saucier, Jackson/Hinds Library System. Photocopy. 3 vols.

Newspaper index that is arranged alphabetically by subject. Few personal names have been included.

Courts, Judges, and Lawyers of Mississippi 1798-1935. Dunbar Rowland. Jackson, MS: Press of Hederman Bros., 1935. 409 pp.

A historical and biographical narrative that gives a brief history of the courts, judges, and lawyers of Mississippi from 1798 to 1935. Of particular note are the data about those who pioneered this profession in the state of Mississippi. Indexed.

Credit Land Sales, 1811–1815: Mississippi Entries East of the Pearl. Richard Stephen Lackey. Hattiesburg, MS. 1975. 222 pp.

This thesis on file at MDAH offers an explanation that will aid the researcher in deciphering credit entry lands for the years 1811 to 1815. Of special note is the appendix that contains an alphabetical compilation of these entries transcribed from the original records.

DAR Patriot Index. National Society of the Daughters of the American Revolution. Washington, DC: National Society of the Daughters of the American Revolution, 1966.

An index to the DAR files of American Revolution patriots that have been identified and then verified by their organization. Included in the index is the patriot's name, dates of birth and death, name of wife or husband, rank, state of residence or service, and notation of existence of pension application. The years of service covered are from 1774 to 1783.

Digested Summary and Alphabetical List of Claims Which Have Been Presented to the House of Representatives From the First to the Thirty-first Congress, Exhibiting the Action of Congress on Each Claim, With References to the Journals, Reports, Bills, etc., Elucidating Its Progress. The House of Representatives. Baltimore, MD: Genealogical Publishing Co., Inc., 1970. 3 vols.

Indexes records found in the National Archives that pertain to private land claims brought before Congress. Some of the information on these congressional lists include name of claimant, object or nature of claim, the congressional session, page of journal, and how it was disposed of by both the Senate and the House. The researcher should remember that these are abbreviated entries and do not give all of the information found in the case files. However, the complete records are available to the public at the National Archives.

Dr. Dromgoole's Yellow Fever Heroes, Honors, and Horrors of 1878. J.P. Dromgoole. Louisville, KY: John P. Morton and Company, 1879. 179 pp.

This publication offers an extensive explanation of the 1878 epidemic along with an alphabetized listing of those who died of yellow fever in the United States. Mississippi towns are included. No index.

Early Inhabitants of the Natchez District. Norman E. Gillis. Privately printed, 1963. 152 pp.

A volume that provides a useful start in gathering information about territorial census records in Mississippi. The book's five sections contain references to English land grants from 1768 to 1779, the Spanish census of 1792, inhabitants of the Natchez District in 1810 and 1816, and inhabitants outside the Natchez District in 1816. Even though much of the material for this work came from secondary sources cited by the author, it is still a highly recommended work. One disadvantage is that there is a separate index for each segment instead of a single alphabetical index.

Early Settlers of Mississippi As Taken From Land Claims in the Mississippi Territory. Walter Lowrie, ed. Reprint. Easley, SC: Southern Historical Press, Inc. 1986. Washington: Duff Green, 1834. (Pagination is lifted from original.)

A work that gives biographical material taken from the original land grants and claims pertaining to the Mississippi Territory. The historical text reveals name and age of claimant, earlier places of residence, names of relatives, exact location of claims, and present residence. A valuable resource reprinted from a portion of the *American State Papers* that relates only to the Mississippi Territory. The advantage in using this book is that it includes a complete full name index.

The Epidemic of 1878 in Mississippi. J. L. Power. Jackson, MS: Clarion Steam Publishing House, 1879. 216 pp.

Contains an inclusive state listing by town of individuals who died of Yellow Fever during the 1878 epidemic. A separate portion of the book includes biographical tributes originally published as obituaries from local newspapers. Unfortunately, names have not been included in the index.

Family Records: Mississippi Revolutionary Soldiers. Mississippi Society, Daughters of the American Revolution. Privately printed, 1956. 457 pp.

This book makes available a collection of family records belonging to Revolutionary War soldiers or their widows who lived in Mississippi. Although each entry gives important genealogical data, the researcher needs to remember that the information compiled in this source which was submitted by families, is not based on official documents. References have been included whenever given by the family. Arranged alphabetically and indexed.

Family Trails. Jackson, MS: Quarterly of Historical and Genealogical Association of Mississippi, 1977-
   A journal that includes genealogical information from different counties in Mississippi. No index available at MDAH.

First Settlers of the Mississippi Territory; Grants Taken from the American State Papers—Class VIII Public Land, Volume I 1789–1809.   St. Louis, MO: Ingmire Publications, 1982. 120 pp.
   A useful source that compiles both Spanish and English land grants of the Mississippi Territory. The text portion of this book was extracted from the *American State Papers*. Indexed.

"Genealogical Research in Mississippi." Ruth Land Hatten. Appears in the journal *National Genealogical Society Quarterly* 76 (March 1988): pp. 25–51.
   This journal article provides useful information to the Mississippi genealogist both from a historical perspective as well as its inclusion of genealogical resources pertaining to Mississippi.

Genealogical Research Methods and Sources.   Kenn Stryker-Rodda. Washington, DC: The American Society of Genealogists, 1983. 2 vols.
   In volume 2, the chapter "Mississippi" by Richard Lackey offers a useful overview of the state along with noteworthy genealogical resources.

Genealogies in the Library of Congress: A Bibliography.   Marion J. Kaminkow, ed. Baltimore, MD: Magna Carta Book Company, 1981. 2 vols.
   A bibliography of genealogical sources found in the Library of Congress. The fact that the books in the listing can only be used in this library is an inconvenience; however, the researcher may be able to locate and borrow them on interlibrary loan through a local library. Also, some of the family histories recorded on microfilm can be borrowed directly from the Library of Congress. Check for published supplements to this work.

Grassroots of America.   Phillip W. McMullin. Salt Lake City, UT: Gendex Corporation, 1972. 489 pp.
   Indexes material found in the *American State Papers* regarding land grants and claims that are generally considered complicated to research or hard to access. The historical notes provide a helpful explanation of these documents and tell how they are of historical and genealogical worth. This

publication leads to such information as the land claimant, names of children and wives, relatives, and previous residence. Covers the years 1789 to 1837.

Guide to Genealogical Research in the National Archives. National Archives and Records Administration. Washington, DC: National Archives Trust Fund Board, 1985. 304 pp.

An excellent resource guide to those records generated by the federal government and housed in the National Archives. Some of the information described includes census, military, naturalization, pension, public land, passenger arrival lists, claims, court, and bounty land records. Clear explanation is given as to how to get use of these records either by mail or by visiting the institution. The many illustrations and tables enhance this book's appeal to a researcher learning the use of genealogical primary source material. Indexed.

A Guide to the Contents of the Mississippi United Methodist Advocate, 1947– 1974. Rush Glenn Miller, Jr., ed. Jackson, MS: The Mississippi United Methodist Advocate, n.d. 138 pp.

Designed for both the historical and genealogical researcher, this source indexes the state's Methodist newspaper from 1947 to 1974. Those items indexed include obituaries, memorials, church appointments, college graduates, and conference proceedings. Refers the researcher to volume, issue, and page number.

Guide to Vital Statistics Records in Mississippi. Work Projects Administration. Jackson, MS: The Mississippi Historical Records Survey, 1942. 2 vols.

A survey of historical records done by the Works Progress Administration that is recognized as a reliable guide to information relating to vital records. Material found in the first volume pertains to public records; the second volume is an inventory of church records. The researcher should note that these inventories were done in 1942, and the information is useful but not current.

The Handy Book for Genealogists. George B. Everton, Sr. Logan, UT: The Everton Publishers, Inc., 1971. 298 pp.

Exactly as its title implies, this is a useful guide that gives general historical and geographical background about each state. It provides a listing of the counties along with such information as when the county was formed and from what parent county or territory, what the county seat is, and what census schedules are available. A standard source well known to genealogists, this book offers quick and easy direction for the researcher. Arranged alphabetically by state.

History of Mississippi: The Heart of the South. Dunbar Rowland. Chicago, IL: The S.J. Clarke Publishing Company, 1925. 4 vols.

This work is a detailed history of Mississippi. A well-documented narrative, it is comprehensive in scope and provides historical and genealogical information by one of the state's best known and most highly regarded historians. Contains the Colonial Census of 1792 for the Natchez District extracted from the Spanish Provincial Records. The last two volumes are devoted to biographical material about select early Mississippians with descriptions that provide some family history. Each volume is indexed separately.

Hometown, Mississippi. James F. Brieger. Privately printed, 1980. 557 pp.

A handy guide that provides an extensive listing of Mississippi places with a brief historical passage for each entry. It is of particular importance to the researcher interested in locating communities that no longer exist. It also includes railroad spurs and flag stops that had fairly short existences. The author does not identify sources used for the publication, but it is probable that the chief source of information is the WPA files. Arrangement of this collection is alphabetical by county and includes two indexes to provide access. The first index is simply an alphabetical list of towns, but the second is an alphabetical list of towns whose names have changed, with both the old name and the new one.

*Index to the Laws of the Mississippi Territory. Charles Pearce. Jackson, MS: Mississippi Department of Archives and History, 1985. 131 pp.

An unpublished index to the laws passed by the Mississippi Territory legislature from the years 1802 to 1816. A brief annotation regarding each law is included with its assembly, session, date when it was passed, and page indicating where the actual law may be found. Divorce proceedings and name changes are some of the legislative actions included that would be of genealogical interest.

Index of Mississippi Session Acts 1817–1865. Rena Humphreys and Mamie Owen. Jackson, MS: Tucker Printing House, 1937. 345 pp.

A guide that indexes the laws of Mississippi from early statehood days until the end of the Civil War. Before 1859 all divorce proceedings in Mississippi were introduced as private bills in the legislature. This publication gives the researcher an index to those actions and other legislative proceedings regarding name changes.

Index to Naturalization Records Mississippi Courts 1798–1906. Work Projects

Administration. Jackson, MS: Old Law Naturalization Records Project, 1942. 250 pp.

This work is the result of a WPA-funded project in which all Mississippi county court records were searched for any material relating to naturalization proceedings. Abstracts were created from court minutes and dockets to provide access to these earlier records. These entries lead to the location of declarations of intention, petitions, and minutes. In addition, there is a listing of oaths of allegiance in the Natchez District for the years 1798 to 1799 and a listing of confederate naturalization in Mississippi. Arranged alphabetically by county and then by name with the inclusion of a general name index.

Index to Private Claims and Field Notes in Mississippi. n.d.

A useful index found at MDAH that provides access to the private land claim records located within the secretary of state land record collection. While the sections are basically arranged by land district, the most helpful would be section two in which the claimants are listed alphabetically with the roll number where the claims may be found. The information given includes the name of the claimant, legal description of the land, certificate or patent number, and sometimes a plat.

Indian Treaties, 1778–1883. Charles J. Kappler. New York, NY: Interland Publishing Inc., 1972. 1,099 pp.

A publication of treaties that may be useful to the Native American genealogist since names are listed. It also may aid in the understanding of these early land transactions.

Inventory of the Church and Synagogue Archives of Mississippi: Jewish Congregations and Organizations. Work Projects Administration. Jackson, MS: Mississippi State Conference B'nai B'rith, 1940. 41 pp.

Through personal interviews and primary source material, this work documents and publishes inventories of Jewish congregations and organizations in Mississippi before 1940. Entries are arranged chronologically by congregation giving general historical information, a bibliography of each assembly, and a detailed inventory of records. A reliable source with useful genealogical information. Index includes only county names and is generally not helpful.

Jews in Early Mississippi. Leo E. Turitz and Evelyn Turitz. Jackson, MS: University Press of Mississippi, 1983. 134 pp.

This is a compilation of selected family stories and photographs focusing on the years from the 1840s to the early twentieth century. Although not comprehensive, it does give an idea of the historical development of the Jewish community in Mississippi and also contains information that the genealogist would find interesting. Arrangement is by town; includes a good index.

The Journal of Mississippi History.   Jackson, MS: Mississippi Historical Society, 1939–   . Quarterly.

A scholarly journal of historical purpose that contains some articles useful to the family historian. Although each volume is indexed separately, every twenty years a cumulative index was created which currently spans the years 1939 to 1979. Articles consisting of lists of personal names were not indexed but may be found at the beginning of each cumulative index volume. Some of these articles include transcriptions of early censuses, wills, qualified voter records, and marriage and death notices. Many of these are cross-referenced in the MDAH card catalog.

Kinfolks.   Picayune, MS: R.F. Lovell, 1989–

A journal publication that focuses on genealogical information for Hancock, Harrison, Jackson, Pearl River, Marion, George, and Stone counties. Sometimes includes information on adjoining areas of Louisiana and Alabama. Index not available at MDAH.

Known Military Dead During the War of 1812.   Clarence Stewart Peterson. Baltimore, MD: Genealogical Publishing Co., 1992. 74 pp.

A good source for the genealogist looking for ancestors who died in the War of 1812.

Legislative Handbook, Mississippi.   Secretary of State's Office. 1924–

Published annually, this handbook contains biographical sketches of each member of the legislative session. Although some issues are missing, MDAH has copies covering the years 1924 to 1984.

Library Catalog: Family Histories and Genealogies.   National Society Daughters of the American Revolution. Washington, DC: Daughters of the American Revolution, 1982. 2 vols.

A bibliographic listing of the complete book holdings of the DAR Library in Washington, D.C. Although the works found here cannot be borrowed from this library, the researcher may be able to locate a circulating copy from another library. One disadvantage of this source is that the alphabetical listing was computer generated in such a way that it can be confusing to use.

Lineage Charts of the Mississippi Genealogical Society. Mississippi Genealogical Society. Privately printed, 1991. 468 pp.

This compilation of lineage charts was submitted by society members. Indexed.

List of Pensioners on the Roll January 1, 1883. United States Pension Bureau. Baltimore, MD: Genealogical Publishing Co., 1970. 5 vols.

A reprint of the 1883 edition that contains pension application information. Gives name, cause for pension, post office address, rate of pension per month, and date of original allowance. Indexed.

Map Guide to the U.S. Federal Censuses, 1790–1920. William Thorndale and William Dollarhide. Baltimore, MD: Genealogical Publishing Co., Inc., 1987. 420 pp.

Corresponding to the census enumeration periods, this standard guide shows county boundaries for each state at each ten-year interval. The book's format of county line changes superimposed over the present county lines give the researcher an immediate comprehension of boundary changes. The years that appear begin in 1790 and end in 1920.

Marriages and Deaths from Mississippi Newspapers. Betty Couch Wiltshire. Bowie, MD: Heritage Books, Inc., 1987–1990. 4 vols.

The first volume abstracts and indexes newspaper articles concerning marriage and death notices in the northern portion of Mississippi from 1837 to 1863. Provides pertinent information while citing its source. Some births and divorces have been included but were not the focus of the publication. The second volume indexes and abstracts newspapers found primarily in the southern portion of Mississippi for the years 1801 to 1850. It was intended as a complementary publication to the first volume with much the same type of information. Covering the years 1813 to 1850, the third volume indexes and abstracts more newspapers from the southern half of Mississippi including new material not found in the previous volumes. Information for the fourth volume came from newspapers printed in the southern portion of Mississippi, but refers to all areas of the state as well as portions of Louisiana and a few other states. All entries cite newspapers that may be obtained from the newspaper microfilm collection at MDAH. Each volume is indexed separately.

Military Annals of Mississippi: Military Organizations Which Entered the Service of the Confederate States of America. J.C. Rietti. Spartanburg, SC: The Reprint Company, Publishers, 1976. 245 pp.

This publication is a reprint edition that was created from the original confederate personnel files. Arranged by regiment. Well indexed.

Military History of Mississippi 1803–1898.   Dunbar Rowland. Spartanburg, SC: The Reprint Company, Publishers, 1978. 650 pp.

This book, first published in 1908, is a definitive work of Mississippi military participation for the years 1803 to 1898. It is a carefully done compilation based on manuscripts, diaries, letters, newspapers, veteran questionnaires, and other private and public papers. Chronologically arranged by war and campaigns, it reveals some names of veterans along with a historical account of the military units. Of particular importance is its comprehensive treatment of the Civil War effort and those who took part. The introduction explains that there are gaps due to incomplete original records and that some redundancy may be found in the historical detail of units. Nevertheless, this is a highly regarded work by an author who is recognized as an authority on Mississippi history.

Miscellaneous Records of Southeast Mississippi.   Jean Strickland and Patricia N. Edwards. Privately printed, 1988. 165 pp.

Selected chancery court and cemetery records from Wayne, Greene, George, Clarke, Jasper, and Jackson counties. Indexed.

Mississippi, as a Province, Territory and State, with Biographical Notices of Eminent Citizens.   J.F.H. Claiborne. Baton Rouge, LA: Louisiana State University Press, 1964. 545 pp.

Historical account of Mississippi's growth into statehood. The narration includes many personal names that are included in the book's index. This source is also found in MDAH's biographical index.

Mississippi Baptist Preachers.   L.S. Foster. St. Louis, MO: National Baptist Publishing Co., 1895. 750 pp.

A composite of biographical sketches of Baptist ministers in Mississippi prior to 1895. Arranged alphabetically. Available on microfiche at MDAH.

Mississippi Biographical Abstracts.   Jean Strickland. Privately printed, 1990. 143 pp.

A single-volume source that abstracts genealogical information from the biographical sketches found in the *Official and Statistical Registers of the State of Mississippi.* The years covered are 1904 to 1921. Indexed.

Mississippi Cemetery and Bible Records.   Mississippi Genealogical Society. Jackson, MS: Mississippi Genealogical Society, 1954–1980. 18 vols.

This series contains tombstone inscriptions recorded in cemeteries throughout the state as well as family Bible records submitted by members. The MDAH non-book card catalog provides an index to the cemeteries and Bible records within this source. Each volume has its own index as well.

Mississippi: Comprising Sketches of Counties, Towns, Events, Institutions, and Persons, Arranged in Cyclopedic Form. Dunbar Rowland. Spartanburg, SC: The Reprint Company, Publishers, 1976. 4 vols.

Reprint of the 1907 edition. Includes useful historical background on Mississippi towns and counties. Also offers a good explanation of historical influences within the state, such as the Yellow Fever Epidemic. The third volume is devoted to biographical sketches of early Mississippians. Arranged alphabetically.

Mississippi Confederate Grave Registrations. Betty Couch Wiltshire. Bowie, MD: Heritage Books, Inc., 1991. 2 vols.

A handy index that provides ready access by its alphabetical arrangement of Mississippi Confederate grave registrations. Information appearing in this work includes soldier's name, service unit, years of birth and death, county and state of birth, and county where buried. The dates of death covered are from the Civil War until 1930.

Mississippi County Court Records. May Wilson McBee. Privately printed, 1958. 94 pp.

Transcription of selected county records. Dates covered are not indicated but most appear to be early nineteenth century. The counties included are Wilkinson, Jefferson, Claiborne, Warren, Hinds, Holmes, and Harrison. Indexed by county.

Mississippi Court Records, 1799–1835. J. Estelle Stewart King. Privately printed, 1969. 193 pp.

Transcription of selected court records considered to have information of a genealogical nature for Mississippi counties formed during this period. Indexed.

Mississippi Court Records from the Files of the High Court of Errors and Appeals 1799–1859. Mary Louise Flowers Hendrix. Privately printed, 1950. 372 pp.

Biographical data may be obtained through documents found in high court files from the probate courts of each county. This particular volume generally abstracts and indexes cases relating to will administration, property settlement, guardianship, and divorce cases. By referring the researcher to the actual case found in the Mississippi archives, it offers a way to find missing genealogical connections. The researcher needs to be aware that all cases cited are not in MDAH. Indexed.

Mississippi Daughters and Their Ancestors. Mississippi Daughters of the American Revolution. Privately printed, 1979. 509 pp.

Arranged alphabetically by name of organization and then by member's name. Information given in first part includes maiden name, husband's first name, address, ancestor, ancestor's name, rank, state of service, and national number. Second part of work is arranged alphabetically by ancestor with further genealogical data. Indexed only by ancestor's name.

Mississippi Daughters of the American Revolution Genealogical Records. 1934–104+ vols.

This series is published periodically and includes all types of records of genealogical worth such as Bible records, cemetery inscriptions, lineage forms, church papers, and wills. A cumulative typescript index for the years through 1986 compiled by Marie Hays offers access to this large collection of data. Each volume is also indexed.

Mississippi Genealogical Exchange. Jackson, MS: Mississippi Genealogical Society, 1955–1986.

This genealogical journal was published quarterly. Each issue contains a descriptive table of contents. Index not available at MDAH.

Mississippi Genealogy and Local History. Shreveport, LA: Norman E. Gillis, 1968.

A genealogical journal that makes available published Mississippi material. No index available at MDAH.

Mississippi Geographic Names Information System. Alphabetical List. U.S. Geological Survey. Norman, OK: University of Oklahoma, n.d. 449 pp.

Provides information leading to exact locations of communities, towns, cities, counties, cemeteries, schools, and various other geographic designations. Arranged alphabetically by place giving county, map coordinates, and map number. The map number refers to the town name that guides the researcher to a map in MDAH.

Mississippi Index of Wills, 1800–1900. Betty Couch Wiltshire. Bowie, MD: Heritage Books, Inc., 1989. 224 pp.

A worthwhile resource that provides access to wills and gives name of the testator, the year the will was probated, and the county where it was recorded. Compilation of this genealogical material came primarily from will books, but other sources of information included inventory books and marriage records. Citation appears with each entry.

Mississippi Masonic Death Records, 1819–1919. Thomas G. S-Wixon and Jean Strickland. Moss Point, MS: Thomas G. S-Wixon and Jean Strickland, 1991. 3 vols.

A compilation of death records taken from the Masonic Lodge annual reports. Arranged alphabetically and indexed.

Mississippi Physicians Roster. Jackson, MS: Mississippi State Board of Health, 1939–1952. 2 vols.

Bound booklets listing physicians and their town of residence published each year by the state board of health. Covers the years 1939 to 1952. No index.

Mississippi Provincial Archives 1763–1766: English Dominion, Letters and Enclosures to the Secretary of State from Major Robert Farmar and Governor George Johnstone. Dunbar Rowland. Nashville, TN: Press of Brandon Printing Company, 1911. 560 pp.

This volume is a published collection of a portion of the original papers of the English Provincial Records dating from 1763 to 1781. However, the researcher should note that this book covers only the years 1763 to 1766. These papers cover the term of British Dominion over what is now the state of Mississippi when it was ruled by England during its early development. The material contains letters and enclosures pertaining to the governing of Colonial Mississippi and cites many individual names that are included in its index. The remaining unpublished transcripts are available to the public in Official Records at MDAH.

Mississippi Provincial Archives French Dominion 1701–1763. Collected, edited, and translated by Dunbar Rowland and A.G. Sanders; revised and edited by Patricia Kay Galloway. Baton Rouge, LA: Louisiana State University Press, 1927–1984. 5 vols.

A published collection of original papers of the French Provincial Records that date from 1701 to 1763. The translation of this documentary series tracks the colonization and development of what would later become the state of Mississippi. The material highlights the period of the French and Indian War and offers information regarding matters that dealt with Indian diplomacy and trade, the Choctaw Civil War, and tribal structure of both the Chickasaw and Choctaw. A description of these papers may be found in the *Fifth Annual Report of the Mississippi Department of Archives and History, 1905–1906*, pp. 61–151. Original records are housed in Paris, France at the Archives of the Ministry of the Marine. Each volume is indexed.

Mississippi Records. Gulfport, MS: A. Anderson, J. Hetchler, 1989-
   A quarterly journal containing information about Mississippi genealogy. An index is published separately.

The Mississippi Society of the National Society Sons of the American Revolution. Jackson, MS: n.d. 4 sets.
   As given to MDAH, these applications to the Sons of the American Revolution were bound and made available to researchers. The applications are arranged alphabetically by the soldier's name and give extensive family history information both in data and narrative form. Since there is no single index, each of the four sets must be checked for an ancestor's name.

Mississippi Territory in the War of 1812. Mrs. Dunbar Rowland. Baltimore, MD: Genealogical Publishing, Co., 1968. 249 pp.
   In this historical narrative, the researcher will find names of Mississippians who fought in the War of 1812 along with unit name and rank. Arranged by unit. Indexed.

*Mississippi Union List of Newspapers. Kathleen Hutchison, ed. Printed by the Mississippi Department of Archives and History. 1990. 376 pp.
   A computer-generated listing created with the help of grant funding from the National Endowment of the Humanities and the Mississippi Department of Archives and History as part of the United States Newspaper Project. An unpublished but comprehensive guide to newspaper holdings in Mississippi courthouses, academic and public libraries, and MDAH. Arranged alphabetically by state, town, and then by newspaper title. Contains several indexes so that the collection can be used according to title, date, subject, or institution.

Natchez Colonials: A Compendium of the Colonial Families of Southwest Mississippi 1716–1800. Johnnie Andrews, Jr. Prichard, AL: Bienville Historical Society, 1986. 105 pp.
   Resources pertaining to eighteenth-century Natchez appear infrequently. This work is a compilation of some two hundred sources, the objective being to bring together selected data about colonial individuals and families in the Natchez area. Source is cited for each entry, and an index is included.

The Natchez Court Records, 1767–1805. May Wilson Mcbee. Baltimore, MD: Genealogical Publishing Co., Inc., 1979. 635 pp.

A single-volume source of the original seven "letter" books that contained the court records of the Natchez District for the years 1767 to 1805. This district included the area that later formed the five Mississippi counties of Wilkinson, Adams, Jefferson, Claiborne, and Warren. Translated and abstracted primarily from provincial records, this work contains a wealth of genealogical information. Compiled first by "letter" book and then chronologically, this resource is also well indexed.

Newspaper Notices of Mississippians, 1820–1860. Mississippi Genealogical Society. Privately printed, 1960. 152 pp.

This publication consists of a series put into book form of newspaper notices that originally appeared in the *Journal of Mississippi History*, volumes 28 to 31. Included are references to marriages, obituaries, and estate notices from the years 1820 to 1860. The original notice may be found in the Mississippi archives newspaper files. Name indexed.

The Northeast Mississippi Historical and Genealogical Society Quarterly. Tupelo, MS: Northeast Mississippi Historical and Genealogical Society, 1980-

A journal publication that contains genealogical information for Benton, Tippah, Alcorn, Prentiss, Tishomingo, Union, Lee, Pontotoc, Chickasaw, Monroe, and Itawamba counties. No index found at MDAH.

The Order of the First Families of Mississippi 1699–1817. Charles Owen Johnson. Ann Arbor, MI: Edwards Brothers, 1981. 381 pp.

A book of Mississippi family lineages for those whose ancestors lived in the state before December 10, 1817. Verification has been made for each entry, which also includes some biographical data about that ancestor along with a family chart. Well indexed.

Passports of Southeastern Pioneers, 1770–1823: Indian, Spanish and Other Land Passports for Tennessee, Kentucky, Georgia, Mississippi, Virginia, North and South Carolina. Dorothy Williams Potter. Baltimore, MD: Gateway Press, Inc., 1982. 449 pp.

This work compiles and indexes national land passports that were issued to those passing through Native American lands or foreign-held land for the period 1770 to 1823. More specifically it pertains to Indian, Spanish, and other land passports for Tennessee, Kentucky, Georgia, Mississippi, Virginia, and North and South Carolina. The narrative summary gives such information as reason for travel, references of good character, and sometimes even a physical description. A helpful genealogical source as well as an interesting read. Indexed.

Pension Roll of 1835. United States Pension Bureau. Baltimore, MD: Genealogical Publishing Co., 1968. 4 vols.

Published copy that is a reprint of the 1835 edition. Gives pensioner's name, rank, unit, age, and often the death date. Southern states are found in volume 3. Indexed.

Personnel of the Civil War. William Frayne Amann. New York: Thomas Yoseloff, 1957. 2 vols.

An important source that clarifies one of the more confusing aspects of researching Civil War records by providing a guide to the translation of the nickname of a unit into the official name. Since a military unit may have been known by several different names, this guide is helpful in distinguishing each of those by cross-referencing local designations. Arranged alphabetically.

Publications of the Mississippi Historical Society. Franklin L. Riley, ed. Oxford, MS: Printed for the Society, 1898. 14 vols.
Publications of the Mississippi Historical Society. Centenary Series. Dunbar Rowland, ed. Jackson, MS: Printed for the Society, 1916. 5 vols.

Although these scholarly articles are generally historical in nature, many include useful genealogical information. Each volume has a table of contents, and MDAH has a bound typescript index. Some of the articles have been cross-referenced in the MDAH card catalog.

Records of the Bureau of Refugees, Freedmen and Abandoned Lands: Mississippi (volume 123, pp. 2–57).

Photocopies of the original records pertaining to Mississippi. No preface, introduction, or index.

Researcher's Guide to American Genealogy. Val D. Greenwood. 2nd ed. Baltimore, MD: Genealogical Publishing Co., Inc., 1990. 609 pp.

A well-known comprehensive guide that teaches the fundamentals of genealogical research. Methods of research are examined and instruction given in basic library use. However, the book's greater appeal exists in the in-depth explanation of primary sources, such as census schedules, wills, probate, court, church, land, and vital records. The 1974 edition had a chapter on Canada that has not been included in this volume. This edition adds chapters on genealogical evidence, personal computers, and the family historian. An excellent source. Indexed.

Selected Records of the War Department Relating to Confederate Prisoners of War 1861–65. National Archives. unpaged.

A printed guide to this series of microfilm rolls indicates the type of information available for each prison camp and the roll where the information may be found. Although taken from various official records, the primary portion of the material forming this source came from documentation created by the individual prisons that was later turned over to the Commissary General's Office of Prisoners. Of particular note to the researcher is the register of prisoners' deaths. This guide is not cataloged and is found in the microfilm room at MDAH.

State and County Boundaries of Mississippi. Work Projects Administration. Jackson, MS: The Mississippi Historical Records Survey, 1942. 152 pp.

Information regarding state and federal land legislation. This guide presents, in summary form, all the laws affecting the boundaries of the state of Mississippi, the counties in the state, and the judicial districts that were changed either by law, treaty, or proclamation. Sources of information are well documented. Indexed by county with index number referring to the paragraph number, not the page number.

Survey of Records in Mississippi Court Houses. Mississippi Genealogical Society. Privately printed, 1957. 180 pp.

Although outdated, this work does provide important holdings information about surviving court records in each Mississippi courthouse. Indicates available documents such as land records, orphans and probate court records, wills, estate papers, and tax lists. Most of these public papers may be found in the microfilm collection at MDAH.

The Territorial Papers of the United States: The Territory of Mississippi, 1798–1817. Compiled and edited by Clarence Edwin Carter. Washington, D.C.: U.S. Government Printing Office, 1937. 815 pp.

A collection of official papers and correspondence about the organization of the Mississippi Territory through its plan for statehood. Included are such aspects as territorial division, land administration, development of the postal system, and internal politics. These papers were compiled from the archives of the departments of state, treasury, war, interior, and post office, the manuscripts division of the Library of Congress, and House files in Washington, D.C. Genealogical information may be found in the lists of names attached to different types of petitions within this publication. Offers an extensive name index and is one of the sources found in the MDAH biographical index.

Tracing Your Ancestry: A Step-by-Step Guide to Researching Your Family History. F. Wilbur Hembold. Birmingham, AL: Oxmoor Press, 1976. 210 pp.
A good "how-to" book for the beginning genealogist.

The War of the Rebellion: a Compilation of the Official Records of the Union and Confederate Armies. Gettysburg, PA: National Historical Society, 1972. 129 vols.
A reprint of military records of the Civil War appearing in three series and published originally by the government in 1880. Papers arranged chronologically from both Confederate and Union Armies include such items as reports, letters, telegrams, and general orders. An extensive single volume index refers the researcher to volume and series. The original version, *Official Records of the Union and Confederate Armies*, is available on microfilm at the National Archives.

*WPA Cemetery List. Works Progress Administration. Photocopy.
An unpublished listing that documents the location of public and private cemeteries. Under each county name the cemeteries are listed in alphabetical order with a designation as to whether they are black or white. Includes coordinates such as township, range, and section that can be used in conjunction with state highway county maps. Typed copy located at MDAH reference desk.

Yellow Fever Epidemic of 1878. Mary Lois Ragland and Kathy Ragland Renfroe. Privately printed, 1987. 55 pp.
A single-volume source that offers a listing of those who died of yellow fever during the epidemic of 1878. Information was taken from Powers' *Epidemic of 1878 in Mississippi*, the Fisher Funeral Home records, and entries from the local newspaper during that time period. The counties included are Claiborne, Hinds, Lauderdale, Madison, Montgomery, Pike, Warren, Washington, and Yazoo as well as some Louisiana towns. In addition, there is a listing of physicians who died of yellow fever. Alphabetically arranged.

TWO

Census and Mortality Schedules for Mississippi

1820 Census of Mississippi. McEllhiney and Thomas. Pass Christian, MS: Willo Publishing Company, 1964. 201 pp.

Indexes names appearing in Mississippi's first federal census taken in 1820. All sixteen counties formed at the time of statehood are included. Arranged by county with maps included. Indexed.

1830 Choctaw Roll: "Armstrong Roll." Larry S. Watson. Laguna Hills, CA: Histree, 1985. 3 vols.

Presents the documentation of the Treaty of Dancing Rabbit Creek giving not only the treaty itself but the proceedings surrounding it. The census of native Americans known as the Armstrong Roll is included and indexed. The information is divided by Choctaw district (Nitakachi, Mushulatubbe, and Leflore) and includes names of Choctaw tribal members, whites who married Choctaw natives, and slaves. This publication holds particular significance for genealogists and historians because the treaty was the last major land concession made by Native Americans to the Europeans in Mississippi. Each volume is separately indexed.

1890 Mississippi Census Index. Ronald Vern Jackson, W. David Samuelsen, and I. Vern Jackson. North Salt Lake, UT: Accelerated Indexing Systems International Inc., 1985. 96 pp.

Indexes only that portion of the federal census schedule that enumerated union veterans. Physical format and arrangement is the same as other publications done by AIS.

ACCELERATED INDEXING SYSTEMS, INC.

Accelerated Indexing Systems is a publishing company that has used computer technology to index original population schedules for federal censuses from 1790 to 1870. The published indexes for Mississippi appear from 1820 to 1870, covering the earliest federal census taken for the state until the WPA Soundex coding began for the 1880 census. Valuable introductory information gives chronological data regarding territories, states, and counties along with useful historical description of federal census taking. However, the address listing of major library and genealogical collections is not current. The AIS publications pertaining to Mississippi federal census schedules are as follows:

> *Mississippi, 1820.* Ronald Vern Jackson. North Salt Lake, UT: Accelerated Indexing Systems International, Inc., 1981. 124 pp.

> *Mississippi, 1830 Census Index.* Ronald Vern Jackson. North Salt Lake, UT: Accelerated Indexing Systems International, Inc., 1976. 28 pp.

> *Mississippi, 1840 Census Index.* Ronald Vern Jackson. Bountiful, UT: Accelerated Indexing Systems, Inc., 1976. 389 pp.

> *Mississippi, 1850 Census Index.* Ronald Vern Jackson. Bountiful, UT: Accelerated Indexing Systems, Inc., 1977. 199 pp.

> *Mississippi, 1860 Census Index.* Ronald Vern Jackson. Bountiful, UT: Accelerated Indexing Systems, Inc., 1985. 362 pp.

> *Mississippi, 1870 Census Index.* Ronald Vern Jackson. North Salt Lake, UT: Accelerated Indexing Systems, Inc., 1988. 979 pp.

Other publications by AIS are found elsewhere in this listing; these pertain to the indexing of mortality schedules and state census records.

Early Inhabitants of the Natchez District. Norman E. Gillis. Privately printed, 1963. 152 pp.

A volume that provides a useful start in gathering information about territorial census records in Mississippi. The book's five sections contain references to English land grants from 1768 to 1779, the Spanish census of 1792, inhabitants of the Natchez District in 1810 and 1816, and inhabitants outside the Natchez District in 1816. Even though much of the material for this work came from secondary sources cited by the author, it is still a highly recommended work. One disadvantage is that there is a separate index for each segment instead of a single alphabetical index.

Early Mississippi State Census and Vital Statistic Records. Donna Pannell. Jackson, MS: Mississippi Department of Archives and History, 1986. 201 pp.

This unpublished source indexes Mississippi's state census records. These documents sometimes provide names missed by federal enumerators for identical years. Although the book claims to cover the years 1818 to 1829, the actual years indexed are from 1818 to 1825. The second portion contains vital statistical information that has limited value, with only the name of the head of the household given. This work is important for those researching the years between federal census enumerations.

Mississippi 1810. Ronald Vern Jackson. Salt Lake City, UT: Accelerated Indexing Systems International, Inc., 1983. 79 pp.

Indexes territorial census schedules giving full name, county, and portion of territory. Arranged alphabetically.

Mississippi 1820 Census. Irene S. and Norman E. Gillis. Baton Rouge, LA: Norman E. Gillis, 1963. 147 pp.

A printed variation of this census schedule by a reliable compiler. Monroe County is not included and the residents of the city of Natchez are identified apart from those of Adams County. Arranged alphabetically.

Mississippi 1820–1825. Ronald Vern Jackson. Salt Lake City, UT: Accelerated Indexing Systems International, 1986. 58 pp.

Index to state census that gives full name, county, and year. Townships are not listed. Helpful though incomplete since it only indexes filmed items. Arranged alphabetically.

Mississippi 1830 Census. Irene S. and Norman E. Gillis. Shreveport, LA: Irene S. and Norman E. Gillis, 1965. 236 pp.

A printed variation of the original census schedule that gives head of household, county of residence, and statistical information pertaining to those living within the household. Enumerations for Pike County are missing from the original schedules, but this index uses extant tax records of 1831 as supplementary material. Residents from the city of Natchez are identified separately from those of Adams County. In addition, an appendix gives residents of the Indian Nation in Simpson County. Arranged alphabetically.

124 Descriptive Profiles of Printed Sources

Mississippi 1830/1837. Ronald Vern Jackson. Salt Lake City, UT: Accelerated Indexing Systems International, Inc., 1986. 63 pp.

State census index that gives name and county. Only township indicated is Natchez. A useful guide though incomplete in that it indexed only those items on microfilm. Arranged alphabetically.

The Mississippi 1850 Census Surname Index. Norman and Irene Gillis. Shreveport, LA: Norman E. Gillis, n.d. 521 pp.

Refers the researcher to the 1850 federal Mississippi census by family number. Because this census year did not list slaves individually, the index includes only native and foreign born residents. Arranged consecutively by number with a surname index. Print is easier to read than the AIS indexes.

Mississippi 1850 Mortality Schedules. Irene S. Gillis. Shreveport, LA: Norman E. Gillis, 1973. 59 pp.

A compilation of data taken from the mortality schedule of 1850. Only deaths of whites are included since only the given names of African-Americans are found on the originals. Also, contains an appendix with a listing of Mississippi physicians. Arranged alphabetically.

Mississippi 1853 State Census Index. Ronald Vern Jackson. North Salt Lake, UT: Accelerated Indexing Systems International, 1988. 251 pp.

Useful though incomplete in that it indexes only the microfilmed records. Arranged alphabetically.

Mississippi 1860 U.S. Census Index. Kathryn Rose Bonner. Privately printed, n.d. 3 vols.

A three-volume index of the 1860 census that usually gives the county abbreviation and page number along with the individual name. If a page number is not included, then the county name is indicated. Census information for free and slave inhabitants of Hancock, Washington, and Sunflower counties are missing. There are names found in this index that have not been listed in the AIS index. The user explanation found in volume 2 and the easy-to-read print make this work a popular index.

Mississippi 1866 State Census Index. Ronald Vern Jackson. North Salt Lake, UT: Accelerated Indexing Systems International, 1988. 158 pp.

A helpful guide though incomplete since it only indexes filmed items. Arranged alphabetically.

Mississippi: Index to the United States Census of 1840. Santa Ana, CA: G.A.M. Publications, 1970. 2 vols.

Transcription of federal census schedule divided into two volumes, southern district and northern district. This finding aid references the head of household to the page number of original census schedule. Arranged by county with surname index found in each volume.

Mortality Schedules: *Mississippi 1850 Mortality Schedule, Mississippi 1860 Mortality Schedule, Mississippi 1870 Mortality Schedule, Mississippi 1880 Mortality Schedule.* Ronald Vern Jackson, ed. Bountiful, UT: Accelerated Indexing Systems, Inc., n.d. 4 vols.

Indexes the original mortality schedules for the years 1850, 1860, 1870, and 1880. Information found in these volumes reflects data collected before June 1 of that census year. Each work consists of the person's name, county and state of residence when death occurred, age, sex, month of death, place of birth, and a code indicating cause of death. Occupation is also given, if shown on the original census schedules. Because enumeration was not always consistent, the researcher will find that some data is missing. Arranged alphabetically.

United States. Commission to the Five Civilized Tribes. Index to the Final Rolls of Citizens and Freedmen of the Five Civilized Tribes in Indian Territory. Photocopy. n.d. 4 parts.

Index to the final rolls of citizens and freedmen of the Five Civilized Tribes in Indian Territory: Choctaw, Cherokee, Creek, Chickasaw, and Seminole. Appears in four parts that are photocopied from the microfilm version.

THREE

Mississippi County Sources

ADAMS COUNTY

Adams County, Mississippi, 1860–1900. Nicholas Russell Murray. Hammond, LA: Hunting For Bears, n.d. 142 pp.

Computer-generated listing of marriage records. Gives names and date of marriage but does not provide reference to marriage record book or page number. Includes a few records for 1803, 1805, and 1806.

Adams County, Mississippi, Marriages 1802–1859. Irene S. and Norman E. Gillis. Shreveport, LA: Norman E. Gillis, 1976. 92 pp.

Transcription of original records. Indexed.

Adams' Light Infantry, Natchez, Mississippi. Privately printed, April 26, 18??. Unpaged.

Lists names of soldiers in the Confederate units from Natchez. No index.

The Black Experience in Natchez 1720–1880. Ronald L.F. Davis. Washington, DC: National Park Service, 1993. 236 pp.

A resource that tracks the historical development of the black community in Natchez. The genealogical information may be found primarily in the list of "tables" included. Among the records are those pertaining to slave sales during the Spanish period, free black and white households, black-related newspaper items from 1857 to 1890, black political leaders from

1865 to 1890, and baptisms of black refugees and soldiers. Although not indexed, the table of contents does provide a useful guide.

Confederate Memorabilia. Mary Groves Barker. Washington, MS: Esperanza Publications, 1979. 107 pp.

This publication consists of Confederate records for Adams, Claiborne, Franklin, Jefferson, and Wilkinson. Pension lists are also included for Adams and Claiborne. Arranged by county, but no index.

Death Records, Natchez, 1839–1856. Interment Reports, Natchez, 1885–1909. Death Records, Natchez, 1857–1909. Burial Locations, Natchez (by name). Burial Locations, Natchez (by lot number). Confederate Army Records. Chancery Court Records, Deed Books 4-I. MDAH has volume 1, which covers December 29, 1839, to December 27, 1856. Most of the information came directly from city record books, with a few items taken from newspaper articles. Appearing in computer printout form, this work presents much genealogical data in one source.

Early Will Records of Adams County, Mississippi. Compiled by Mary G. Barker, Mavis Oliver Feltus, and Diane A. Stockfelt. 1975. 130 pp.

Includes genealogical data abstracted from wills, as well as some biographical narrative. Appears in two parts and is indexed separately.

The History of the Descendants of the Jersey Settlers of Adams County, Mississippi. Frances Preston Mills, ed. Privately printed, 1981. 2 vols.

A wealth of genealogical information about some of the early families of Adams county. Indexed.

Index. Heads of Families. 1830 Census. Adams County. Jane Melton. 16 pp. Typescript.

Marriages Celebrated at Natchez, Mississippi, and Data Recorded in the St. Louis Parish Church (now St. Louis Cathedral of New Orleans). Marriage Register "A" (1720–1730). 11 pp.

Typescript. Gives date along with name of parents of bride and groom.

Marriages in Deed Books. Index. Deeds Book I. Adams County, Mississippi. Gordon Wells. 1962. 4 pp.

Typescript. An index.

Monuments in the Natchez City Cemetery. 1821–1981. The Genealogical Committee Natchez Historical Society. Natchez, MS: McDonald's Printers, 1982. 247 pp.

Index not included.

Name Index to Monuments in the Natchez City Cemetery. Mary Fisher. Privately printed, 1984. Unpaged. Typescript.

The Natchez Court Records, 1767–1805. May Wilson McBee. Baltimore, MD: Genealogical Publishing Co., Inc., 1979. 635 pp.

A single-volume source of the original seven "letter" books that contained the court records of the Natchez District for the years 1767 to 1805. This district included the area that later formed the five Mississippi counties of Wilkinson, Adams, Jefferson, Claiborne, and Warren. There is a wealth of genealogical information in this work that was translated and abstracted primarily from provincial records. Compiled first by "letter" book and then chronologically, this resource is also well indexed.

Natchez Rifles Company E, 4th Louisiana Battalion Civil War. n.d. Unpaged.

Photocopy of index cards listing Mississippians who served in this Louisiana company during the Civil War. No index.

A Partial List of Private Cemeteries in Natchez, Adams County, Mississippi. Sarah and Bob Shumway. Vidalia, LA. 1987. 115 pp.

Generally, a compilation of the lists taken from the WPA work and the DAR series. Also includes records of interments from September 2, 1819 to January 20, 1822 with interment records for blacks to January 2, 1834. Surname index.

ALCORN COUNTY

Alcorn County, Mississippi, 1870–1900. Nicholas Russell Murray. Hammond, LA: Hunting for Bears, Inc., n.d. 197 pp.

Computer-generated listing of marriage records. Gives names and date of marriage but does not provide reference to marriage record book or page numbers. Title information incorrect in that the publication actually contains marriage records for the years 1842 to 1900. Arranged alphabetically.

Alcorn County, Mississippi, Cemetery Records. Thomas P. Hughes, Jr., and Jewel B. Standefer. Privately printed, 1971. 239 pp.

Arranged by cemetery. Index included.

History of Alcorn County, Mississippi. Alcorn County Historical Association. Dallas, TX: National Share Graphics, Inc., 1983. 645 pp.

Information for this county history came from personal recollections and secondary source material. Includes separate section of family histories. Index refers to each story section, not page number.

AMITE COUNTY

Amite County and Liberty, Mississippi. Sesqui-Centennial Commemorating 150 Years of Progress. Privately printed, 1959. Unpaged.
Typical "celebration" booklet filled with interesting bits of genealogical information. No index. Difficult to use.

Amite County, Mississippi, 1699–1865. Albert E. Casey. Privately printed, 1948. 4 vols.
A four-volume work that includes many types of public records, private papers, and church records; provides genealogies of some families. Good index to a wealth of information.

Amite County, Mississippi, 1810–1899. Nicholas Russell Murray. Hammond, LA: Hunting for Bears, n.d. 190 pp.
Computer-generated listing of marriage records. Gives names and date of marriage but does not provide reference to marriage record book or page number. Arranged alphabetically.

Amite County, Mississippi, Cemeteries. J. Paul Mogan, Jr. and Kathryn Cole Mogan. Osyka, MS: An Armadillo Book, 1982. 483 pp.
These entries consist of data copied from the grave sites plus information gathered from other types of records or newspaper files. Includes maps and index.

Farewell to This Day; The Diary of Miss Frances Ann Cain of Zion Hill, Mississippi, 1856–1858. J. Paul Mogan, Jr. and Kathryn Cole Mogan. Privately printed, 1983. 116 pp.
Transcription of early diary that contains references to many family names and local happenings. Indexed.

ATTALA COUNTY

Attala County, Mississippi, 1892–1900. Nicholas Russell Murray. Hammond, LA: Hunting for Bears, Inc., n.d. 117 pp.
Computer-generated listing of marriage records. Gives names and date of marriage but does not provide reference to marriage record book or page number. Arranged alphabetically.

Attala County, Mississippi, Cemeteries. Marymaganos McCool Fenwick. Privately printed, 1988. 403 pp.
Indexed.

Attala County, Mississippi, Pioneers. Betty Couch Wiltshire. Bowie, MD: Heritage Books, Inc., 1991. 238 pp.

The documentation for this publication comes from various types of records and covers the years 1834 to 1865. Information comes from such sources as tax lists for selected years, newspaper notices, marriages and divorce records, court cases, business transactions, public auctions, sheriffs' sales, crime reports, and delinquent taxpayers. As in previous works the author includes genealogies of families for the year 1860 and earlier. This is a reliable source that is indexed and well researched.

Confederate Pension Records of Attala County, Mississippi. 6 pp. Typescript. An index.

Early Attala Records. Joyce William Sanders. 1972. 37 pp.

Abstracts from early Attala newspapers relating to deaths, marriages, and land sales. Does not include an index.

Kosciusko-Attala History. Kosciusko-Attala Historical Society. Privately printed, n.d. 314 pp.

General county history offering genealogical information. A separate typescript index is available that provides easy access to names.

A Place Called Sallis in Attala County, Mississippi. Anne Hughes Porter. Privately printed, 1982. 420 pp.

A collection of various types of genealogical material offering a substantial amount of information about the people of this town. Indexed.

BENTON COUNTY

Benton County, Mississippi, 1871–1900. Nicholas Russell Murray. Hammond, LA: Hunting for Bears, n.d. 81 pp.

A computer-generated listing of marriage records. Gives names and date of marriage but does not provide reference to marriage record book or page number. Arranged alphabetically.

Cemeteries of Benton County, Mississippi. Don Martini and Bill Gurney. Ripley, MS: Old Timer Press, 1985. 115 pp.

Arranged by cemetery and then alphabetically. Includes surname index.

BOLIVAR COUNTY

1860 Federal Population Census. Bolivar County, Mississippi. John C. Green III. Privately printed, 1984. 65 pp.

A computer-generated index.

Bolivar County, Mississippi. Nicholas Russell Murray. Hammond, LA: Hunting for Bears, n.d. 127 pp.

A computer-generated listing of marriage records. Gives names and date of marriage but does not provide reference to marriage record book or page number. Inclusive dates not indicated. Arranged alphabetically.

Cleveland; A Centennial History 1886–1986. Linton Weeks. Privately printed, 1985. 237 pp.

Good town history for genealogical research. Contains early family histories along with an appendix of listings relating to military records, postmasters, clubs, education and government officials. Indexed.

Early Mississippi Records: Bolivar County. Volume 1, 1836–1861; Volume 2, 1866–1904; Volume 8, 1866–1900. Katherine Clements Branton and Alice Clements Wade, eds. Privately printed, 1988. 3 vols.

A three-volume series that contains several types of records including probate papers, mortality schedules, naturalization records, newspaper abstracts, census schedules, and deed books. Spans the period from 1836 to 1904. Each volume is indexed separately.

History of Bolivar County, Mississippi. Wirt A. Williams, ed. Jackson, MS: Hederman Brothers, 1948. 634 pp.

A good county history with listings of names cited from public records. This source focuses primarily on family histories. Well indexed.

Homecoming at Mound Bayou, Mississippi, With Some of the Education History of We Americans of African Heritage. Milburn J. Crowe, ed. Privately printed, 1982. Unpaged.

Compiled from secondary sources and includes some early family histories. No index.

Journal of the Bolivar County Historical Society. Cleveland, MS: The Society, 1977– 8 vols.

A journal devoted to genealogical and historical articles for this county. Index not available at MDAH.

Mound Bayou, Mississippi, Centennial Celebration July 6–12, 1987. Milburn J. Crowe, ed. Privately printed, 1987. Unpaged.

A publication created for the town's centennial celebration that offers some items of genealogical interest. No index.

The Negro at Mound Bayou. A.P. Hood. Nashville, TN: A.M.E. Sunday School Union, 1910. 122 pp.

Gives black genealogical information along with historical text about the development of this all-black community. No index.

Calhoun County, Mississippi, 1923–1935. Nicholas Russell Murray. Hammond, LA: Hunting for Bears, n.d. 44 pp.

A computer-generated listing of marriage records. Gives names and date of marriage but does not provide reference to marriage record book or page number. Arranged alphabetically.

The Cherry Hill-Poplar Springs Reid Community in Calhoun County, Mississippi. Monette Morgan Young. Privately printed, 1985. 186 pp.

Focuses primarily on family history of this community. Well indexed.

Index to Marriage Records, Calhoun County, Mississippi, Colored, February 13, 1923 and August 9, 1970. 58 pp.

Typescript. Arranged alphabetically.

Land Patents. Calhoun County, Mississippi, Book III. Imogene Springer. Houston, MS: Chickasaw County Historical Genealogical Society, 1989. 25 pp.

Transcription from the Pontotoc Land District tract book. Indexed.

Carroll County Cemetery Records. Mrs. Lawrence H. Bibus. 105 pp.

Typescript. Indexed.

Carroll County, Mississippi, 1834–1885. Nicholas Russell Murray. Hammond, LA: Hunting for Bears, n.d. 94 pp.

A computer-generated listing of marriage records. Gives names and date of marriage but does not provide reference to marriage record book or page number. Arranged alphabetically.

Carroll County, Mississippi, Abstracts of Wills 1834–1875, Divorces 1857–1875. Betty Couch Wiltshire. Bowie, MD: Heritage Books, Inc., 1987. 69 pp.

Abstracts and indexes wills and divorces for years given in title. This same information has been included in a later publication.

Carroll County, Mississippi, Pioneers with Abstracts of Wills, 1834–1875 and Divorces, 1857–1875. Betty Couch Wiltshire. Bowie, MD: Heritage Books, Inc., 1990. 293 pp.

A reliable source that focuses on the early residents of Carroll County from its beginning to 1850. This volume consists of abstracts of land plats, probate records, personal tax rolls, and the 1850 slave schedule from the federal census. Additionally, the volunteers in the Mexican War are listed with the inclusion of genealogies of forty-three early families. The wills and divorces published in this book appeared in an earlier volume that is now out of print. Indexed.

History of Carroll County. William Franklin Hamilton. Privately printed, n.d. 98 pp.

Most of the information in this interesting publication seems to have come from newspaper articles. The author served as a corporal during the Civil War and later was sheriff of the county. This work not only includes families and an explanation of relationships but in some cases gives a general description of the individual. A separate typescript index was created by MDAH to provide access for the researcher.

Marriage Records II District Carroll County, Vaiden, Mississippi, 1873–1920. Willie Boyett Hunter. Privately printed, n.d.

Arranged chronologically. Does not have an index.

Military Annals of Carroll County. W.F. Hamilton. Carrollton, MS: The Conservative Print, 1906. 76 pp.

A pamphlet listing company and names of soldiers who served in the Confederacy for this county. Additional information is given regarding those who served in the Mexican War and the Spanish-American War. No index.

Vaiden Heritage. Vaiden Garden Club. Florence, MS: Messenger Press, 1976. 280 pp.

General town history. Although there is no index, this work does have a table of contents that offers some guidance in its use.

CHICKASAW COUNTY

The 1860 Census of Chickasaw County, Mississippi. Jeanne Robey Felldin and Charlotte Magee Tucker. Tomball, TX: Census Reprints, 1978. 185 pp.

A photographic reproduction of the original handwritten census entries of 1860. Generally hard to decipher. Surname index included.

Chickasaw County, Mississippi, 1863–1900. Nicholas Russell Murray. Hammond, LA: Hunting for Bears, n.d. 68 pp.

A computer-generated listing of marriage records. Gives names and date of marriage but does not provide reference to marriage record book or page number. Arranged alphabetically.

Chickasaw Times Past. Houston, MS: West Chickasaw County Historical and Genealogical Society, 1982–

Journal published by the Chickasaw County Historical and Genealogical Society. Index not found at MDAH.

A History of Chickasaw County, Mississippi. Chickasaw County Historical and Genealogical Society. Dallas, TX: Curtis Media Corporation, 1985. 625 pp.

The information in this county history came primarily from personal recollections and secondary sources. A separate section devoted to family histories is of genealogical interest. Index refers to story name rather than page number.

Houlka: Yesterday, Today. Rad Harrill Reed. Privately printed, 1914. 154 pp.

A large portion of this book contains biographical material of genealogical interest. No index.

The Land Owners. Chickasaw County, Mississippi, 1836–1852. Book II. Imogene Springer. Houston, MS: Chickasaw County Historical Genealogical Society, 1989. 157 pp.

Transcription of recorded land records. Indexed.

The People. Chickasaw County, Mississippi, 1836–1852. Book I. Imogene Springer. Houston, MS: Chickasaw County Historical Genealogical Society, 1989. 126 pp.

A transcription of tax assessments, state census records, the mortality schedule of 1850, federal census records, and other official county documents. Indexed.

Records of Monroe, Lowndes, and Chickasaw Counties, Mississippi. Elizabeth C. Jones. Privately printed, n.d. 137 pp.

The Chickasaw County portion of this publication indexes early will and estate papers. Also includes selected county records for Monroe and Lowndes counties. Indexed.

CHOCTAW COUNTY

Choctaw County Chronicles: A History of Choctaw County, Mississippi, 1830–1973. J. P. Coleman. Spartanburg, SC: The Reprint Company, Publishers, 1981. 483 pp.

Worthwhile general county history that provides easy access through good indexing and a thorough table of contents. Originally printed in 1973.

Choctaw County, Mississippi, 1881–1900. Nicholas Russell Murray. Hammond, LA: Hunting for Bears, n.d. 64 pp.

A computer-generated listing of marriage records. Gives names and date of marriage but does not provide reference to marriage record book or page number. Arranged alphabetically.

Choctaw County, Mississippi, Cemeteries. Hazel Crenshaw Garrett and Louis Taunton. Louisville, MS: G & T Publishers, 1990. 391 pp. Indexed.

Index Choctaw County, Mississippi, Census of 1850. Jane Melton. 31 pp. Typescript.

Index to Heads of Families and Other Adults Choctaw County, Mississippi, Census of 1850. Jane Melton. 1962. 31 pp. Typescript.

CLAIBORNE COUNTY

Claiborne County, Mississippi, 1816–1827. Nicholas Russell Murray. Hammond, LA: Hunting for Bears, 1981. 111 pp.

A computer-generated listing of marriage records. Gives names and date of marriage but does not provide reference to marriage record book or page number. Arranged alphabetically.

Claiborne County, Mississippi: The Promised Land. Katy McCaleb Headley. Port Gibson, MS: Claiborne County Historical Society, 1976. 542 pp.

A comprehensive county source that contains information obtained from cemeteries, military records, doctors' papers, and early settlers, as well as other genealogical material. Indexed.

Confederate Memorabilia. Mary Groves Barker. Washington, MS: Esperanza Publications, 1979. 107 pp.

This publication consists of Confederate records from Adams, Claiborne, Franklin, Jefferson, and Wilkinson. Pension lists are also included for Adams and Claiborne. Arranged by county but does not have an index.

Death Notices from Port Gibson, Mississippi, Reveille, August 19, 1926. 32 pp.

Transcription of newspaper notices but not in any arranged form. Typescript. No index.

CLARKE COUNTY

Clarke County, Mississippi, Index: Probate Court, Court Minutes Volume 8, April 1867-July 1870. Glennie W. Kamper. Meridian, MS: Lauderdale County Department of Archives and History, Inc., 1988. 31 pp.

Printed name index resulting from a page-by-page search of the original court records.

Clarke County, Mississippi, Index: Probate Minutes and Wills, Volume II, 1839 to 1846. Glennie W. Kamper. Meridian, MS: Lauderdale County Department of Archives and History, Inc., 1988. 14 pp.
An index to court records compiled from a page-by-page examination.

Clarke County, Mississippi, Marriage Record Book B. Period: 1865–1867, White. Glennie Kamper. Meridian, MS: Lauderdale County Department of Archives and History, Inc., 1989. 34 pp.
An index.

Clarke County, Mississippi, Tax Rolls and Census 1835–1866. Jean Strickland and Patricia N. Edwards. Privately printed, 1990. 186 pp.
The tax rolls for the years 1842, 1844, 1846, 1847, 1849, and 1850 are missing. Includes index.

History of Clarke County, Mississippi: Wills 1834–1900, Land Grants and Cemetery Records 1834–1915. H. H. Daniel. Privately printed, n.d. 77 pp.
A transcription of records that also includes an index.

CLAY COUNTY

Clay County, Mississippi, 1874–1900. Nicholas Russell Murray. Hammond, LA: Hunting for Bears, n.d. 156 pp.
A computer-generated listing of marriage records. Gives names and date of marriage but does not provide reference to marriage record book or page number. Arranged alphabetically.

The History of Clay County. Richie Norwood Franks. Privately printed, 1982. 167 pp.
General county history with a name index.

History of Clay County, Mississippi. Clay County Historical Book Committee. Dallas, TX: Curtis Media Corporation, 1988. 862 pp.
General county history created from personal recollections and secondary source material. Includes separate section of family histories. Index refers to story section, not page number.

Oral History Interview Transcripts, Tombigbee Historic Townsites Project. James M. McClurken and Peggy Uland Anderson. Washington, D.C.: U.S. Department of Interior, 1981. 8 vols.

An eight-volume printed work of a federally funded oral history project. Well indexed with useful genealogical material.

COAHOMA COUNTY

Clarksdale and Coahoma County: A History. Linton Weeks. Clarksdale, MS: Carnegie Public Library, 1982. 265 pp.
Offers genealogical information with accounts of early family settlers and connections. Appendix contains various listings. Indexed.

Coahoma County, Mississippi, 1868–1900. Nicholas Russell Murray. Hammond, LA: Hunting for Bears, n.d. 2 vols.
A computer-generated listing of marriage records. Gives names and date of marriage but does not provide reference to marriage record book or page number. Arranged alphabetically.

COPIAH COUNTY

Copiah County, Mississippi, 1823–1875. Nicholas Russell Murray. Hammond, LA: Hunting for Bears, n.d. 132 pp.
A computer-generated listing of marriage records. Gives names and date of marriage but does not provide reference to marriage record book or page number. Arranged alphabetically.

Copiah County, Mississippi, 1830 Census. Isom Stephens. 18 pp.
Typescript.

Hazlehurst. Copiah County, Mississippi. Hartwell Cook, ed. Privately printed, 1985. 382 pp.
County history created from personal recollections and secondary source material. Family information included. No index.

Marriage Records, Copiah County, Mississippi, 1823–1843. Marie Luter Upton. Privately printed, 1958. 59 pp.
Transcription of marriage records. Indexed.

Marriage Records, Copiah County, Mississippi, 1844–1859. Mary E. Thomas. Privately printed, n.d. 124 pp.
Transcription of marriage records. Indexed.

COVINGTON COUNTY

Cemetery Census: Covington County, Mississippi, and Surrounding Counties. Mrs. Archie Pickering and Mrs. Mart Rogers. Privately printed, 1976. 256 pp.

A separate typescript index is available at MDAH.

Church Records of Covington County, Mississippi, Presbyterian and Baptist. Jean Strickland and Patricia N. Edwards. Privately printed, 1988. 147 pp.
Indexes early church records. Inclusive years not given though it seems to refer primarily to the first half of the nineteenth century.

Confederate Records: Covington, Wayne, and Jones County. Jean Strickland and Patricia N. Edwards. Privately printed, 1987. 140 pp.
Combines three county Confederate records in one source. The information from records concerning Covington County was taken from handwritten forms that include more genealogical information than is usually found in the later conventional pension applications.

Covington County, Mississippi, 1904–1924. Nicholas Russell Murray. Hammond, LA: Hunting for Bears, 1981. 39 pp.
A computer-generated listing of marriage records. Gives names and date of marriage but does not provide reference to marriage record book or page number. Arranged alphabetically.

Covington County, Mississippi, Tax Rolls 1819–1846. Jean Strickland and Patricia N. Edwards. Privately printed, 1990. 177 pp.
A transcription of county records. Tax rolls are missing for the years 1826, 1830, 1836, 1842, 1844, and 1845. Index included.

Mount Olive: Yesterday and Today. Sandra Boyd. Privately printed, 1987. 52 pp.
General town history with an unexpected inclusion of grade school students for the years 1903 and 1904. No index.

Who Married Whom, Covington County, Mississippi. Jean Strickland and Patricia N. Edwards. Privately printed, 1991. 209 pp.
Includes only white marriages. Indexed.

DESOTO COUNTY

DeSoto Cemetery Inscriptions. J.B. Bell and Mildred M. Scott. Hernando, MS: Genealogical Society of DeSoto County, Mississippi, n.d. 293 pp.
Indexed.

DeSoto Descendants. Hernando, MS.: Genealogical Society of DeSoto County, 1982– .
Newsletter of the Genealogical Society of DeSoto County. No index found at MDAH.

Hernando Historic Windows 1836–1986.   J.B. Bell. Privately printed, 1986. 100 pp.
   Includes genealogical family charts. Indexed.

Index 1870 Federal Census. DeSoto County, Mississippi.   Genealogical Society of DeSoto County, Mississippi. Hernando, MS. 1984. Unpaged. Indexed.

Our Heritage: DeSoto County, Mississippi.   Pam McPhail Ivy, ed. Memphis, TN: Myers, 1979. 210 pp.
   General county history that includes family histories. A separately bound index is available at MDAH.

FORREST COUNTY

Forrest County, Mississippi, 1906–1920.   Nicholas Russell Murray. Hammond, LA: Hunting for Bears, n.d. 105 pp.
   A computer-generated listing of marriage records. Gives names and date of marriage but does not provide reference to marriage record book or page number. Arranged alphabetically.

Forrest County, Mississippi, Tombstone Inscriptions (western part of old Perry County, Mississippi).   South Mississippi Genealogical Society. Hattiesburg, MS: South Mississippi Genealogical Society, 1986. 680 pp.
   Includes a brief history of each church and its location. Indexed.

History of Morriston, Mississippi: From Its Beginnings in 1862 Before the Civil War to 1988.   Alice Moore, Arlice Moore, and Leonard L. Slade, Jr. Baltimore, MD: Gateway Press, Inc., 1988.
   Community history that includes some family histories. No index.

FRANKLIN COUNTY

Franklin County, Mississippi, 1817–1899.   Nicholas Russell Murray. Hammond, LA: Hunting for Bears, n.d. 80 pp.
   A computer-generated listing of marriage records. Gives names and date of marriage but does not provide reference to marriage record book or page number. Arranged alphabetically.

Franklin County, Mississippi, Cemeteries.   J. Paul Mogan, Jr., and Kathryn Cole Mogan. Osyka, MS: Armadillo Book, 1982. 310 pp.
   Indexed.

Franklin County, Mississippi, Marriages.   Mildred Ezell. Privately printed, n.d. 178 pp.

Transcription of early marriage records. Two periods not included are from 1809 to April 10, 1818, and from June 1, 1826, to August 29, 1832. Indexed.

Heads of Families and Other Adults in Franklin County, 1850.   Lamar Laufair. 1960. 12 pp.

Typescript. An index.

History of Franklin County, Mississippi, from 1809 to 1899.   W.W. Lambright. McComb, MS: Special Job Office Print., 1899. 100 pp.

Gives listings of public as well as federal census information. Also includes family histories. Difficult to use since there is no index.

GEORGE COUNTY

By the Rivers of Water: History of George County, Mississippi.   W. Harvell Jackson. Privately printed, 1978, 1982. 2 vols.

Interesting county history with a strong emphasis on early family histories. Difficult to use as there is no index.

Four Centuries on the Pascagoula: History, Story, and Legend of the Pascagoula River Country.   Cyril Edward Cain. Spartanburg, SC: The Reprint Company, Publishers, 1983. 2 vols.

Based on reliable primary source material, this publication provides a comprehensive historical account of Jackson and George counties. Although the book was originally printed in 1953, the initial writing began as early as 1937. The second volume includes primarily family history information that is of particular interest to the genealogist. A well-indexed and well documented county history.

George County, Mississippi, 1911–1925.   Nicholas Russell Murray. Hammond, LA: Hunting for Bears, 1981.

A computer-generated listing of marriage records. Gives names and date of marriage but does not provide reference to marriage record book or page number. Arranged alphabetically. Appears in the same volume with Pearl River and Stone counties.

George County, Mississippi, Cemetery Records.   Ben and Jean Strickland. Privately printed, 1984. 2 vols.

Both the WPA list of cemeteries and a highway map were used to locate cemeteries included in this source. The researcher should remember that all of George County was once in what is now Jackson County. Index and map included.

Obituaries, Marriages and Celebrations of Jackson and George Counties, Mississippi. Betty Clark Rodgers. Pascagoula, MS: Jackson County Genealogical Society, 1989. 275 pp.
Contains biographical data taken from selected newspaper articles from the 1800s to the 1930s. Indexed.

Records of George County, Mississippi. Death Records 1912–1945. Mary Childress Rouse. Privately printed, 1983. 210 pp.
Transcription of state death records. Indexed.

GREENE COUNTY

Cemetery Records of Greene County, Mississippi. Book A. Book B. Ben and Jean Strickland. Privately printed, 1982. 133 pp. 140 pp.
The transcribing of these cemetery records is particularly important because of the destruction of early county records due to courthouse fires. All cemeteries are included that were found in printed sources such as the WPA list and state highway department maps. Book A covers the northern half of the county; and Book B covers the southern portion. Well indexed.

Greene County, Mississippi, 1875–1910. Nicholas Russell Murray. Hammond, LA: Hunting for Bears, n.d. 54 pp.
A computer-generated listing of marriage records. Gives names and date of marriage but does not provide reference to marriage record book or page number. Arranged alphabetically.

Records of Greene County, Mississippi: 1812–1820 Tax Rolls, 1816 Territorial Census, Cemetery Records. Ben and Jean Strickland. Privately printed, 1980. 2 vols.
Each volume has an index.

Records of Greene County, Mississippi: 1840 Census, 1846 Land Commissioner's Book, 1853 State Census. Ben and Jean Strickland. Privately printed, 1982. 94 pp.
Indexed.

Who Lived Where. Greene County, Mississippi. Book of Original Entry. Jean Strickland and Patricia N. Edwards. Privately printed, 1989. 166 pp.
This publication abstracts the original tract books. Includes helpful material about land acquisition in Mississippi. Indexed.

Who Married Whom. Greene County, Mississippi. Patricia N. Edwards and Jean Strickland. Privately printed, 1984. 124 pp.

Provides a listing of Greene County residents taken primarily from census records and tax rolls in the years 1820 to 1880. Information given includes name, place and year of birth, military record, year of marriage, and spouse. Also, contains some contributions from individual researchers. Indexed.

GRENADA COUNTY

Cemeteries of Grenada County, Mississippi, and Surrounding Areas. Frances G. Martin. Privately printed, 1987. 2 vols.

Provides genealogical information taken from Grenada County tombstones. The first volume includes old family cemeteries, and the second focuses on known white cemeteries. This work is indexed by name with an additional geographic index that shows place of origin for many of the county's early settlers. Contains a special inclusion of those cemeteries relocated by the federal government in 1946.

Grenada County, Mississippi, 1870–1900. Nicholas Russell Murray. Hammond, LA: Hunting for Bears, n.d. 20 pp.

A computer-generated listing of marriage records. Gives names and date of marriage but does not provide reference to marriage record book or page number. Arranged alphabetically.

The History of Grenada County. Privately printed, 1985. 192 pp.

Shows family histories in alphabetical sequence. No index.

A History of Grenada County. J.C. Hathorn. Privately printed, n.d. 229 pp.

General county history with separate typescript index.

HANCOCK COUNTY

Hancock County Census of 1880. Ernest A. Carvin. 1980. 202 pp.

A typed copy of the original census schedule. Includes an index.

Hancock County, Mississippi, 1853–1895. Nicholas Russell Murray. Hammond, LA: Hunting for Bears, n.d. 76 pp.

A computer-generated listing of marriage records. Gives names and date of marriage but does not provide reference to marriage record book or page number. Arranged alphabetically.

Catholic Church Records. Diocese of Biloxi, Mississippi. Anne S. Anderson. Biloxi, MS: L.W. Anderson Genealogical Library, 1991. 374 pp.

Arranged alphabetically by name. Refers the researcher to baptisms, marriages, deaths and burials in the diocese for 1843 to 1900.

Harrison County, Mississippi, 1841–1886. Nicholas Russell Murray. Hammond, LA: Hunting for Bears, n.d. 74 pp.

A computer-generated listing of marriage records. Gives names and date of marriage but does not provide reference to marriage record book or page number. Arranged alphabetically.

Harrison County, Mississippi. 1860 census. Julia Cook Guice, ed. Biloxi, MS: Community Development Department, 1982. 109 pp.

Transcription of original census schedule in column arrangement. Indexed.

Harrison County, Mississippi. 1870 Census. Julia Cook Guice, ed. Biloxi, MS: Community Development Department, 1981. 166 pp.

Transcription of original census schedule in column arrangement. Indexed.

History of Harrison County, Mississippi. John H. Lang. Gulfport, MS: The Dixie Press, 1936. 303 pp.

Although this book is more historical than genealogical, several name listings are found throughout the work. Contains a separate chapter of biographies that give family information. General index with inclusion of few names.

History of Pass Christian. R.J. Caire and Katy Caire. Pass Christian, MS: Lafayette Publishers, 1976. 122 pp.

General town history. Offers a table of contents for general access but no index.

Marriages: Harrison County, Mississippi, 1841–1899. Julia Cook Guice. Privately printed, n.d. 103 pp.

Indexed by surname.

*Pass Christian Birth Certificates. Otto L. Stephens III. Jackson, MS: Mississippi Department of Archives and History, 1987. 191 pp.

This unique source is a compilation of midwife certificates recorded before the year 1912 when the state of Mississippi first required them by law. Arranged in two sections, first by mother's name and then by father's name. The name of the child is not given.

Rosalie and Radishes: A History of Long Beach, Mississippi.   Mary Ellen Alexander. Gulfport, MS: Dixie Press, 1980. 130 pp.

The focus for this work is historical, but some family history is found in the chapter about early settlers. Appendix includes listings of town officials and ministers. No index.

State of Mississippi, County of Harrison: Data Taken from Gravestones of Soldiers Interred Beauvoir Shrine Cemetery, Beauvoir Shrine, Mississippi, Serving Confederate States of America.   Beauvoir Chapter, No. 621, Mississippi Division, United Daughters of the Confederacy. Privately printed, n.d. Unpaged.

The spine of this publication reads *Register of Confederate Dead.* Gives location of gravestone, description, and inscription of gravestone.

HINDS COUNTY

Complete Directory of the City of Vicksburg, Also Business Directories of Yazoo City, Jackson, and Natchez, with Other Useful Information.   Vicksburg, MS: A.C. Tuttle, 1877. 240 pp.
Indexed.

Heads of Families and Other Adults in Hinds County, Mississippi 1850.   Jane Melton. 1959. 44 pp.
Typescript. An index.

Hinds County, Mississippi, 1820–1900.   Nicholas Russell Murray. Hammond, LA: Hunting for Bears, n.d. 95 pp.

A computer-generated listing of marriage records. Gives names and date of marriage but does not provide reference to marriage record book or page number. Arranged alphabetically.

Hinds County, Mississippi, Marriage Records 1823–1848.   Clara Wright Forrest. Privately printed, 1957. 144 pp.
Indexed.

Hinds County, Mississippi, Will Book I 1822–1854.   Clara Wright Forrest. Privately printed, 1959. 72 pp.
Indexed.

Index to Estates I.   Mary C. Cunningham. 1960. 68 pp.

Typescript. Indexes land transactions that were probated from 1826 to 1854.

Jackson Death Certificates (1909–1912). Anne S. Lipscomb. Jackson, MS: Mississippi Department of Archives and History, 1987. 105 pp.

A transcription of original death records from the city of Jackson that are now located at MDAH. This unpublished source is a listing of pertinent data relating to death certification before such records were required by law. Arranged alphabetically.

The Old Cemeteries of Hinds County, Mississippi: From 1811 to the Present. Mary Collins Landin. Utica, MS: Hinds History Books, 1988. 539 pp. Indexed.

Some Cemetery Records. Hinds, Scott, Smith. Jeanne Louise Johnston. Unpaged.

Typescript. Includes only select cemeteries.

The Story of Jackson: A History of the Capital of Mississippi 1821–1951. William D. McCain. Jackson, MS: J.F. Hyer Publishing Company, 1953. 2 vols.

Although historical in nature, the second volume is devoted wholly to biographical material about city leaders. Arranged alphabetically in sequence. Indexed.

HOLMES COUNTY

Bethesda, Pleasant Ridge, Spring Hill and Others. Holmes County, Mississippi. Myrtis Irene Siddon. 1975. 25 pp.
Typescript.

Census. Holmes County, Mississippi. 1865. N.d. Unpaged.

Photocopies of handwritten sheets. Includes only free white inhabitants. Hard to read and no index.

Goodman, Mississippi. Holmes County 1865–1986. Magnolia Club. Privately printed, 1986. 94 pp.

Inclusion of family histories that are arranged in alphabetical order. No index.

The History of Tchula 1830–1954, Including Census Records of Tchula Beat, Holmes County, Mississippi: 1850, 1869, 1870, 1880. Margaret Grafton Peaster. Privately printed, 1954. 32 pp.

The genealogical value of this work is found in the listing of census data for the years 1850 to 1880. No index.

Holmes County, Mississippi, 1894–1920. Nicholas Russell Murray. Hammond, LA: Hunting for Bears, n.d. 60 pp.

A computer-generated listing of marriage records. Gives names and date of marriage but does not provide reference to marriage record book or page number. Arranged alphabetically.

HUMPHREYS COUNTY

From Greasy Row to Catfish Capital. Mrs. Jon Cerame. Oxford, MS: Rebel Press, Inc., 1978. 153 pp.

General town and county history that does give information about early pioneers and settlers. Difficult to use with no index.

Humphreys County, Mississippi, 1918–1925. Nicholas Russell Murray. Hammond, LA: Hunting for Bears, n.d. 53 pp.

A computer-generated listing of marriage records. Gives names and date of marriage but does not provide reference to marriage record book or page number. Arranged alphabetically.

ISSAQUENA COUNTY

Early Mississippi Records. Issaquena County, Sharkey County. 1868–1906. Vol. 5. Katherine Branton and Alice Wade, eds. Privately printed, 1986. 203 pp.

Provides listings for Sharkey and Issaquena counties from various sources including church and county records, newspapers, and cemeteries. Though the information is not comprehensive, this publication does make select sources available in one volume. General index included.

Early Records of Mississippi: Issaquena and Washington Counties. Katherine Branton. Privately printed, 1982. 3 vols.

Several kinds of public records have been abstracted into this three-volume series. Included are marriage records, wills, medical licenses, newspaper notices, an index to apprenticeships, estate papers, and others. Although not inclusive, these records date from 1827 to 1926. Each volume includes an index.

Issaquena County, Mississippi, 1866–1900. Nicholas Russell Murray. Hammond, LA: Hunting for Bears, Inc., n.d. 123 pp.

Computer-generated listing of county marriage records. Gives names and date of marriage but does not provide reference to a marriage record book or page number. Arranged alphabetically.

ITAWAMBA COUNTY

1850 Census. Itawamba County, Mississippi. 164 pp.
Typescript. Arranged as appears on census sheets. Indexed.

Cemetery Markings. Itawamba County, Mississippi. Betty Burton-Cruber. Amory, MS: The Amory Advertiser, n.d. 558 pp.
Indexed by surname.

Cemetery Records of Old Bethel Cemetery and Temple Cemetery, Itawamba County, Mississippi. Mr. and Mrs. Charles Booth, Pat Booth, and Marilyn Kucera. 6 pp.
Typescript.

First United States Census of Itawamba County, Mississippi, 1840. Henry McRaven, 1964. 25 pp.
Typescript. Transcription of original census schedule.

Itawamba: A History. Forrest F. Reed. Nashville, TN: Reed and Company, 1966. 186 pp.
County history with a general index that does not include names. Additional section contains family genealogies.

Itawamba County, Mississippi, 1837–1900. Nicholas Russell Murray. Hammond, LA: Hunting for Bears, Inc., n.d. 215 pp.
Computer-generated listing of county marriage records. Gives names and date of marriage but does not provide reference to a marriage record book or page number. Arranged alphabetically.

Itawamba Settlers. Tupelo, MS: R.A. Turner, 1981-
A journal that publishes genealogical information about Itawamba County. Annual index.

Marriage Records of Itawamba County, Mississippi, 1837–1866 with Heads of Families, 1840 Federal Census. Betty Ann Burton Gruber. Memphis, TN: The Milestone Press, 1973. 100 pp.
Typescript.

JACKSON COUNTY

The Chronicle Star and Moss Point Advertiser, Pascagoula, Mississippi, Obituaries Index. 19 pp.

Typescript.

Chronicle Obituaries Index 1963 and 1964.   Pascagoula, Mississippi. 12 pp. Typescript.

Confederate Records: Jackson County, Mississippi.   Jean Strickland and Patricia N. Edwards. Privately printed, 1988. 178 pp.
This volume contains copies of the pension applications made by confederate veterans in Jackson County. When two or three applications appeared for one person, these were combined into one form. Indexed.

Confederate Records: Jackson County, Mississippi, Widows.   Jean Strickland and Patricia N. Edwards. Privately printed, 1989. 184 pp.
This book is a transcription of the pension applications made by widows of Confederate veterans. No information has been excluded from the original records. The pensioners for the years 1900, 1919, 1936, and 1937 are listed. Indexed.

Four Centuries on the Pascagoula: History, Story, and Legend of the Pascagoula River Country.   Cyril Edward Cain. Spartanburg, SC: The Reprint Company, Publishers, 1983. 2 vols.
Based on reliable primary source material, this publication provides a comprehensive historical account of Jackson and George counties. Although the book was originally printed in 1953, the initial writing began as early as 1937. The second volume includes principally family history information that is of particular interest to the genealogist. A well-indexed and well-documented county history.

Grove Cemetery, Jackson County, Mississippi.   H. Grady Howell. 1981. 7 pp. Typescript.

The History of Jackson County, Mississippi.   Jackson County Genealogical Society. Pascagoula, MS: Lewis Printing Service, 1989. 438 pp.
The major portion of this narrative is family histories. Indexed.

Jackson County, Mississippi, 1875–1900.   Nicholas Russell Murray. Hammond, LA: Hunting for Bears, n.d. 88 pp.
A computer-generated listing of marriage records. Gives names and date of marriage but does not provide reference to a marriage record book or page number. Arranged alphabetically.

Jackson County, Mississippi, Death Records. Volume 1, 1912–1937.   Melba Goff Allen. Pascagoula, MS: Jackson County Genealogical Society, 1990. 140 pp.

The entries for this volume were taken from death and funeral home records. Surname index included.

Journal of the Jackson County Genealogical Society. Pascagoula, MS: Jackson County Genealogical Society, 1984– .
A journal with a genealogical focus. No index found at MDAH.

Miscellaneous Records of Jackson County, Mississippi. Vol. 1. Betty Clark Rodgers. Pascagoula, MS: Jackson County Genealogical Society, 1990. 152 pp.
This work offers access to information through a variety of records such as a physicians' and pharmacists' license book, assorted land deeds, swamp land certificates, and other legal papers covering the years 1821 to 1890. In addition, there is a detailed journal that recorded births and deaths along with other community activities for the time period between the years 1875 to 1928. Includes a general index.

The Mississippi Press Index. Obituaries 1966–1973, 1974–1979, 1980–1981. 3 vols.
Photocopied from the typed bound copy of newspapers. Alphabetically arranged by year.

Ocean Springs, 1892. Regina B. Hines. Pascagoula, MS: Lewis Printing Co., 1979. 78 pp.
Some family history is included in this primarily historical account. Difficult to use without an index.

Requiem. Jackson County Genealogical Society. Pascagoula, MS: Lewis Secretarial and Printing Services, 1969. 3 vols.
A publication of Jackson County cemetery records. Indexed.

JASPER COUNTY

Cemeteries. Jasper County, Mississippi. 6 pp.
Typescript. Includes only Garlandsville Cemetery.

East Mississippi Source Material (newspaper abstracts). Vol. 1. Richard S. Lackey. Privately printed, 1968. 30 pp.
Abstracts taken from an early newspaper published in the town of Paulding during the years 1845 and 1846. Does not include an index.

History of Jasper County, Mississippi: Cemetery Records, 1834–1910, Index of Wills and Land Grants, 1834–1905. H.H. Daniel. Privately printed, 1970. 106 pp.

Indexed.

Jasper County, Mississippi. 1840 and 1850 Federal Census. 1866 State Census. Patricia N. Edwards and Jean Strickland. Privately printed, 1986. 176 pp.
A transcription of the original census schedule.

Jasper County, Mississippi, 1906–1923. Nicholas Russell Murray. Hammond, LA: Hunting for Bears, Inc., n.d. 37 pp.
Computer-generated listing of marriage records. Gives names and date of marriage but does not provide reference to a marriage record book or page number. Arranged alphabetically.

Jasper County, Mississippi. Index to 1850 Census. Jane Melton. 1963. 18 pp.
Typescript.

Jasper County, Mississippi. Tax Rolls 1834–1856. Jean Strickland and Patricia N. Edwards. Privately printed, 1990. 125 pp.
Since the tax rolls for 1844 to 1852 no longer exist, they are not included in this volume. Indexed.

JEFFERSON COUNTY

Christ Church (Church Hill, Jefferson County, Mississippi). Register of Burials and Marriages. Mrs. L.R. McGehee. 21 pp.
Typescript. Arranged chronologically by date of burial and sometimes gives age and residence. Marriages are also arranged chronologically.

Index to Minutes of the Orphans' (Probate) Court of Jefferson County, Mississippi, January 23, 1830-November 24, 1834. Laura D. S. Harrell. 18 pp.
A name listing that refers to orphans court proceedings and includes not only the name of the person but also the minor children, ward, and administrators involved in the will or estate. Names of slaves have been included in this index. Originally appeared in *Journal of Mississippi History*, volume 33, numbers 3 and 4.

Jefferson County, Mississippi, 1805–1900. Nicholas Russell Murray. Hammond, LA: Hunting for Bears, Inc., n.d. 137 pp.
Computer-generated listing of marriage records. Gives names and date of marriage but does not provide reference to a marriage record book or page number. Arranged alphabetically.

Jefferson County, Mississippi, Index to 1850 Census. James H. McLaurin. 9 pp.
Typescript.

News from Rodney 1845–1840: Notices of Historical and Genealogical Interest from the Newspaper of Rodney, Mississippi. Gordon A. Cotton. Raymond, MS: Keith Printing Co., Inc., 1987. 124 pp.

This volume contains notices pertaining to missing persons, divorces, marriages, estates, deaths, murders, and obituaries. Surname index.

Newspaper Notices from Southern Telegraph (Jefferson County, Mississippi) July 1834–July 1837. Mrs. Wayne Q. Nevels. 28 pp.

Typescript. Arranged chronologically and indexed.

Wills of Jefferson County, Mississippi. Book "A." Gordon Wells. 16 pp.

Typescript. Inclusive years not given.

JEFFERSON DAVIS COUNTY

Cemeteries of Jefferson Davis County, Mississippi (old Lawrence and Covington counties). W. Arnold, Jr., and Elaine Bullock. Privately printed, 1989. 619 pp.

An extensive compilation of information gathered from Jefferson Davis County cemeteries. All cemeteries that are recorded in published works as well as those found through word of mouth are included. Detailed physical description of each cemetery is given along with map coordinates indicating location. Provides two separate name indexes, one for blacks and one for whites. A useful source of information for Jefferson Davis, Lawrence, and Covington counties.

Jefferson Davis County, Mississippi, 1906–1920. Nicholas Russell Murray. Hammond, LA: Hunting for Bears, Inc., n.d. 38 pp.

Computer-generated listing of county marriage records. Gives names and date of marriage but does not provide reference to a marriage record book or page number. Arranged alphabetically.

JONES COUNTY

Confederate Records: Covington, Wayne, and Jones County. Jean Strickland and Patricia N. Edwards. Privately printed, 1987. 140 pp.

Combines Confederate records from these counties in one source. The material regarding Jones County came from rosters of military companies and personal interviews.

The Echo of the Black Horn. Ethel Knight. Privately printed, n.d. 328 pp.

A separate typescript index is available that provides access to the many individual names found throughout this town history.

Educable Children of Jones County, Mississippi, 1896. NSDAR Tallahala Chapter. Privately printed, 1985. 187 pp.

Transcription of public school records that makes available information that was lost with the destruction of the 1890 census. Arranged by district and then alphabetically by parent or guardian. Gives child's name, age, sex, and race. Indexed.

History of Jones County, Mississippi, Church and Cemetery 1830–1915. Index to Land Grants. H.H. Daniel. 95 pp.

Indexed.

Jones County, Mississippi. Nicholas Russell Murray. Hammond, LA: Hunting for Bears, n.d. 38 pp.

A computer-generated listing of county marriage records. Gives names and date of marriage but does not provide reference to a marriage record book or page number. Does not indicate the period of time covered. Arranged alphabetically.

Jones County, Mississippi, Deed Book A and B 1827–1856. Ben and Jean Strickland. Privately printed, 1981. 118 pp.

Abstracts and indexes entries.

Laurel: A History of the Black Community 1882–1962. Cleveland Payne. Privately printed, 1962. 158 pp.

A unique work that focuses on the development of the black middle-class community in this town. Indexed.

Records of Jones County, Mississippi. 1827–1841 Tax Rolls, 1837, 1841, 1853 State Census. Ben and Jean Strickland. Privately printed, 1983. 122 pp.

Indexed.

Who Married Whom. Jones County, Mississippi. Patricia N. Edwards and Jean Strickland. Privately printed, 1986. 195 pp.

A listing of white residents in Jones County taken primarily from the federal census records and county tax rolls from 1830 to 1880. Sources are cited, and the work is indexed.

KEMPER COUNTY

Index to Heads of Families and Other Adults, Kemper County, Mississippi, Census 1850. Jane Melton. 1961. 25 pp.

Typescript.

Kemper County, Mississippi. Nicholas Russell Murray. Hammond, LA: Hunting for Bears, Inc., n.d. 90 pp.

Computer-generated listing of county marriage records. Gives names and date of marriage but does not provide reference to marriage record book or page number. Does not indicate what years are included. Arranged alphabetically.

Kemper County, Mississippi. 1860 Census. Elia Griffin Davis. 1985. 59 pp. Indexed.

Kemper County: The Pioneer Days. Louis Parmer. Livingston, AL: Sumter Graphics, 1983. 215 pp.

General county history that covers the period of time from the mid–1830s to the mid–1880s. Indexed.

Southeast Kemper: Its People and Communities. Louis Parmer. Livingston, AL: Sumter Graphics, 1982. 261 pp.

General county history with information of genealogical notice. Indexed.

The Story of Electric Mills, Mississippi. Eva Ma May. Privately printed, 1970. 153 pp.

A rare find that records the history of a community that no longer exists. Includes names of the deceased for the years 1941 to 1970. No index.

LAFAYETTE COUNTY

Early Settlers of Lafayette County, Mississippi: A Period Study of Lafayette County from 1836–1860 with Emphasis on Population Groups. John Cooper Hathorn. Oxford, MS: Skipwith Historical and Genealogical Society, Inc., 1980. 146 pp.

Originally created as a master's thesis, this publication focuses on the early settlement of Lafayette County. Contains material relating to land sales and ownership, slaves, slave holders, and those who did not own slaves. Includes an appendix that lists landowners in 1850 and 1860. Well documented and indexed.

Family Ties. Skipwith Historical and Genealogical Society. Oxford, MS: Skipwith Historical and Genealogical Society, Inc., 1981–1982. 2 vols.

Transcription of a collection of Bible records and personal letters.

The Heritage of Lafayette County, Mississippi. The Skipwith Historical and Genealogical Society, Inc. Dallas, TX: Curtis Media Corporation, 1986. 642 pp.

Information for this general county history was gathered from personal recollections and secondary sources. Of particular note is the section devoted to family histories. Index refers to the story rather than the page number.

Lafayette County, Mississippi, 1848–1887.   Nicholas Russell Murray. Hammond, LA: Hunting for Bears, Inc., n.d. 81 pp.

Computer-generated listing of marriage records. Gives names and date of marriage but does not provide reference to marriage record book or page number. Arranged alphabetically.

Lafayette County, Mississippi, Cemetery Records.   Skipwith Historical and Genealogical Society. Privately printed, 1978. 2 vols.

Indexed.

Lafayette County, Mississippi, Marriage Bonds. Book 1 through 5 (1848–1881).   Mrs. G.L. Eatman. Oxford, MS: Skipworth Genealogical Society, 1971. 116 pp.

Indexed.

Lafayette County, Mississippi, Original Land Grant Patent Record 1836–1844.   Earl A. Truett. Privately printed, 1986. 191 pp.

An indexed source to land records.

Lafayette County, Mississippi. Probate Court Records: Abstracted from Original Court Dockets (dockets 1 through 730-first 12 boxes) 1836–1858.   Cathering Eaton, Mrs. G.L. Eatman and Earl A. Truett, Jr. Oxford, MS: 1978. 106 pp.

Indexed.

Lafayette County, Mississippi. Will Abstracts 1836–1898.   Joan Goar Bratton and Juanita R. Harwell. Oxford, MS: Skipwith Historical and Genealogical Society, Inc., 1980. 95 pp.

Indexed.

Lafayette County, Mississippi Will Books, 1843–1897: An Index.   Compiled by Rozelle C. Wax. Aberdeen, MS: Allmond Printing Co., 1961. 21 pp.

Arranged alphabetically. A listing of pre-Civil War cemeteries included.

Marriage Bonds of Lafayette County, Mississippi: Transcribed from the Original Records, Old Newspapers and Bible Records.   Sybil Metts Hill, "Nue" Wimbish Turnipseed, and Annette Inman Waite. Oxford, MS: Skipwith Historical and Genealogical Society, 1990. 2 vols.

A transcription of original records, newspapers, and Bible records of white marriages in Lafayette County. Information found in consent forms has been included. Volume one covers the years from 1843 to 1881; volume two, 1882 to 1900. Indexed.

LAMAR COUNTY

Lamar County Heritage. Leonard L. Slade, Sr. Baltimore: Gateway Press, Inc., 1978. 261 pp.
General county history that contains numerous cemetery listings. Arranged alphabetically with no single index.

LAUDERDALE COUNTY

Cemetery Records of Lauderdale County, Mississippi. Vol. 1. Cecilia Nabors Hobgood and Ann Jones Clayton. Privately printed, 1971. 317 pp.
Provides some brief historical information regarding Lauderdale County records and where they may be found. Genealogical information gathered from the cemeteries includes pertinent data along with cemetery inscriptions.

Confederate Pension Record Book A–D. Lauderdale County, Mississippi. James T. Dawson. Meridian, MS: Lauderdale County Department of Archives and History, Inc., 1988. 168 pp.
Abstracts pension applications.

Enumeration of Educable Children: School Census 1885, White and Black. James T. Dawson. Meridian, MS: Lauderdale County Department of Archives and History, 1987. 262 pp.
Transcribes and indexes school records that offer information lost with the destruction of the 1890 census. Arranged by ward and then alphabetically by parent. Includes name of child, age, sex, and race.

History, Board of Police, 1832–1870, Board of Supervisors, 1870–1992. Jim Dawson. Meridian, MS: Lauderdale County Department of Archives and History, Inc., 1992. 51 pp.
Includes names of members of the board of police and board of supervisors. Typescript with no index.

Lauderdale County, Mississippi. 1835–1848 Tax Rolls, 1853 State Census. Ben and Jean Strickland. Privately printed, 1986. 221 pp.
Indexed.

Lauderdale County, Mississippi, 1842–1900. Nicholas Russell Murray. Hammond, LA: Hunting for Bears, Inc., 1982. 171 pp.

Computer-generated listing of county marriage records. Gives names and date of marriage but does not provide reference to marriage record book or page number. Arranged alphabetically.

Lauderdale County, Mississippi. 1858 Land Roll (Taxes) Book. James T. Dawson. Meridian, MS: Lauderdale County Department of Archives and History, Inc., 1987. 61 pp.
Arranged alphabetically.

Lauderdale County, Mississippi, 1870 Census Index. Mollie Lide Monk. Meridian, MS: Lauderdale County Department of Archives and History, Inc., 1987. Unpaged.
Arranged as appears on census sheets. Index included.

Lauderdale County, Mississippi. 1878 Land Roll (Taxes) Book. James T. Dawson. Meridian, MS: Lauderdale County Department of Archives and History, 1987. Unpaged.
Arranged alphabetically.

Lauderdale County, Mississippi. Confederate Pension Applications. James T. Dawson. Meridian, MS: Lauderdale County Department of Archives and History, Inc., 1988. 98 pp.
Some additional material such as letters is found along with abstracted information. Indexed.

Lauderdale County, Mississippi, Marriage Record Book A. James T. Dawson. Meridian, MS: Lauderdale County Department of Archives and History, Inc., 1987. 49 pp.
Covers the years 1839 to 1845.

Lauderdale County, Mississippi, Marriage Record Book A-1, 1851–1867. James T. Dawson. Meridian, MS: Lauderdale County Department of Archives and History, Inc., 1987. 60 pp.
Arranged alphabetically.

Lauderdale County, Mississippi. Motion Docket—Circuit Court 1838-1841. James T. Dawson. Meridian, MS: Lauderdale County Department of Archives and History, Inc., 1987. 53 pp.
Entries abstracted from original source. Arranged alphabetically.

Lauderdale County, Mississippi. Probate Court Docket 1846-1847. James T. Dawson. Meridian, MS: Lauderdale County Department of Archives and History, Inc., 1987. 18 pp.
Entries are abstracted from original source records. Arranged alphabetically.

Lauderdale County, Mississippi. Probate Court Docket 1852-1855. Index. James T. Dawson. Meridian, MS; Lauderdale County Department of Archives and History, Inc., 1988. 58 pp.

Apart from expected information, this index includes the first names of slaves.

Lauderdale County, Mississippi. Probate Court Minutes 1849–1852. Index. James T. Dawson. Meridian, MS: Lauderdale County Department of Archives and History, Inc., 1987. 35 pp.

Arranged alphabetically.

Lauderdale County, Mississippi. Probate Court Minutes Book "G" 1855–1856 Index. James T. Dawson. Meridian, MS: Lauderdale County Department of Archives and History, Inc., 1987. 30 pp.

Arranged alphabetically.

Lauderdale County, Mississippi. Probate Court Record Book "C" 1847–1851 Index. James T. Dawson. Meridian, MS: Lauderdale County Department of Archives and History, Inc., 1987. Unpaged.

Arranged alphabetically.

Lauderdale County, Mississippi. Probate Court Record Book "D" 1851–1853. James T. Dawson. Meridian, MS: Lauderdale County Department of Archives and History, Inc., 1987. 99 pp.

Arranged alphabetically.

Lauderdale County, Mississippi. Probate Records Book "E" 1853–1855 Index. James T. Dawson. Meridian, MS: Lauderdale County Department of Archives and History, Inc., 1987. 66 pp.

Arranged alphabetically.

Lauderdale County, Mississippi. Probate Record Book "F" 1855–1856 Index. James T. Dawson. Meridian, MS: Lauderdale County Department of Archives and History, Inc., 1987. 121 pp.

Arranged alphabetically.

Lauderdale County, Mississippi. Probate Court Record Book "G" 1856–1858 Index. James T. Dawson. Meridian, MS: Lauderdale County Department of Archives and History, 1987. 72 pp.

Arranged alphabetically.

Lauderdale County, Mississippi. Taxable Lands March 1, 1841. James T. Dawson. Meridian, MS: Lauderdale County Department of Archives and History, Inc., 1987. 13 pp.

Information from records found in the Augusta land office in Augusta, Mississippi. Arranged alphabetically.

Paths to the Past: An Overview History of Lauderdale County, Mississippi. Laura Nan Fairley and James T. Dawson. Meridian, MS: Lauderdale County Department of Archives and History, 1988. 207 pp.

A publication that presents an extensive county history complete with material of genealogical interest. Indexed.

A Transcription of the 1840 Census for Lauderdale County, Mississippi. Fred W. Edmiston. Privately printed, 1983. Unpaged.

Indexed by family number.

LAWRENCE COUNTY

1830 Census of Lawrence County, Mississippi. Isom Stephens. 11 pp. Typescript.

Cemetery Records of Lawrence County, Mississippi, 1810–1988. Lawrence County Historical Society. Privately printed, 1989. 450 pp.

A useful compilation of cemeteries giving pertinent data taken from tombstones along with a listing of WPA cemeteries and of markers for veterans of early wars. Index and map included.

Compiled Cemetery Records of Lawrence County, Mississippi. Mrs. Wendell C. Russell. Hattiesburg, MS: University of Southern Mississippi, 1979. Unpaged.

Arranged by cemetery. Black cemeteries included. No general index.

Index to Heads of Families and Other Adults, Lawrence County, Mississippi Census of 1850. Jane Melton. 1961. 13 pp. Typescript.

Lawrence County, Mississippi, 1818–1899. Nicholas Russell Murray. Hammond, LA: Hunting for Bears, Inc., n.d. 106 pp.

Computer-generated listing of marriage records. Gives names and date of marriage but does not provide reference to marriage record book or page number. Arranged alphabetically.

Lawrence County, Mississippi, Marriages 1818–1879. Maxie Ruth Hedgepeth Brake. Shreveport, LA: Norman E. Gillis, 1970. 81 pp.

Cites sources and is indexed.

Marriage Records. Lawrence County, Mississippi. 1818–1838. Marie Luter Upton. 1970. 56 pp.

Actually contains the years 1817 to 1838.

Records of Lawrence County, Mississippi. John Paul Smith. Privately printed, 1984. 3 vols.

The first volume does not give the researcher the exact dates covered, though most entries are from 1860 to 1870. A separate index listing slaves is included. The second volume contains abstracted entries that appeared originally in a deed book for the years 1815 to 1826 and tax rolls for the years 1818 and 1825. Of particular note are the birth and death records for the years 1823 and 1824. The third volume abstracts entries from deed books covering the years from 1826 to 1840 and provides references to the original record. Each volume is indexed separately.

Selected Documents from 101 Chancery Court Cases, Lawrence County, Mississippi, 1815–1845. John Paul Smith. Privately printed, 1984. 3 vols.

This three-volume series is a combination of photocopies and transcriptions of original public records. The cases are listed numerically and are indexed. Also includes a separate slave index.

LEAKE COUNTY

1850 Census, Leake County, Mississippi, Index. Jane Melton. 17 pp. Typescript.

The History of Leake County, Mississippi: Its People and Places. Mac and Louise Spence. Dallas, TX: Curtis Media Corporation, 1984. 358 pp.

Useful genealogical information may be found in this county history that includes a separate section devoted to family histories. Index refers to each story section rather than page number.

Leake County, Mississippi, 1836–1900. Nicholas Russell Murray. Hammond, LA: Hunting for Bears, Inc., n.d. 161 pp.

Computer-generated listing of marriage records. Gives names and date of marriage but does not provide reference to marriage record book or page number. Arranged alphabetically.

LEE COUNTY

Lee County, Mississippi, 1816–1910. Nicholas Russell Murray. Hammond, LA: Hunting for Bears, Inc., n.d. 218 pp.

Computer-generated listing of marriage records. Gives names and date of marriage but does not provide reference to a marriage record book or page number. Arranged alphabetically.

Lee County, Mississippi, Cemetery Records, 1820–1979. Northeast Mississippi Historical and Genealogical Society. Columbus, MS: Blewett Company, 1981. 458 pp.

Gives location and condition of cemetery as well as brief general historical comments. A map is included that indicates location of cemetery. Indexed.

Lee County, Mississippi, Marriage Records 1867–1901. Mertice Finley Collins. 1981. 117 pp.
Indexed.

The Life and Times of Saltillo. The Saltillo History Committee. Fulton, MS: The Itawamba County Times, Inc., 1979. 352 pp.
General town history. Indexed.

LEFLORE COUNTY

Index to the W.P.A. History of Greenwood and Leflore County, Mississippi. Mrs. Charles Wells and Mrs. Blanche Williams. 31 pp.

Typescript. Easy-to-read subject and name index to the historical data produced by the Works Progress Administration in the 1940s. Refers to original papers housed in Official Records in MDAH.

Marriage Records. Sunflower County-Leflore County, Mississippi. Hester R. Lowe. 1956. 56 pp.

Marriage records for Leflore County covering the years 1860 to 1871. No index.

LINCOLN COUNTY

Cemetery Record. Mr. and Mrs. Cletos Goza. Brookhaven, MS: New Prospect Baptist Church, 1982. 23 pp.

Typescript listing those who are buried in Prospect Baptist Church Cemetery. Arranged alphabetically.

Lincoln County, Mississippi, 1893–1913. Nicholas Russell Murray. Hammond, LA: Hunting for Bears, n.d. 76 pp.

Computer-generated listing of marriage records. Gives names and date of marriage but does not provide reference to a marriage record book or page number. Arranged alphabetically.

Lincoln County, Mississippi: Its People 1875–1895. Volume 1. Yvonne M. McGlothing. Privately printed, 1988. 228 pp.

Abstracts genealogical information taken from Brookhaven newspapers from 1875 to 1895. Indexed.

Some Cemeteries of Lincoln County. Unpaged.
Typescript. Arranged by cemetery and then alphabetically by name.

LOWNDES COUNTY

1850 Census. Lowndes County, Mississippi, Including Free, Slave, Mortality and Agricultural Schedules. Betty Wood Thomas. Columbus, MS: Blewett Company, n.d. 205 pp.
Combines free, slave and mortality schedules into one alphabetical arrangement. The agriculture schedule is separate.

By the Flow of the Inland River: The Settlement of Columbus, Mississippi, to 1825. Samuel H. Kaye, Rufus Ward, Jr., and Carolyn B. Neault. Privately printed, n.d. 109 pp.
A town's history through the year 1825. Indexed.

Cemeteries of Lowndes County, Mississippi. Rolfe B. Chase. Privately printed, n.d. 4 parts.
Although not all cemeteries are included, there is still a wealth of useful genealogical information. The material found in these four volumes pertains mostly to white cemeteries, but some black data has been recorded. Indexed.

Evidence of Births, Marriages, and Deaths in Lowndes County, Mississippi, 1830–1987. Margaret E. Webb and Lida E. Logan. Privately printed, 1990. 393 pp.
Brings together in one source material relating to births, marriages, and deaths of individuals before 1912, when state law began to require documentation of such records. The data came from both private sources and public records. Some of the sources of information are funeral home records, mortality schedules, Confederate records, and orphans court records. Entries include documents pertaining both to whites and blacks and are indexed.

Friendship Cemetery, Columbus, Mississippi: Tombstone Inscriptions and Burial Records. James W. Parker. Columbus, MS: Lowndes County Department of Archives and History, 1979. 2 vols.
Indexed.

A History of Columbus, Mississippi, During the 19th Century. Dr. W. L. Lipscomb. Birmingham, AL: Press of Dispatch Printing Co., 1909. 167 pp.

A well-researched town history that records the building of a community during the 1800s. Many personal names, both black and white, are included as the narrative traces the development of schools, churches, and professions, and tells of early settlers. An additional section contains the Civil War rosters. Separate typescript index.

Index to Source Material for Mississippi History, Lowndes county, volume 44, parts 1 and 2. Sadie Simon. 62 pp.

Many personal names have been included in this typescript index. Makes records available that were created by the Works Progress Administration in the 1940s. Original papers are found in Official Records at MDAH.

Lowndes County, Mississippi, 1830–1900. Part 2. Nicholas Russell Murray. Hammond, LA: Hunting for Bears, Inc., n.d. 362 pp.

Computer-generated listing of marriage records. Gives names and date of marriage but does not provide reference to marriage record book or page number. Arranged alphabetically.

Lowndes County, Mississippi. Will books 1 and 2, 1858–1905. Betty Wood Thomas. Columbus, MS: Blewett Company, 1979. 46 pp.

Refers to page numbers in will books.

Mississippi Marriages. Betty Wood Thomas. Columbus, MS: Blewett Company, 1980. 2 vols.

Includes marriage records for Monroe County for 1821 to 1858 and marriage records for Lowndes County for 1830 to 1868. Arranged alphabetically.

Mississippi Wills. Betty Wood Thomas. Columbus, MS: Blewett Company, 1982. 79 pp.

Indexes wills for Lowndes County from 1830 to 1859 and wills for Monroe County from 1820 to 1830. Also includes some orphans court records for Monroe County. Indexed.

Private Land Claims. Cash Entry Abstracts of Columbus Land Office, Columbus, Mississippi. n.d.

Bound typescript. Contains abstracts for researchers interested in land records before Mississippi was a part of the United States. Refers to documents found in the General Land Office and the Bureau of Land Management. Indexed.

Records of Land Patents, Lowndes County, Mississippi, 1820–1842. Columbus, MS: The Columbus-Lowndes Genealogical Society, 1988. 83 pp.

Transcription of land records.

Records of Monroe, Lowndes, and Chickasaw Counties, Mississippi. Elizabeth C. Jones. Privately printed, n.d. 137 pp.

County records in this publication that relate to Lowndes County are indexes to wills and estate papers for the early to mid-nineteenth century. Also includes selected county records for both Monroe and Chickasaw counties. Indexed.

MADISON COUNTY

Cemeteries. Madison County, Mississippi. Mr. and Mrs. S.S. Howess, Mr. and Mrs. Patrick W. Johnson, Mr. and Mrs. Richard Anthony Horne. Unpaged.

Typescript. Arranged by cemetery. No index and no set form of arrangement.

Heads of Families and Other Adults in Madison County, 1850. Jane Melton. 1959. 22 pp.

Typescript.

The Land Between Two Rivers: Madison County, Mississippi. Carol Lynn Mead. Canton, MS: Friends of the Madison County-Canton Public Library, 1987. 404 pp.

A worthwhile comprehensive county history that includes a separate section devoted to family histories. Indexed.

Madison County Confederates: Muster Rolls of Confederate Soldiers from Madison County, Mississippi. H. Grady Howell, Jr. 1981 var. pp.

Contains only a partial listing of muster rolls of each company. Not indexed.

Madison County, Mississippi, 1835–1900. Part 2. Hammond, LA: Hunting for Bears, Inc., n.d. 276 pp.

A computer-generated index for marriage records.

Marriage Records, Madison County, Mississippi. Book "E" 1830–1836. Book "F" 1835–1847. R.C. and Marie Luter Upton. Privately printed, n.d. 42 pp. Indexed.

Minutes of the Orphans Court. Madison County, Mississippi Territory. 147 pp.

Mimeographed transcription that covers the period between January 10, 1810, and October 19, 1819. Indexed.

MARION COUNTY

Abstracts of Deeds. Marion County, Mississippi: Containing Deeds, Marks and Brands, Bonds, Mortgages, and Deeds of Gift. E. Russ Williams, Jr. Privately printed, 1962. 103 pp.

Abstracts of deeds for the years 1818 to 1840. Contains copy of the index from the county deed book for the years 1812 to 1818. General index included.

History of Marion County, Mississippi. Marion County Historical Society. Marceline, MO: Walsworth Publishing Company Inc., 1976. 198 pp.

Distinct styles of writing appear in this volume, since each topic had a different author. General county history created as a bicentennial project. Indexed.

Index to Heads of Families and Other Adults, Marion County, Mississippi, Census of 1850. 9 pp.

Typescript.

Marion County, Mississippi, 1812–1899. Nicholas Russell Murray. Hammond, LA: Hunting for Bears, Inc., n.d. 100 pp.

Computer-generated listing of marriage records. Gives names and date of marriage but does not provide reference to marriage record book or page number. Arranged alphabetically.

Marion County, Mississippi. 1870 Census Surname Index. Mary Fisher. 1985. 59 pp.

Typescript.

The Marion County, Mississippi, Cemetery Record. Stanley W. Arnold, Jr. and Louise Anderson. Privately printed, 1988. 686 pp.

Provides a useful research tool for those examining genealogical data in Marion County. Index for blacks and whites included.

Marriage Records. Marion County, Mississippi. 1812–1860. Mrs. Robert Chester Upton. Privately printed, 1958. 61 pp.

Indexed.

Orphan Court Records (Abstracts of Wills and Estates) 1812–1859. E. Russ Williams, Jr. Bogalusa, LA: E. Russ Williams, Jr., 1962. 108 pp.

Indexed.

Records of Marion County, Mississippi. E. Russ Williams, Jr. Privately printed, n.d. 122 pp.

A transcription of various public records of this county. Included are the 1860 census, the 1850 and 1860 mortality schedules, listing of Confederate volunteers, muster roll of Captain Mayson's company, and tax lists for 1813 and 1825. Indexed.

Records of Marion County, Mississippi: 1850 Federal Census, 1816 Territorial Census, the Old Road Books (Part 1 1812–1818, Part 2 1818–1823). E. Russ Williams, Jr. 1965. 105 pp.
The "road books" referred to in the title were actually the minutes of the orphans court. Indexed.

MARSHALL COUNTY

Cemeteries of Marshall County, Mississippi. Bobby Mitchell. Ripley, MS: Old Timer Press, 1983. 116 pp.
Indexed.

Index to 1860 Marshall County, Mississippi, Census. Bobby Joe Mitchell. Ripley, MS: Old Timer Press, 1981. 29 pp.

Marriages of Marshall County, Mississippi. Ripley, MS: Old Timer Press, 1986. 2 vols.
Arranged alphabetically.

Marshall County, Mississippi, Marriages 1836–1860. Helen Bowling McKnight. 101 pp.
Typescript. Indexed.

Marshall County, Mississippi, 1866–1900. Nicholas Russell Murray. Hammond, LA: Hunting for Bears, Inc., n.d. 2 vols.
Computer-generated listing of marriage records. Gives names and date of marriage but does not provide reference to marriage record book or page number. Arranged alphabetically.

MONROE COUNTY

1848 Tax Assessment Roll. Aberdeen, Athens, Carmargo, Cotton Gin Port and Monroe County, Mississippi. Lillian Plant Nickles. 1960. 21 pp.
Arranged alphabetically. No index.

A Brief History of Aberdeen and Monroe County, Mississippi 1821–1900. Bertie Shaw Rollins. Privately printed, 1957. 128 pp.

This source was compiled from original public and private papers along with newspaper accounts. Each entry gives citation of source. Separate typescript index is available at MDAH.

A History of Monroe County, Mississippi.   Monroe County Book Committee. Dallas, TX: Curtis Media Corporation, 1988. 968 pp.

Information for this county history came from personal recollections and secondary source material. Includes a separate section of family histories. Index refers to story section, not page number.

Marriage Book 4, Monroe County, Aberdeen, Mississippi.   Lillian Plant Nickles. 40 pp.

Typescript. Arranged alphabetically.

Mississippi Marriages.   Betty Wood Thomas. Columbus, MS: Blewett Company, 1980. 2 vols.

Includes marriage records for Monroe County from 1821 to 1858 and marriage records for Lowndes County from 1830 to 1868. Arranged alphabetically.

Mississippi Wills.   Betty Wood Thomas. Columbus, MS: Blewett Company, 1982. 79 pp.

Indexes wills for Lowndes County from 1830 to 1859 and for Monroe County from 1820 to 1830. Also includes some orphans court records for Monroe County. Indexed.

Monroe County, Mississippi, 1821–1900.   Part 1. Hammond, LA: Hunting for Bears, Inc., n.d. 164 pp.

A computer-generated listing of marriage records. Gives names and date of marriage but does not provide reference to marriage record book or page number. Arranged alphabetically.

Monroe County, Mississippi, 1860 Census.   Lillian Mann. 182 pp.

Arranged as appears on census schedule found on microfilm copy. Indexed.

Monroe County, Mississippi, Deeds Books 1, 2, and 3.   Betty Wood Thomas. Columbus, MS: Blewett Company, n.d. 127 pp.

Indexed.

Monroe County, Mississippi, Marriages: Marriage Book No. 1—1821–1825; Marriage Book No. 2—1834–1850.   Elizabeth C. Jones. Privately printed, n.d. Var. pp.

Arranged alphabetically.

Mother Monroe: A Series of Historical Sketches of Monroe County.   Dr. W. A. Evans. *Pioneer Times in Monroe County: From a Series of Letters Published in the Aberdeen Weekly 1877 and 1878.* W. B. Wilkes. *Who's Who in Monroe County Cemeteries.* Dr. W. A. Evans. Aberdeen, MS: Mother Monroe Publishing Company, 1979. 153 pp.

A reprint of newspaper articles that is a compilation of various types of primary source material. Includes a single index.

A Place Called Darracott.   Ruth Basinger Morgan. Aberdeen, MS: Allmond Printing Company, 1978. 88 pp.

General town history rich in names. One portion contains family charts. No index.

Records of Monroe, Lowndes, and Chickasaw Counties, Mississippi.   Elizabeth C. Jones. Privately printed, n.d. 137 pp.

County documents relating to Monroe County include orphans court records from 1821 to 1829, wills from 1836 to 1860, and abstracts of estate papers; also estate and will records for Chickasaw and Lowndes counties. Indexed.

Roster of Cemeteries and of Persons in Marked Graves in Monroe County, Mississippi.   1938. 271 pp.

Typescript. Arranged by cemetery and includes an index.

Something Good about the Thirties.   Sam Wilburn Crawford. Aberdeen, MS: Allmond Printing Co., 1983. 313 pp.

Local history that covers the decade of the 1930s. The index includes the many names found throughout the narrative.

MONTGOMERY COUNTY

History of Montgomery County.   Dallas, TX: Curtis Media Corporation, 1993. 612 pp.

County history drawing on personal recollections and secondary source material. Separate section includes family histories. Index refers to each story section rather than page number.

Montgomery County Men and Women in the Armed Forces of the United States of America, World War II.   N.d. Unpaged.

A commemorative booklet containing biographical information on all those who served during World War II from Montgomery County. No index. Photos included.

Montgomery County, Mississippi.   Hammond, LA: Hunting for Bears, Inc., n.d. 111 pp.

A computer-generated listing of marriage records. Dates covered not indicated. Gives names and date of marriage but does not provide reference to marriage record book or page number. Arranged alphabetically.

NESHOBA COUNTY

Neshoba County Cemetery Records.   Compiled by Neshoba County Historical Society. Cullman, AL: The Gregath Company, 1987. 412 pp. Indexed.

Neshoba County, Mississippi, Marriages 1877–1889.   Lucille Simms Mallon. 34 pp.

Arranged alphabetically and includes an index.

Neshoba County, Mississippi, 1912–1920.   Nicholas Russell Murray. Hammond, LA: Hunting for Bears, Inc., n.d. 42 pp.

A computer-generated listing of marriage records. Gives names and date of marriage but does not provide reference to marriage book or page number. Arranged alphabetically.

Neshoba County, Mississippi. Marriages 1877–1889.   Compiled by Lucille Simms Mallon. 34 pp.

An index.

Red Clay Hills of Neshoba: The Early History of Neshoba County, Mississippi. Jenelle B. Yates and Theresa T. Ridout. Privately printed, 1992. 275 pp.

Well-researched county history that also includes genealogical material. Indexed.

NEWTON COUNTY

1838 Personal Tax Roll for Newton County, Mississippi.   Richard S. Lackey. Privately printed, 1968. 6 pp.

A transcription of tax rolls in alphabetical arrangement.

The History of Newton, Mississippi, 1860-1988.   Nancy Katherine Williams. Newton, MS: The Newton Record, 1989. 231 pp.

General town history that does include information of genealogical interest. Indexed.

Newton County, Mississippi. 1860 Census and Slave Schedule.   Bonnie Morse. Mobile, AL: Bonnie Morse, 1984. 257 pp.

Arranged as appears on census schedule. Indexed.

Newton County, Mississippi, 1872–1900. Nicholas Russell Murray. Hammond, LA: Hunting for Bears, Inc., n.d. 69 pp.
Computer-generated listing of marriage records. Gives names and date of marriage but does not provide reference to marriage record book or page number. Arranged alphabetically.

United States Land Patent Record Index, Newton County, Mississippi-Book #39. Richard S. Lackey. 1967. 3 pp.
An index in typescript form.

NOXUBEE COUNTY

Abstracts of Death Notices from the Macon Beacon (Macon, Mississippi) 1871–1912. E.Q. Richards. 1982. 70 pp.
Abstracted death notices taken from the newspaper *Macon Beacon.* Surname index included.

Abstracts of Wills of Noxubee, County, Mississippi, 1834, 1910, and Index to Cases. Lucille M. Reeves, ed. Macon, MS: Noxubee County Historical Society, 1990. 89 pp.
Along with abstracts of wills, this book offers a general index to estate settlements and guardianships.

Dancing Rabbit: A Book About People, Places and Things in Noxubee County. Broox Sledge. Privately printed, 1986. 306 pp.
Although difficult to use with no index, this book has a table of contents that indicates the varied genealogical material contained therein. Includes public records as well as a personal diary. No specific dates given as to years covered.

Historical Notes of Noxubee County, Mississippi. John A. Tyson. Privately printed, 1928. 340 pp.
Newspaper articles published from 1827 to 1927 that have been compiled into book form. Includes family histories. No index.

Mississippi Marriages. Noxubee County 1834-1869. E.Q. Richards and Louise Jackson Lee. Noxubee County Historical Society, 1975. 102 pp. Indexed.

Noxubee County, Mississippi, 1834–1900. Nicholas Russell Murray. Hammond, LA: Hunting for Bears, Inc., n.d. 80 pp.

A computer-generated listing of marriage records. Gives names and date of marriage but does not provide reference to marriage record book or page number. Arranged alphabetically.

Noxubee County, Mississippi, Marriages.   Macon, MS: Noxubee County Historical Society, 1979. 3 vols.

Transcribed from county record books for the years 1834 to 1930. Indexed.

Tombstone Inscriptions of Noxubee County, Mississippi.   E.Q. Richards. Macon, MS: Noxubee County Historical Society, 1975. 305 pp.

A listing of inscriptions from white cemeteries. Indexed.

OKTIBBEHA COUNTY

Cemetery Records of Oktibbeha County, Mississippi.   Compiled by members of the Oktibbeha County Genealogical Society and Interested Citizens of the County. Starkville, MS: The Oktibbeha County, Mississippi, Genealogical Society, 1969. 222 pp.

Indexed.

Families of Oktibbeha County, Mississippi, 1850.   Katie-Prince Ward Esker. Privately printed, n.d. 246 pp.

Compiles and indexes the 1850 federal census schedule for Oktibbeha County.

Federal Land Sales in Oktibbeha County, Mississippi.   Katie-Prince Ward Esker. Privately printed, 1944. 153 pp.

This publication makes the information extracted from land records more readily available to the researcher. Indexed.

Oktibbeha County, Mississippi, 1863–1900.   Nicholas Russell Murray. Hammond, LA: Hunting for Bears, Inc., n.d. 87 pp.

Computer-generated listing of marriage records. Gives names and date of marriage but does not provide reference to marriage record book or page number. Arranged alphabetically.

PANOLA COUNTY

Cemeteries of North Panola County, Mississippi.   Panola Historical and Genealogical Society. 1980. 52 pp.

Indexed.

History of Panola County, Mississippi. Panola Historical and Genealogical Society. Dallas, TX: Curtis Media Corporation, 1987. 558 pp.

General county history created from personal recollections and secondary source material. Of particular note to the genealogist is the separate section of family histories. Index references each story rather than page.

Panola County, Mississippi. Nicholas Russell Murray. Hammond, LA: Hunting for Bears, Inc., n.d. 62 pp.

A computer-generated listing of marriage records. Dates covered not given. Gives names and date of marriage but does not provide reference to marriage record book or page number. Arranged alphabetically.

The Panola Story. Pan Gens' Historical and Genealogical Society of Panola County. Quarterly.

Journal containing genealogical information about Panola County.

South Panola County, Mississippi, Cemeteries and Addenda for Other Cemeteries of Panola County. Panola Historical and Genealogical Society. 1981. 63 pp.

Arranged by cemetery and then alphabetized by name. Surname index included.

PEARL RIVER COUNTY

Lower Pearl River's Piney Woods: Its Land and People. John Hawkins Napier III. Oxford, MS: University of Mississippi, 1985. 227 pp.

Historical account of this area; includes early families. Well indexed.

Pearl River County, Mississippi, 1890–1918. Nicholas Russell Murray. Hammond, LA: Hunting for Bears, 1981. Var. pag.

A computer-generated listing of marriage records. Gives names and date of marriage but does not provide reference to marriage record book or page number. Arranged alphabetically. Appears in same volume with George and Stone counties.

Pearl River County Veterans. N. Christian Smoot and Charles E. Jones. Privately printed, n.d. 214 pp.

Provides reference to county military records. No index.

Pearl River County Veterans II: War Stories and Sea Tales. N. Christian Smoot. New York, NY: Rivercross Publishing, 1992. 421 pp.

A detailed source in narrative text about veterans and their families. Unique in that it chronicles generations of families from one war to another. Arranged chronologically by war beginning with the War of 1812 through Operation Desert Storm. Interesting source but no index.

Cemetery Records of Perry County, Mississippi.   Ben and Jean Strickland. Moss Point, MS. 1986. 215 pp.
Cemeteries for whites and blacks included. Indexed.

Perry County, Mississippi, 1877–1912.   Nicholas Russell Murray. Hammond, LA: Hunting for Bears, n.d. 50 pp.
A computer-generated listing of marriage records. Gives names and date of marriage but does not provide reference to marriage record book or page number. Arranged alphabetically.

Records of Perry County, Mississippi: 1820-1830 Tax Rolls, 1822–1823 Birth and Death Schedules, 1831–1840 Tax Rolls.   Ben and Jean Strickland. Privately printed, 1979. 2 vols.
Arranged alphabetically. Dates given are inclusive for the information provided, but publication does not provide records for every year.

Records of Perry County, Mississippi: 1831–1840 Tax Rolls.   Ben and Jean Strickland. Privately printed, 1979. 54 pp.
Actually transcribes the tax rolls for 1833, 1835, and 1837 to 1840. Each year is arranged alphabetically.

Records of Perry County, Mississippi: 1841–1847 Tax Rolls, 1845 and 1853 State Census.   Ben and Jean Strickland. Moss Point, MS. 1982. 76 pp.
Indexed.

Who Married Whom Perry County, Mississippi.   Jean Strickland and Patricia N. Edwards. Privately printed, 1985. 156 pp.
Transcription of marriage records. Indexed.

Abstracts of Obituaries from the Minutes of the Magee's Creek Baptist Association (Mississippi and Louisiana) 1882–1924.   E. Russ Williams, Jr. Privately printed, n.d. 96 pp.
A collection of obituaries taken from church records in the southern part of Pike County; may include a large part of Walthall County. Also includes some reported deaths for parts of Tangipahoa and Washington parishes in Louisiana. Indexed.

Cemetery Inscriptions: Pike County, Mississippi, 1750–1978.   Ray & June Sartin Parich. 1979. 760 pp.
Indexed.

An Historical Sketch of Magnolia, Mississippi, Centennial Celebration Magnolia, Mississippi, 1856–1956. Privately printed, 1956. 120 pp.

Entire volume is devoted to family names and relationships. No index. Difficult to use.

*Index to the W.P.A. Pike County Source Material Compiled by Volunteers of the Junior League of Jackson 1979. Privately printed, n.d. Unpaged.

A good readable index that refers to W.P.A. material held in Official Records at MDAH.

Osyka: A Memorial History 1812–1978. Pike County, Mississippi. Lucy (Wall) Varnado. Owensboro, KY: Cook & McDowell Publications, 1980. 214 pp.

General town history with a separate section that includes family histories. Indexed.

Pike County, Mississippi, 1798–1876: Pioneer Families and Confederate Soldiers, Reconstruction and Redemption. Luke Ward Conerly. Nashville, TN: Brandon Printing Company, 1909. 368 pp.

A wealth of genealogical material may be found within the narration of these family histories. Includes an appendix with the 1816 census, 1820 census, and selected church memberships. Well indexed.

Pike County, Mississippi, 1882–1899. Nicholas Russell Murray. Hammond, LA: Hunting for Bears, Inc., n.d. 68 pp.

Computer-generated listing of marriage records. Gives names and date of marriage but does not provide reference to marriage records book or page number. Arranged alphabetically.

School Census. Serena Abbess Haymon. Privately printed, 1990.

A transcription of the educable children county records that are often used to help fill the gap left by the destruction of the 1890 federal census schedule. Although not a series, there are three volumes printed for Pike County for the years 1890, 1896, and 1900. The books are alphabetically arranged by parent or guardian, giving the child's name, age, sex, and race.

PONTOTOC COUNTY

Complete Index of All Wills and Estate Settlements or Administrations in the Courthouse at Pontotoc, Mississippi, for the Years of 1836–1870. Rozelle C. Wax. 1959.

Wills actually cover years 1836 to 1880. Connects name to probate book number and page. Arranged alphabetically.

From These Hills: A History of Pontotoc County. Callie B. Young, ed. Fulton, MS: Itawamba County Times, 1976. 702 pp.

One of many good histories that were created as a bicentennial project. Valuable genealogical information. Indexed.

Pontotoc County, Mississippi. Nicholas Russell Murray. Hammond, LA: Hunting for Bears, Inc., n.d. 147 pp.

Computer-generated listing of marriage records. Dates covered in this publication are not given. Gives names and date of marriage but does not provide reference to marriage record book or page number. Arranged alphabetically.

Pontotoc County, Mississippi, 1850 Census Index to Heads of Families. Jane W. Melton. 1963. 49 pp.

Typescript.

Pontotoc County, Mississippi, Deed Books 1836–1872, An Index. Rozelle Callaway Wax. Privately printed, 1962. 621 pp.

An index that gives grantor, grantee, date, book, and page number.

Pontotoc County, Mississippi. "Missing marriages" 1867–1880. Hazle Boss Neet. Pontotoc, MS., n.d. 45 pp.

A typescript. Indexed.

Pontotoc County Pioneers. Pontotoc, MS: Hazle Bass Neet, 1980–1986.

A journal relating genealogical information about Pontotoc County.

PRENTISS COUNTY

Cemeteries of Prentiss County, Mississippi. Privately printed, 1981. 271 pp. Well indexed.

History of Prentiss County, Mississippi. The Prentiss County Historical Society Association. Dallas, TX: Curtis Media Corporation, 1984. 457 pp.

County history drawing on personal recollections and secondary source material. Separate section includes family histories. Index refers to each story section rather than page number.

Prentiss County, Mississippi. Nicholas Russell Murray. Hammond, LA: Hunting for Bears, Inc., n.d. 82 pp.

A computer-generated listing of marriage records. Dates covered not given. Gives names and date of marriage but does not provide reference to marriage record book or page number. Arranged alphabetically.

QUITMAN COUNTY

First Marriage License Book and First Will Book of Quitman County, Mississippi. Mrs. John C. Rich and Mrs. James Roseberry. Unpaged.

Typescript. Covers marriage records for 1877 to 1892 and wills for the years 1878 to 1934. The will book section is indexed.

Quitman County, Mississippi, 1877–1900. Nicholas Russell Murray. Hammond, LA: Hunting for Bears, Inc., n.d. 29 pp.

Computer-generated listing of marriage records. Gives names and date of marriage but does not provide reference to marriage record book or page number. Arranged alphabetically.

RANKIN COUNTY

1830 Census, Rankin County, Mississippi. 7 p.
Typescript. Arranged alphabetically.

Cemeteries, Rankin County, Mississippi. n.d. 274 pp.
Typescript. No index included.

Educable Children of Rankin County, Mississippi, 1885 and 1900. Alma Doris Howell. 1973. 10 pp.
Typescript. Transcription of school records that offers information lost with the destruction of the 1890 census. Arranged alphabetically by name of parent or guardian; gives child's age, sex, and race.

Heads of Families and Other Adults, Rankin County, 1850. 17 pp.
Typescript. Indexed.

A History of Rankin County, Mississippi. Rankin County Historical Society. Privately printed, 1984. 311 pp.
General county history that includes a separate section of early family histories. Indexed.

Rankin County, Mississippi, 1828–1900. Nicholas Russell Murray. North Salt Lake, UT: Hunting for Bears, Inc., n.d. 2 vols.
Computer-generated listing of marriage records. Gives names and date of marriage but does not provide reference to marriage record book or page number. Arranged alphabetically.

Rankin County, Mississippi, Cemetery Records 1824–1980. Rankin County Historical Society, Inc. Brandon, MS.: privately printed, 1981. 220 pp.
Surname index.

SCOTT COUNTY

1860 United States Census. Scott County, Mississippi. Jeanne Robey Felldin and Charlotte Magee Tucker. Tomball, TX: Genealogical Publications, 1978. 134 pp.

A photographic reproduction of the original handwritten census of 1860. Generally hard to read. Indexed by surname.

Cemeteries. Scott County, Mississippi.   Unpaged. Typescript. Arranged by cemetery. No index.

Remember Me: Complete Directory of Cemeteries (White) in Scott County, Mississippi.   Delores Pickering Sanders. 1986. 767 pp. Indexed.

Scott County, Mississippi, Marriages: 1872-1900, Books 1–5.   Marilyn Philbert Corley. Forest, MS: Marilyn Philbert Corley, 1987. 166 pp. Indexed.

Some Cemetery Records. Hinds, Scott, Smith.   Jeanne Louise Johnston. Unpaged. Typescript. Includes select cemeteries.

SHARKEY COUNTY

Early Mississippi Records. Issaquena County, Sharkey County. 1868–1906.   Vol. 5. Katherine Branton and Alice Wade, eds. Privately printed, n.d. 203 pp.
   Provides listings for each county from various sources including church and county records, newspapers, and cemeteries. Though the information is not comprehensive, this publication does make select sources accessible in one volume. General index included.

Sharkey County, Mississippi, 1876–1893.   Nicholas Russell Murray. Hammond, LA: Hunting for Bears, Inc., n.d. 107 pp.
   Computer-generated listing of marriage records. Gives names and date of marriage but does not provide reference to marriage record book or page number. Arranged alphabetically.

SIMPSON COUNTY

1860 Census of Simpson County, Mississippi.   Jeanne Robey Felldin and Charlotte Magee Tucker. Tomball, TX: Genealogical Publications, 1978. 95 pp.
   A photographic reproduction of the original handwritten census of 1860. Generally hard to read. Indexed by surname.

Cemeteries, Simpson County, Mississippi.   Unpaged. Typescript. Arranged by cemetery and then alphabetically. No index.

Heads of Families and Other Adults in 1850 Census of Simpson County.   14 pp.

Typescript.

Pleasant Hill Baptist Church Cemetery, Simpson County, Mississippi. Mary Dent Dickerson Deaton and Dara Lane Deaton. Greenwood, MS: 1981. 15 pp.
Transcription. No index.

Sharon Church and Cemetery. Thomas F. Richardson. 30 pp.
Arranged alphabetically.

Simpson County, Mississippi, 1872–1900. Nicholas Russell Murray. Hammond, LA: Hunting for Bears, Inc., n.d. 47 pp.
Computer-generated listing of marriage records. Gives names and date of marriage but does not provide reference to marriage record book or page number. Arranged alphabetically.

SMITH COUNTY

1860 Census of Smith County, Mississippi. Jeanne Robey Felldin and Charlotte Magee Tucker. Tomball, TX: Genealogical Publications, 1978. 141 pp.
Reproduction of original handwritten census records. Surname index included.

Cemeteries, Smith County, Mississippi. 49 pp.
Typescript. No index.

Smith County, Mississippi, 1912–1920. Nicholas Russell Murray. Hammond, LA: Hunting for Bears, Inc., n.d. 34 pp.
Computer-generated listing of marriage records. Gives names and date of marriage but does not provide reference to marriage record book or page number. Arranged alphabetically.

Some Cemetery Records. Hinds, Scott, Smith. Jeanne Louise Johnston. Unpaged.
Typescript. For Smith County includes only Byrd cemetery.

This Is a Reprint of Works Progress Administration (W.P.A.) for Mississippi. Statewide WPA Historical Research Project. Smith County Historical Society, n.d. 392 pp.
This reprint of WPA source material for Smith County offers an alternative to delving into the original material, which is often hard to read. Although this was a history project, there are many names included of genealogical interest. However, there is no index.

STONE COUNTY

Stone County, Mississippi, 1916–1935. Nicholas Russell Murray. Hammond, LA: Hunting for Bears, 1981.

A computer-generated listing of marriage records. Gives names and date of marriage but does not provide reference to marriage record book or page number. Arranged alphabetically. Appears in same volume with George and Pearl River counties.

SUNFLOWER COUNTY

Fevers, Floods and Faith: A History of Sunflower County, Mississippi, 1844–1976. Marie M. Hemphill. Privately printed, 1980. 849 pp.

General county history. Includes an appendix that contains various lists of genealogical interest. Well indexed.

The History of Inverness, Mississippi. Don Carol Bell. Privately printed, 1976. 339 pp.

Some family histories of both blacks and whites included in this town history. No index.

Marriage Records. Sunflower County-Leflore County, Mississippi. Hester R. Lowe. 46 pp.

Marriage records for Sunflower County covers the years 1844 to 1859. No index.

Records of Indianola City Cemetery. Indianola, Mississippi. David Holmes Chapter, National Society Daughters of the American Revolution. 1985. 99 pp.

Indexed.

Sunflower County, Mississippi, 1844–1900. Nicholas Russell Murray. Hammond, LA: Hunting for Bears, Inc., 1981. 116 pp.

A computerized listing of marriage records. Gives names and date of marriage but does not provide reference to marriage record book or page number. Arranged alphabetically.

TALLAHATCHIE COUNTY

Articles from the Tallahatchie Herald 1905 in Chancery Clerk's Office, Charleston, Tallahatchie County, Mississippi. 1971. Unpaged.

Bound photocopies of numerous newspaper articles featuring an "early history" column. Many names are included with explanation of family relationships. No index.

Index to 1907 Tallahatchie County, Mississippi, Enumeration of Confederate Soldiers and Widows.   Sally Adams Lee. Adamsville, TN. 1987. 6 pp.

Tallahatchie County, Mississippi.   Nicholas Russell Murray. Hammond, LA: Hunting for Bears, Inc., n.d. 90 pp.

Computer-generated listing of marriage records. No dates given as to years covered in this publication. Gives names and date of marriage but does not provide reference to marriage record book or page number. Arranged alphabetically.

TATE COUNTY

1890 Replacement Census, Tate County, Mississippi.   Louise C. Fox. Senatobia, MS: The Tate County Genealogical and Historical Society, Inc., 1990. Unpaged.

Information compiled from court dockets, tax books, poll books, school records, pauper lists, and newspapers that replaces data from the 1890 federal census schedule that was destroyed.

C.O. Pate Funeral Home Records 1927–1967.   David Spencer. Privately printed, 1985.

Abstracted entries taken from local funeral home records. Gives name, place, residence, date of death, and cemetery. Arranged alphabetically.

Educable Children: Tate County, Mississippi, 1892.   Rebecca Haas Smith. Senatobia, MS: The Tate County Genealogical and Historical Society, Inc., n.d. 99 pp.

A transcription of school records that provides genealogical information lost when the 1890 census was destroyed. Arranged alphabetically; includes an index for children whose parents or guardians had different surnames.

Educable Children: Tate County, Mississippi, 1885.   Marie Haven Carlton. Senatobia, MS: The Tate County Genealogical and Historical Society, Inc., 1987. 70 pp.

A transcription of original school records that makes available some information lost when the 1890 census was destroyed. Name of child appears alphabetically along with age, sex, name of parent or guardian, and school district.

Educable Children: Tate County, Mississippi, 1894.   Louise C. Fox. Senatobia, MS: The Tate County Genealogical and Historical Society, Inc., 1987. 96 pp.

Transcribes original school records making information available that was lost when the 1890 census was destroyed. Arranged alphabetically by parent; gives child's name, age, sex, and school district. A volume for 1900 has also been printed that gives the same information.

The Heritage of Tate County, Mississippi. Tate County Genealogical and Historical Society, Inc. Dallas, TX: Curtis Media Corporation, 1991. 805 pp.

Information for this county history was gathered from personal recollections and secondary source material. Includes a separate section of family histories. Index refers to each story section rather than page number.

A History of Tate County. Howard Carpenter, ed. Senatobia, MS: B/C Printing Co., 1975. 358 pp.

General county history. Indexed.

Senatobia Centennial Commemorating 100 Years of Progress. Senatobia, MS: Senatobia Centennial, Inc., 1960. 120 pp.

Includes some information of interest to genealogical researchers.

Tate County, Mississippi, 1878–1900. Nicholas Russell Murray. Hammond, LA: Hunting for Bears, Inc., n.d. 60 pp.

Computer-generated listing of marriage records. Gives names and date of marriage but does not provide reference to marriage record book or page number. Arranged alphabetically.

Tate Trails. Senatobia, MS: Tate County Genealogical and Historical Society, 1983– .

A journal of genealogical interest. MDAH does not have an index.

TIPPAH COUNTY

1850 Census-Tippah County, Mississippi. Jane Melton. 1962. 59 pp. Typescript.

1850 Slave Schedule of Tippah County, Mississippi. Tommy Lockhart. Ripley, MS: Tippah County Historical Society, 1976. 34 pp. Typescript in column arrangement.

1860 Census of Tippah County, Mississippi. Ripley, MS: Tippah Old Timer Press, 1981. 256 pp.

Indexed.

1870 Census of Tippah County, Mississippi. Bill Gurney. Ripley, MS: Tippah Old Timer Press, 1981. 210 pp.

Index included.

Biographical Notes from the Files of the Southern Sentinel, 1894. Tommy Lockhart. Ripley, MS: Old Timer Press, 1977. 71 pp.

A compilation of newspaper articles of genealogical interest. Indexed.

Cemeteries of Tippah County. Don Martini and Tommy Lockhart. Ripley, MS: Tippah County Historical Society, 1977. 196 pp.

Arranged by cemetery and then alphabetically by name. Indexed.

Census of 1840. Tippah County, Mississippi. Tommy Lockhart. Ripley, MS: Tippah County Historical Society, Inc., 1976. 33 pp.

Typescript.

The History of Tippah County, Mississippi. Tippah County Historical Society. Dallas, TX: National Share Graphics, Inc., 1981. 722 pp.

Information for this county history comes from personal recollections and secondary sources. A separate section is devoted to family histories. Index refers to story section not page number.

History of Tippah County, Mississippi: The First Century. Andrew Brown. Ripley, MS: Tippah County Historical Society, 1976. 321 pp.

General county history. Indexed.

Marriage Records of Tippah County, Mississippi. Tommy Lockhart. Ripley, MS: Tippah Old Timer Press, 1981. 4 vols.

Marriage records for the years 1858 to 1919. Arranged alphabetically by groom's name. No other index.

News and Journal. Ripley, MS: Tippah County Historical Society, 1977–

This journal was previously published as *Tippah County Historical and Genealogical Society Newsletter.* No index available at MDAH.

Tippah Countians in the Service 1941–1947. W.H. Anderson, ed. Ripley, MS: Southern Sentinel, n.d. Unpaged.

A publication commemorating those who served in World War II from this county. Arranged alphabetically, it includes biographical sketches along with photos.

Tippah County Death Notices. Don Martini. Ripley, MS: Tippah County Historical Society, 1976. 3 vols.

A three-volume work that transcribes obituaries taken from Ripley newspapers from 1837 to 1950. For the years 1861 to 1880 public records such as probate records, administrators' bonds, guardianship bonds, wills and mortality schedules were used in place of newspaper notices. Each abstract cites source of information. Alphabetically arranged.

Tippah County Historical and Genealogical Society Newsletter. Ripley, MS: The Society, 1975–1977.
A journal of genealogical interest. Title changed to *News and Journal.* No index available at MDAH.

Tippah County Land Deeds (1836–1870). Don Martini and Bill Gurney. Ripley, MS: Old Timer Press, 1983. unpaged.
Abstracted land records that also give deed book and page number for those who want complete record. Indexed.

Tippah County, Mississippi, Circuit Court Records 1849–1886. Don Martini. Ripley, MS: Old Timer Press, 1986. 253 pp.
A transcription of early county records. Indexed.

Tippah County, Mississippi, Obituaries, Wills, Estates. Don Martini. Ripley, MS: Tippah Old Timer Press, n.d. 161 pp.
A varied collection of genealogical records that combine to give the researcher an accounting of deaths in this county for the years 1850 to 1950. There is a gap in the records for the years 1836 to 1850. Each record book is indexed separately within the publication.

TISHOMINGO COUNTY

1860 Census of Tishomingo County, Mississippi. Tommy Lockhart. Ripley, MS: Old Timer Press. 412 pp.
Indexed.

Cemeteries of Tishomingo County, Mississippi. Rayma Biggs and Irene Barnes. Iuka, MS: Rayma Biggs and Irene Barnes, 1979. 329 pp.
Indexed.

Down Memory Lane: A History of Iuka, Mississippi, 1900–1915. Autrey William Mangum. Bossier City, LA: Everett's Bindery, 1971. 333 pp.
Primary portion of text is listing of family histories. Arranged alphabetically. No index.

History of Old Tishomingo County, Mississippi Territory. Fan Alexander Cochran. Oklahoma City, OK: Barnhart Letter Shop, 1969. 377 pp.
General county history that includes useful genealogical information. Well indexed.

Marriages of Old Tishomingo County, Mississippi. Irene Barnes. Iuka, MS. 1978. 2 vols.

Volume 1 contains the years 1837 to 1859, volume 2 has 1859 to 1870. General index not included.

Marriages of Tishomingo County, Mississippi, 1870–1922. Irene Barnes. Iuka, MS. 1989. 238 pp.

No general index included.

Tishomingo County, Mississippi, 1830–1900. Nicholas Russell Murray. Hammond, LA: Hunting for Bears, Inc., n.d. 53 pp.

Computer-generated listing of marriage records. Gives names and date of marriage but does not provide reference to marriage record book or page number. Arranged alphabetically.

Tishomingo County, Mississippi. Marriage Bonds and Ministers' Returns January 1842-February 1861. Thomas P. Hughes, Jr. and Jewel B. Standefer. Privately printed, 1973. 217 pp.

Indexed.

TUNICA COUNTY

Oakwood Cemetery West of Tunica, Mississippi, on Hiway #4. Tunica County. Vera Floyd. Senatobia, MS: The Tate County, Mississippi, Genealogical and Historical Society, Inc., 1987. 35 pp.

Indexed.

Tunica County, Mississippi, 1863–1900. Nicholas Russell Murray. Hammond, LA: Hunting for Bears, n.d. 111 pp.

Computer-generated listing of marriage records. Gives names and date of marriage but does not provide reference to marriage record book or page number. Arranged alphabetically.

UNION COUNTY

History of Union County, Mississippi. Union County Historical Committee. Dallas, TX: Curtis Media Corporation, 1990. 458 pp.

County history drawing on personal recollections and secondary source material. A separate section includes family histories. Index refers to each story section, not page number.

Union County, Mississippi, 1870–1900. Nicholas Russell Murray. Hammond, LA: Hunting for Bears, n.d. 65 pp.

Computer-generated listing of marriage records. Gives names and date of marriage but does not provide reference to marriage record book or page number. Arranged alphabetically.

Union County, Mississippi, Cemetery Records. Ish-te-ho-to-pah Chapter of the Daughters of the American Revolution. New Albany, MS: Ish-te-ho-to-pah Chapter, 1980. 314 pp.
Arranged by cemetery and then alphabetically.

WALTHALL COUNTY

The Tombstone Inscriptions of Walthall County, Mississippi. William and Irma Lampton. 1976. 402 pp.
Indexed.

Walthall County, Mississippi, 1914–1931. Nicholas Russell Murray. Hammond, LA: Hunting for Bears, Inc., n.d. 51 pp.
Computer-generated listing of marriage records. Gives names and date of marriage but does not provide reference to marriage record book or page number. Arranged alphabetically.

WARREN COUNTY

Anshe Chesed Cemetery, Vicksburg, Mississippi. Walter and Annie S. Salassi. 1986. 31 pp.
Arranged alphabetically.

Complete Directory of the City of Vicksburg, Also Business Directories of Yazoo City, Jackson and Natchez, with Other Useful Information. Vicksburg, MS: A.C. Tuttle, 1877. 240 pp.
An interesting find that is primarily a listing of names. Indexed.

Fisher Funeral Home Records. Mary Lois Sheffield Ragland. Privately printed, 1985. 18 binders.
A large compilation of funeral home records appearing in several volumes. Includes age, cause of death, and residence of deceased when known, as well as who paid funeral expenses. Although the introduction does indicate that there are missing years, no inclusive dates are given. The copies found in the Mississippi Archives are a photocopy of the original work. Each volume is arranged alphabetically.

The Leading Afro-Americans of Vicksburg, Miss.: Their Enterprises, Churches, Schools, Lodges, and Societies. Vicksburg, MS: Biographical Publishing Co., 1908. 80 pp.

A valuable resource that includes biographical sketches of prominent African-Americans living in Vicksburg towards the end of the nineteenth century. The text portion of this publication, which lists names in reference to local churches, lodges, and societies, may be of genealogical interest. Names of proprietors of businesses are given along with members of their boards of directors. Includes photographs but no index.

Spreading The Word: Mississippi Newspaper Abstracts of Genealogical Interest 1825–1935. Mary Lois S. Ragland. Bowie, MD: Heritage Books, Inc., 1991. 249 pp.

This volume abstracts articles that appeared in Vicksburg newspapers during the years 1825 to 1935. Although most pertain to marriage and death notices, others are included if they provide genealogical information. Well indexed.

Through Open Gates: History, Symbolisms, and Legends of Vicksburg's Cedar Hill Cemetery. Charles Riles. Jackson, MS: Hederman Brothers, 1989. 88 pp.

This publication is of historical interest more than genealogical. However, a few notable persons are included.

Warren County, Mississippi, 1810–1900. Nicholas Russell Murray. Hammond, LA: Hunting for Bears, Inc., n.d. 104 pp.

Computer-generated listing of marriage records. Gives names and date of marriage but does not provide reference to marriage record book or page number. Arranged alphabetically.

Warren County, Mississippi Territory: Tax Rolls 1810–1817.

Partially indexed. Other sections are arranged alphabetically.

With Malice Toward Some: The Military Occupation of Vicksburg, 1864–1865. Gordon A. Cotton and Ralph C. Mason. Vicksburg, MS: Vicksburg and Warren County Historical Society, 1991. 192 pp.

A unique work that covers the years 1864 and 1865 during the Union occupation of Vicksburg, this volume is of particular importance because it gives alphabetized listings taken from the provost marshall's records of day-to-day arrests and imprisonments that contain the names of whites and blacks, Union, Confederate, and civilian. It also features personal recollections given in newspaper accounts. An index was not included.

Words of Stone: From Within Warren County, Mississippi. Mary Hall Rutland. Privately printed, 1984. 3 vols.

Cemetery record data taken from tombstone inscriptions. Indexed.

WASHINGTON COUNTY

Cemetery Records. Belzoni, Mississippi.   Iklanna Chapter D.A.R., 1971.
Paging inconsistent. No index.

Early Records of Mississippi: Issaquena and Washington Counties.   Katherine
Branton. Privately printed, 1982. 3 vols.
Several kinds of public records have been abstracted into this three-
volume series. Included are marriage records, wills, medical licenses, newspaper notices, an index to apprenticeships, estate papers, and others.
Although not inclusive, these records date from 1827 to 1926. Each volume
includes an index.

Leland, Mississippi: From Hellhole to Beauty Spot.   Dorothy Love Turk. Leland Historical Foundation, 1986. 205 pp.
A historical narrative that includes many names with an additional section
on family histories. Well indexed.

*Memoirs of Henry Tillinghast Ireys: Papers of the Washington County Historical
Society, 1910–1915.*   William D. McCain and Charlotte Capers, eds. Jackson, MS: Mississippi Department of Archives and History and Mississippi
Historical Society, 1954. 423 pp.
A worthwhile source compiled from personal recollections, newspaper
notices, and personal papers. The index includes a listing of plantations
that may not be available in other sources.

Old Greenville Cemetery, 1880–1982.   Caledonia Jackson Payne. Leland,
MS: Caledonia Jackson Payne, n.d. 114 pp.
Information taken from the written records kept by the Greenville Ceme-
tery Association. Indexed.

Washington County, Mississippi, 1853–1900.   Nicholas Russell Murray.
Hammond, LA: Hunting for Bears, n.d. 2 vols.
Computer-generated listing of marriage records. Gives names and date
of marriage but does not provide reference to marriage record book or
page number. Arranged alphabetically.

Washington County, Mississippi Territory: 1803–1816 Tax Rolls.   Ben and Jean
Strickland. Milton, FL: Ben and Jean Strickland, 1980. 117 pp.
Indexed.

WAYNE COUNTY

1860 Census of Wayne County, Mississippi.   32 pp.
Typescript.

Confederate Records: Covington, Wayne, and Jones county. Jean Strickland and Patricia N. Edwards. Privately printed, 1987. 140 pp.

A Compilation of Confederate records from three counties. Information regarding Wayne County includes rosters of military companies, narrative sketches of a number of officers, and other material that might be of particular genealogical interest.

History of Wayne County, Mississippi, Churches and Cemetery Records 1800s–1915. H.H. Daniel. Privately printed, n.d. 38 pp.

Includes cemetery data for the years before 1915. Indexed.

Records of Wayne County, Mississippi: Cemetery Records. Jean Strickland and Patricia N. Edwards. Privately printed, 1987. 2 vols. Indexed.

Records of Wayne County, Mississippi: State Census 1816, 1820, 1841, 1845, 1853, 1866. Ben and Jean Strickland. Privately printed, 1981. 65 pp. Indexed.

Records of Wayne County, Mississippi: Tax Rolls 1810–1820. Ben and Jean Strickland. Privately printed, n.d. 72 pp. Indexed.

Wayne County, Mississippi: 1820, 1830, 1840 and 1850 Federal Census, 1821–1829 Tax Rolls. Ben Strickland and Patricia N. Edwards. Privately printed, 1988. 178 pp. Indexed.

Wayne County, Mississippi: 1831–1844 Tax Rolls and Agricultural Census. Jean Strickland and Patricia N. Edwards. Privately printed, 1991. 200 pp.

Arranged chronologically and then alphabetically. Some names found on the agricultural census that do no appear on the federal census. Indexed.

Wayne County, Mississippi, 1881–1900. Nicholas Russell Murray. Hammond, LA: Hunting for Bears, n.d. 46 pp.

Computer-generated listing of marriage records. Gives names and date of marriage but does not provide reference to marriage record book or page number. Arranged alphabetically.

Who Lived Where. Wayne County, Mississippi. Book of Original Entry. Jean Strickland and Patricia N. Edwards. Privately printed, 1989. 161 pp.

This work consists of abstracts taken from the tract book of original land entries from the Bureau of Land Management. It is particularly significant since many of Wayne County's records for the years from early settlement until 1880 were destroyed by fire. Includes index.

Who Married Whom, Wayne County, Mississippi. Jean Strickland and Patricia N. Edwards. Privately printed, 1987. 235 pp.

Includes only caucasian marriages for the years 1816 to 1880. Arranged alphabetically. Indexed.

WEBSTER COUNTY

The History of Webster County, Mississippi. Webster County History Association. Dallas, TX: Curtis Media Corporation, 1985. 503 pp.

Information for this general county history was gathered primarily from personal recollections and secondary sources. A separate section devoted to family histories is of genealogical interest. Index refers to each story name rather than page number.

Some Inscriptions From Tombstones and Markers in Cemeteries of Webster County, Mississippi. William D. McCain. Privately printed, 1986. 4 vols.

Indexed.

Webster County, Mississippi, 1874–1900. Nicholas Russell Murray. Hammond, LA: Hunting for Bears, n.d. 49 pp.

A computer-generated listing of marriage records. Gives names and date of marriage but does not provide reference to marriage record book or page number. Arranged alphabetically.

WILKINSON COUNTY

The Journal of Wilkinson County History: Wilkinson County Cemeteries. Volume 1. Mrs. James V. Gross and Miss Marion Miles. Privately printed, 1990. 347 pp.

Along with expected genealogical data from cemeteries, this publication includes a listing of newspaper obituaries for the years 1823 to 1890, with some years missing. Of additional interest may be those indexes to unidentified footstones and to unmarked graves from Bible records, family members, and church records. One general alphabetical index gives each cemetery listing.

The Journal of Wilkinson County History: Wilkinson County Marriage Records, 1800 to 1924. Linda Gene Felter Carter. Woodville, MS: The Woodville Civic Club, Inc., 1991. 364 pp.

A transcription of marriage records that includes indexes for both bride and groom.

Wilkinson County, Mississippi, 1805–1899. Nicholas Russell Murray. Hammond, LA: Hunting for Bears, n.d. 162 pp.

Computer-generated listing of marriage records. Gives names and date of marriage but does not provide reference to marriage record book or page number. Arranged alphabetically.

The Woodville Republican: Mississippi's Oldest Existing Newspaper. Volume I: December 18, 1823-December 17, 1839. O'levia Neil Wilson Wiese. Bowie, MD: Heritage Books, Inc., 1990. 275 pp.

This publication abstracts relevant genealogical information found in existing issues of the *Woodville Republican*. No entries are found for the year 1832 since no issues are in existence. Arrangement is chronological and a surname index has been included.

WINSTON COUNTY

The Centennial History of Winston County, Mississippi. William T. Lewis. Pasadena, TX: Globe Publishers International, 1972. 216 pp.

This is the publication of a manuscript that was written in 1876. Although there is no index, this source's genealogical value comes from its many listings of names.

Early Deeds of Winston County, Mississippi. 6 pp.

Typescript. Arranged alphabetically.

Marriage Records of Winston County, Mississippi. Volume I. 1834–1880. Winston County Genealogical and Historical Society. Privately printed, 1984. 240 pp.

Arranged alphabetically by groom's name. Includes bride index.

Tomb Records of Winston County, Mississippi. Josie Worthy Holman. Louisville, MS: Josie Worthy Holman, 1966. 368 pp.

Includes surname index.

Winston County and Its People: A Collection of Family Histories. Nancy Randolph Parkes. Louisville, MS: The Winston County Genealogical and Historical Society, 1980. 320 pp.

A wealth of genealogical material is gathered in this single volume of family histories.

Winston County, Mississippi. Nicholas Russell Murray. Hammond, LA: Hunting For Bears, Inc., n.d. 132 pp.

A computer-generated listing of marriage records. Years of inclusion not indicated. Gives names and date of marriage but does not provide reference to marriage record book or page number. Arranged alphabetically.

Winston County, Mississippi, Marriages 1834–1880.   Lucille Simms Mallon. N.d. 46 pp.

Each marriage "book" is indexed separately within this single-volume work.

YALOBUSHA COUNTY

Abstract of Yalobusha County, Mississippi, Will Book A (1800–1857).   C. Blair Morgan. Memphis, TN: C.B. Morgan, 1980. Unpaged.

Annotations of will entries for years 1808 to 1857. Arranged alphabetically.

Records of Yalobusha County, Mississippi.   Frances L. Turnage and Edith W. McLarty. Privately printed, n.d.

Information taken from will book A; however, there is no explanation as to what years are included.

Yalobusha County History.   The Heritage Committee of the Yalobusha Historical Society. Dallas, TX: National Share Graphics, Inc., 1982.

General county history taken from personal recollections and secondary source material. A separate section is devoted to family histories. Index refers to each story section rather than page number.

Yalobusha County, Mississippi, 1833–1900.   Nicholas Russell Murray. Hammond, LA: Hunting for Bears, Inc., 1981. 117 pp.

A computer-generated listing of marriage records. Gives names and date of marriage but does not provide reference to marriage record book or page number. Arranged alphabetically.

Yalobusha County, Mississippi, Cemetery Records.   Coffeeville, MS: The Yalobusha County Historical Society, 1979. 2 vols.

Indexed.

Yalobusha County, Mississippi, Cemetery Records: Oakhill Cemetery, Water Valley, Mississippi.   130 pp.

Arranged alphabetically.

Yalobusha County, Mississippi, Marriage Records 1833–1900.   Pauline Casey Briscoe. 1981. 232 pp.

Transcription of marriage records. Indexed.

Yalobusha County, Mississippi, Original Land Patents Books 1 and 2, 1833–1853. Francis Marion Duke III and Chris B. Morgan. Privately printed, 1981. 209 pp.

This publication presents an easier approach to land research through the transcription of these patents. Includes a helpful overview of land transactions for this county along with an index.

Yalobusha Pioneer. Yalobusha County Historical Society. 1977–1989.

A journal of genealogical interest. Published seasonally. Index not available at MDAH.

YAZOO COUNTY

Complete Directory of the City of Vicksburg, Also Business Directories of Yazoo City, Jackson and Natchez, with Other Useful Information. Vicksburg, MS: A.C. Tuttle, 1877. 240 pp.

An interesting find containing listings of names. Indexed.

Glimpses of Yazoo City 1867–1916, 1920, 1925. Mary Elizabeth Bedwell. Privately printed, 1981. 178 pp.

An annotated transcription of newspaper entries for the years noted in title. The topical index provides little assistance to the researcher.

Marriage Records. Yazoo County, Mississippi. Nina Pepper. Privately printed, 1965. 4 vols.

Transcription of marriage records for the years 1845 to 1870. Indexed.

Records of Cemeteries wherein Confederate Veterans are Interred and Records of Confederate Grave Markers, Yazoo County, Mississippi. United Daughters of the Confederacy, Jefferson Davis Chapter No. 216. Privately printed, n.d. Unpaged.

Arranged by cemetery with each entry certified by name of individual giving information. Indexed.

Roster and Sketches of the Several Military Companies Which Were in Regular Service of the Confederate States during the Civil War from Yazoo County, Miss. Yazoo Camp, 176, Confederate Veterans of Yazoo City, Miss. Yazoo City, MS: Waller Printing Co., 1905. 21 pp.

Pamphlet that lists names of soldiers within each unit obtained from muster rolls and personal recollections. Indexed by military company and then arranged alphabetically.

Yazoo County, Mississippi, 1845–1900. Nicholas Russell Murray. Hammond, LA: Hunting for Bears, Inc., n.d. 220 pp.

A computer-generated listing of marriage records. Gives names and date of marriage but does not provide reference to marriage record book or page number. Arranged alphabetically.

Yazoo County, Mississippi, 1850 U.S. Census and Marriages. Diane Ryans Roos. Bowie, MD: Heritage Books, Inc., 1990. 135 pp.

Census information is an actual transcription, and marriage information is taken from several unlisted sources. Indexed.

Yazoo County Story. Yazoo Historical Association. Fort Worth, TX: University Supply and Equipment Company, 1958. 184 pp.

General county history that offers some genealogical interest. Indexed.

Yazoo: Its Legends and Legacies. Harriet DeCell and JoAnne Prichard. Yazoo City, MS: Yazoo Delta Press, 1976. 515 pp.

A well-documented narrative of a county's historical development. The appendix includes detailed genealogical data from primary sources, along with an inclusion of family histories, written from material provided by the families. Indexed.

Appendix

Mississippi (by county)

Adams
Judge George W. Armstrong Library
S. Commerce and Washington
P. O. Box 1406
Natchez, MS 39121

LDS Family History Center
Lower Woodville Road
Natchez, MS 39121

Attala
Attala County Library
201 South Huntington Street
Kosciusko, MS 39090

Bolivar
Bolivar County Library
104 South Leflore Avenue
Cleveland, MS 38732

Chickasaw
Houston Carnegie Library
104 West Madison
P. O. Box 186
Houston, MS 38815

Forrest
William D. McCain Library and
    Archives

University of Southern Mississippi
Box 5148
Southern Station
Hattiesburg, MS 39406-5148
(Richard Lackey genealogical
    collection; census records from
    southern states; newspapers
    on microfilm which they will
    interlibrary loan)

Hattiesburg Area Historical Society
127 West Front Street
P. O. Box 1573
Hattiesburg, MS 39403

LDS Family History Center
US 11 South
Hattiesburg, MS 39401

Harrison
Biloxi Public Library
217 Lameuse Street
Biloxi, MS 39530-4298

L. W. Anderson Genealogical
    Library
William Carey College
P. O. Box 1647

Gulfport, MS 39502

Gulfport-Harrison County Library
1300 21st Avenue
P. O. Box 4018
Gulfport, MS 39502

LDS Family History Center
Klein Road at David
Gulfport, MS 39502

Hinds

Baptist Historical Commission
Mississippi College
P. O. Box 51
Clinton, MS 39060

Eudora Welty Library
300 N. State Street
Jackson, MS 39201

J. B. Cain Archives of Mississippi
   Methodism
Millsaps College
Millsaps-Wilson Library
1701 N. State Street
Jackson, MS 39210

Catholic Diocese of Jackson Archives
Chancery
237 East Amite Street
P. O. Box 2248
Jackson, MS 39205

Mississippi Library Commission
P. O. Box 10700
Jackson, MS 39289-0700

LDS Family History Center
1301 Pinehaven Road
Clinton, MS 39056

Mississippi Veterans Home
4607 Lindberg Drive
Jackson, MS 39209

Department of Environmental
   Quality
Geology Office

2380 Highway 80 West
Southport Center
Jackson, MS 39204
(maps available for purchase)

Jackson

Moss Point City Library
4401 McInnis Avenue
Moss Point, MS 39563

Ocean Springs Municipal Library
525 Dewey Avenue
Ocean Springs, MS 39564

Jackson-George Regional Library
3214 Pascagoula Street
Pascagoula, MS 39567

Jasper

Bay Springs Municipal Library
5th Avenue
Drawer N
Bay Springs, MS 39422

Jones

Laurel-Jones County Library
530 Commerce Street
Laurel, MS 39440

Lauren Rogers Museum of Art
   Library
5th Avenue at 7th Street
P. O. Box 1108
Laurel, MS 39441

Kemper

DeKalb Library
Corner of Bell and Main Streets
P. O. Box 710
DeKalb, MS 39328

Lafayette

Skipwith Historical and Genealogical
   Society
Oxford-Lafayette County Public
   Library
Bramlett Boulevard

P. O. Box 1382
Oxford, MS 38655

Lauderdale
Lauderdale County Department of
   Archives and History
410 21st Avenue - Annex
P. O. Box 5511
Meridian, MS 39302

Lee
Lee County Library
219 Madison Street
Tupelo, MS 38801

Leflore
Greenwood-Leflore Public Library
405 W. Washington
Greenwood, MS 38930-4297

Cottonlandia Museum
Highway 82 West
Greenwood, MS 38930

Lincoln
Lincoln County Public Library
100 South Jackson Street
P. O. Box 541
Brookhaven, MS 39601

Lowndes
Lowndes County Library System
Columbus Public Library - Archives
314 N. Seventh Street
Columbus, MS 39701

LDS Family History Center
708 Airline Road
Columbus, MS 39701

Monroe
Evans Memorial Library
105 North Long Street
Aberdeen, MS 39746

Neshoba
Neshoba County Public Library

230 Beacon Street
Philadelphia, MS 39350

Noxubee
Noxubee County Library
103 East King Street
Macon, MS 39341

Oktibbeha
Mississippi State University
Mitchell Memorial Library
P. O. Drawer 5408
Mississippi State, MS 39762
(newspapers on microfilm which they
   will interlibrary loan)

Panola
Batesville Public Library
106 College Street
Batesville, MS 38606

Pearl River
Margaret Reed Crosby Memorial
   Library
900 Goodyear Boulevard
Picayune, MS 39466

Pike
Pike-Amite-Walthall Library
114 State Street
McComb, MS 39648

Pontotoc
Pontotoc County Library
111 North Main Street
Pontotoc, MS 38863

Prentiss
George E. Allen Library
Highway 45 West and Church Street
Booneville, MS 38829

Rankin
Brandon Public Library
1475 West Government Street
Brandon, MS 39042

Scott
Forest Public Library
210 South Raleigh Street
P. O. Box 737
Forest, MS 39074

Simpson
Magee Public Library
120 Northwest 1st Street
Magee, MS 39111

Smith
Floyd J. Robinson Memorial Library
P. O. Box 266
Raleigh, MS 39153

Sunflower
Sunflower County Library
201 Cypress Drive
Indianola, MS 38751

Tippah
Ripley Public Library
308 North Commerce
Ripley, MS 38663

Tishomingo
Iuka Public Library
204 North Main Street
Iuka, MS 38852

Union
Jennie Stephens Smith Library
219 King Street
P. O. Box 846
New Albany, MS 38652

Walthall
Walthall County Library
707 Union Road
Tylertown, MS 39667

Warren
Old Courthouse Museum
1008 Cherry Street
Vicksburg, MS 39180
Warren County-Vicksburg Public
  Library
700 Veto Street
Vicksburg, MS 39180

Washington
William Alexander Percy Library
341 Main Street
Greenville, MS 38701

Yazoo
Ricks Memorial Library
310 N. Main Street
P. O. Box 575
Yazoo City, MS 39194

RESOURCES OUT OF STATE

Alabama
Alabama Department of Archives and
  History
624 Washington Avenue
Montgomery, Alabama 36130

Samford University
Harwell Goodwin Davis Library
800 Lakeshore Drive
Birmingham, Alabama 35229

Birmingham Public Library
2100 Park Place
Birmingham, Alabama 35203

District of Columbia
National Archives
Central Reference Section
7th and Pennsylvania Avenue, NW
Washington, D.C. 20408

Georgia
Georgia Department of Archives and History
330 Capitol Avenue, SE
Atlanta, Georgia 30334
National Archives - Southeast Region
1557 St. Joseph Avenue
East Point, Georgia 30344

Illinois
American Medical Association
535 N. Dearborn Street
Chicago, Illinois 60610
American Medical Association
Library and Archives
P. O. Box 10623
Chicago, Illinois 60610

Indiana
Allen County Public Library
900 Webster Street
P. O. Box 2270
Fort Wayne, Indiana 46801
(largest genealogical collection in a public library in the United States)

Kansas
U.S. Department of Commerce
Bureau of the Census
Pittsburg, Kansas 66762

Louisiana
Louisiana State Archives and Records Services
P. O. Box 94125
1515 Choctaw Drive
Baton Rouge, Louisiana 70804
The Historic New Orleans Collection
533 Royal Street
New Orleans, Louisiana 70130

Missouri
Military Personnel Records
9700 Page Boulevard
St. Louis, Missouri 63132

North Carolina
North Carolina Division of Archives and History
109 East Jones Street
Raleigh, North Carolina 27611

South Carolina
South Carolina Department of Archives and History
1430 Senate Street
Columbia, South Carolina 29201
University South Caroliniana Society
South Caroliniana Library
University of South Carolina
Columbia, South Carolina 29208

Tennessee
Tennessee State Library and Archives
403 Seventh Avenue North
Nashville, Tennessee 37219

Texas
Dallas Public Library
1515 Young Street
Dallas, Texas 75201
Clayton Library
Center for Genealogical Research
5300 Caroline
Houston, Texas 77004
National Archives - Southwest Region
501 West Felix, Building 1
Fort Worth, Texas 76115

Utah
Church of Jesus Christ of Latter-day Saints
Family Research Library
35 North West Temple Street
Salt Lake City, Utah 84150
(largest private genealogical collection in the world)

Virginia
Bureau of Land Management
Eastern States Office
7450 Boston Boulevard
Springfield, Virginia 22153

Index